Seventy Years of Best Sellers

70 YEARS OF

BEST SELLERS

1895-1965

ALICE PAYNE HACKETT

 R. R. BOWKER COMPANY

NEW YORK · LONDON · 1967

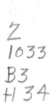

We shall not busy ourselves with what men ought to have admired, what they ought to have written, what they ought to have thought, but with what they did think, write, admire.

—A HISTORY OF CRITICISM

by George Saintsbury

Contents

FOREWORD
to "50 Years of Best Sellers"

THE TERM "BEST SELLER" was coined and came into common use because it filled a need. A term was needed to describe what were not necessarily the best books but the books that people liked best. For a long time people have been interested in what other people read and why. If we are studying what books were popular in any period of our history, it is important to know not only what people could have read, or should have read, but what they did read. The record of what books a great many people have bought and read is a part of the social history of those people.

The books which have been important from a literary standpoint have been recorded in many volumes of literary criticism. Many of those books have had large and continuing sales, though some have only been appreciated years after they were published. These great books are the products in which any country must take great pride. On the other hand the record of best sellers of the hundred or more years during which book publishing has been an active industry in this country has not heretofore been adequately made. The record is only in part literary history. A literary classic is a book which continues to be important to succeeding generations of readers. Some of the best sellers of each decade have done that; many more have not. The lists covering a fifty-year period which this volume includes will make interesting material for study. Whether or not literature of continuing value is to be found among the best sellers, the lists provide significant insight into the thinking and emotions of a people. The trends of such reading may have more significance than a casual glance indicates.

How many copies any book has sold is recorded on the files of its publisher, and business records are not readily unearthed. Fortunately, however, the comparative sales of books year by year for the last half century have been kept systematically. The closing of this fifty year period makes a natural occasion for printing the record. The sales totals of books are more difficult to gather and to verify, but such figures, insofar as they have ever been printed, have become part of the historical files of the *Publishers' Weekly* office. Alice Payne Hackett, who has had so much to do with the development and completeness of these files, has pursued for her book every figure that could be verified by the files or records in the publishing offices.

Fifty Years of Best Sellers will open up to the student and bookman new fields for speculation. Perhaps students of literary history will try to chart the evolution of public taste from these records and writers of tomorrow's best sellers find, in these titles of the past, some clue to the perennial elements of popular appeal.

FREDERIC G. MELCHER

1946

FOREWORD
to "60 Years of Best Sellers"

THE PROMPT recognition which was accorded ten years ago to Alice Hackett's records and comments on best sellers and the demand which has followed for a continuation of her figures and analysis has shown that such records have an interest to widely different groups of people—to the book trade, of course, but also to reminiscent readers and to students of public taste and social history. This continuation of the yearly lists is now accompanied by an expansion of earlier information which Miss Hackett has gathered by persistent contacts with many sources and to these annual lists has been added a greatly extended group of classified lists which enhance the popular interest and usefulness of the book.

FREDERIC G. MELCHER

August 1956

FOREWORD
to "70 Years of Best Sellers"

Soon after Alice Hackett graduated from Wellesley she joined the staff of the *Publishers' Weekly* as an editor. And soon she developed a special interest in the phenomenon of the best seller. She applied her considerable talent for research to the subject and has made *Publishers' Weekly* the prime source of information about best sellers. She also originated the *Publishers' Weekly* Forecasts to which she continues to contribute. She has made of the term best seller at once something glamorous and a practical measure.

The first edition of this book, in 1945, was the first attempt to gather in one place American best seller records. Its scope was much enlarged in the second, 1955, edition. Proliferation of books during the past ten years has necessitated this new edition, which, as it brings the records of seventy years up to date, is most welcome.

MILDRED C. SMITH

August 1967

A Guide To Best Sellers

A GUIDE TO BEST SELLERS

IT IS the purpose of this book as of its predecessors, *Fifty Years of Best Sellers* and *Sixty Years of Best Sellers,* to present as completely as possible the facts and figures about American best sellers during the period in which their records have been preserved, to interpret and comment to some extent upon the statistics and the trends, but not to evaluate them from a literary point of view.

There is always a great deal of interest and curiosity about best-selling books among members of the general reading public as well as among those concerned with publishing, selling and publicizing books. The lists and figures of this book constitute an attempt to answer the questions of such interested people. In view of the recurrent controversies about the best-seller system, which usually hinge upon the complaint that best seller lists draw attention only to a few books to the disadvantage of what are possibly more worthy books, it must be pointed out that this book is not designed to glorify the best seller *per se,* but simply to give the facts. As long as newspapers and magazines find best seller lists attractive features for their readers, the best seller will be with us. Even if there were no organized best seller lists, notable sales for certain books would be news. When books become conspicuous for fast and unusually large sales, people who are not ordinarily book buyers or not commonly book readers become aware of them, even buy them. Sales of themselves stimulate sales. Sales records of books have become more and more important in relation to the sales of subsidiary rights, especially movie rights. Sometimes sales records assume exaggerated importance in this field of subsidiary rights, which some publishers admit is the present life blood of book publishing.

The term best seller is comparative rather than absolute; there is no fixed figure which a book's sales must reach in order for it to be considered a best seller. A book may be the best seller in one store or one city. It may be the best seller over the whole country for a month, a year, five years, or for a century. The words used to designate such a book have become so established in our language and are so often loosely used that "best seller" too often becomes synonymous with "book," especially in circles outside the book industry. Advertisers, magazine, radio and television writers, attempting to adhere to fair standards when mentioning books, often query major review media, libraries, trade magazines, book associations and others as to whether a certain book may honestly be called a best seller. In the office of *Publishers' Weekly,* the book trade magazine where much of the material for this present volume was developed, it has become the practice to answer such questions in the affirmative if a book has appeared on one of its monthly best seller lists, which are based upon bookstore surveys. The book is a best seller for at least the moment at which the question is asked. But is the book of the moment or month a best seller as *David Copperfield* or *Gone with the Wind* is a best seller? In the pages following I have attempted to illustrate the various stages of best sellerdom.

The reason why the story of best sellers begins in 1895 is that it was in that year that the first best seller lists were printed in the United States. Harry Thurston Peck, editor of the literary magazine *The Bookman,* which was founded in that year, began to run each month the lists of the best-selling books in a number of large cities. By 1902, the term "best seller" was well established, mainly through the publicity derived from *The Bookman's* lists, as a term specifically applied to books. About 1903 the magazine set the limit of its monthly list of titles at six and called the lists "the six best sellers." From these *Bookman* lists were formulated the annual best seller lists in this book from 1895 up to 1912 when the *Publishers' Weekly* lists were begun. There were few and scattered records of best-selling books previous to 1895. There are occasional lists to be found in early literary magazines, some in *Publishers' Weekly,* and a few lists of the most popular reading matter in public libraries, but all these give the effect of rather random reporting. Without any methodical listing of best sellers in the years previous to 1895, it is impossible to arrive at exact figures of sales for the books of preceding centuries. A list of "Early Best Sellers," most of which have been read for more than a century, is included in this book. It has been checked by a number of authorities, and, while it may possibly not be complete, the titles on it comprise a valid body of best sellers published before 1895.

The first edition of this book covered the years from 1895 to 1945, the second from 1895 to 1955. Since then there have been tremendous changes in the business of bookselling and publishing. During and just after World War II more books could have been sold than were available. This was because of paper quotas, shortages in other materials, and other wartime restrictions. Children's books, especially, sold as fast as they could be placed on sale, for one reason because the metals used in making toys for children were in even shorter supply than paper. All books sold very well in spite of these limitations placed upon their manufacture. There were fewer titles published but those that were published and were successful sold out all available printings. At about the time that paper restrictions began to be lifted book clubs boomed. The major clubs had been in existence for a number of years but it was not until the postwar period that all their monthly selections sold into the hundreds of thousands. "You

2

could sell almost any book during the war years," said Harry Scherman, founder of the Book-of-the-Month Club. The Book-of-the-Month Club distributed a total of 7,011,936 books in 1950. Its membership had hit an all-time peak of 920,000 in 1947. Since then it has declined. The club estimates sales of 700 million books in its history. In its fiscal year of 1950 the Literary Guild sent out about 8,800,000 books, in 1966, 6,500,000. Compare these figures with those which had been estimated by Maxwell Aley as to the book market twenty years previously. He wrote in *Publisher's Weekly* in 1931, that there were "one million habitual book buyers, one million more occasional buyers and beyond that a vague but large number who buy one or two books a year."

The big totals piled up by the book clubs in the war and postwar periods had a tremendous effect on the overall best seller lists, the three lists in this book that include books that have sold from 750,000 to one million or more copies in the past seventy years. Many books of this mid-century have displaced the favorites of the century's early years that once were close to the top of the lists. New titles added to the list of hardcover best sellers (750,000 or more) were, in many cases, the result of book club sales. At the same time, new readers for older books, the result often, in this case, of paperback sales, have brought some titles published in the early years into the overall best seller picture, for example, *The Red Badge of Courage,* originally published in 1895.

Because of the popularity of books in the Armed Services Editions, issued in paperback and distributed to men and women in the U.S. Armed Services during World War II, the book trade hoped that the many new readers of books thus created would continue to read in the postwar years and that the book boom of the late '40's and early '50's would continue. The distribution of the Armed Services Editions certainly stimulated new readership. It was not, however, the new readers of the World War II period and immediate postwar years who created the very large increase in book production and sales of the 1950's and early 1960's. This increase was due to the coming of age of new generations brought up on paperbacks, in other words, a combination of "the paperback revolution" and the "population explosion."

The paperbound book was not exactly an innovation in the trade. In the nineteenth century paperbound "dime novels" had big sales, and flourished for years thereafter. There were also many experiments in later years to launch paperbound lines. It was not until 1939 that the 25-cent paperbound book came into its own. Its success was attributed to new methods of cheaper manufacture, to new methods of distribution through the magazine wholesaler system providing new outlets, and to improved literary quality of the books chosen for reprint in paper covers. The price of paperbacks has long since risen above the original 25-cent tag. As

3

longer, more impressive novels and nonfiction titles were reprinted in paper-back, prices had to rise. So-called "quality" or trade paperbacks, sold like hardbound titles instead of by mass merchandising, became more and more in demand. These were often priced at two and three dollars or more. Textbooks are not within the scope of this book. The increase in their production and sale is well known. School supplementary reading, how-ever, is undoubtedly a factor in the sales of paperbacks of literary quality, reflected on these lists. Related as well, must be the increase in the number of reference books among the million-copy sellers, including dictionaries, both English and foreign language. With school populations rising, the future of such useful books seems unlimited.

When the first edition of this book appeared, paperbound books were established but had not yet attained the enormous sales that came later on. There was only one "overall" best-seller list, 1895-1945, in *Fifty Years of Best Sellers*. Hardbound books, including the reprints at 75 cents and $1 which sold well up to the 1940's, and paperbound books were all included on this one list. Paperbound sales account for the place of only a few books on this first list—titles like *See Here, Private Har-grove* and *The Pocket Book of War Humor*. That list, made in 1944, was, on the whole, not greatly affected by paperbound book sales. Since then the whole picture has changed. Paperbound sales, both reprints of hard-cover editions and paperback "originals," books which made their first appearance in paper covers, account for the majority of titles.

In the second edition and in this volume the overall best seller lists were arranged in three sections: combined (both hardcover and paper-back); hardbound alone; and paperback alone. Students of the book business and students of literary taste and social history will find what books have sold to bookstore and book club customers, what titles have sold to the so-called mass market. The evidence is not quite what one might expect. While great numbers of detective, some western stories and some sensational fiction on the list are due to paperback sales, it is also true that paperback distribution accounts for the appearance of such authors as John Steinbeck, William Faulkner, J. D. Salinger, Katherine Anne Porter, and James Joyce in this million-copy list.

Naturally the sales figures on these three lists are much larger than those on the first lists, and, naturally, all three lists, especially the com-bined list and the paperback list are much longer than they were ten or twenty years ago. The minimum sales figure on the original 1895-1945 list was arbitrarily set at one-half million copies. On two of the present lists the minimum is one million; on the hardbound list, 750,000. Title pro-duction has more than doubled in the past twenty years. Ten years ago Robert Frase, then economic consultant and associate director of the

4

American Book Publishers Council, pointed out that the population pattern ought soon to affect the book business favorably even if it had not yet affected it as much as had been expected. The slow rate of increase in sales, if not in title production in the postwar decade was illustrated by figures Mr. Frase quoted for trade books sold in 1929 and in 1954. The figures for both years were practically the same, about 70,000,000 copies. Book club sales, however, rose from about two million to 50 million; paperbacks from zero to 190 million; juveniles from 37 million to 95 million. By 1963 300 million paperbacks a year were produced. The American Book Publishers Council report for what was roughly the second postwar decade, 1957-1965, was based upon dollar volume of sales. The increases during this period were 8.1 per cent for adult hardbound books, 8.7 per cent for paperbacks, and 12.7 per cent for children's books.

Among trade books the topmost sold in even greater quantities than they did previously, but for the run-of-the-mill books the situation has not been so happy. Highly publicized novels, children's books and topical nonfiction particularly have normally attained high sales. The novel or nonfiction title that might be worthwhile but was not particularly outstanding had a rougher road. Because of increasing manufacturing costs and the decrease in rental libraries, which once absorbed a creditable number of the ordinary romances and novels designed for a few hours' diversion, it was difficult for the publisher to sell the unassuming book profitably. Fortunately both authors and publishers do not have to live on book sales alone. The sales of subsidiary rights, i.e., rights to use a book as the basis of a movie, television show, or condensation, are today essential both to author and publisher. Other subsidiary returns to authors and publishers are magazine serialization, secondary serialization, play production, book club distribution (there are many types of specialized book clubs in addition to the half-dozen big general ones), publication in foreign countries, and, of course, paperback reprint.

Readers may wonder why many, if not most, of the best sellers on the three overall lists do not appear on the annual lists of best sellers, 1895 through 1966, and, conversely, why many of the titles on the yearly lists do not appear on the overall best seller lists. This situation illustrates the difference between the best seller of the year and the all-time best seller. These annual lists as compiled by *Publishers' Weekly* are primarily for the interest of the retail bookseller. They do not include book club sales or sales in paperbound reprint editions. They are intended to show the reading tastes of the book buyers who actually go to a store to select books, not of those who buy by mail or pick up random reading from newsstands. Most of the novels on the annual lists of recent years sell a

5

minimum of about 75,000 copies, the nonfiction, 100,000 copies. This is for a single year. In most cases these titles never reach the overall lists without additional book club sales and/or paperback sales.

The reason why many of the books on the all-time lists do not appear on the yearly lists is, in general, the same. In the case where book club or paperback sales do not enter into the situation the books must have sold steadily, piling up sales over many years until they reach the big totals that put them on these lists. Nonfiction, such as cook books and other books of information, are good examples of such perennial popularity.

The yearly lists are more interesting for the student of social history and literary taste than are the overall lists. They reflect events and crises in history over seventy years as well as changing mores—from Pollyanna to Polly Adler, from *Beside the Bonnie Briar Bush* (1895) to *Valley of the Dolls* (1966). There are books on these lists that have made history and influenced American thinking. Consider *The Honorable Peter Stirling* by Paul Leicester Ford, *The Pit* by Frank Norris, *The Jungle* by Upton Sinclair, *Mr. Britling Sees It Through* by H. G. Wells, *The Economic Consequences of the Peace* by John Maynard Keynes, *The Plastic Age* by Percy Marks, *Mother India* by Katherine Mayo, *Looking Forward* by Franklin D. Roosevelt, *It Can't Happen Here* by Sinclair Lewis, *The Grapes of Wrath* by John Steinbeck, *For Whom the Bell Tolls* by Ernest Hemingway, *Berlin Diary* by William L. Shirer, *The White Cliffs* by Alice Duer Miller, *You Can't Do Business with Hitler* by Douglas S. Miller, *Victory Through Air Power* by Major Alexander P. de Seversky, *They Were Expendable* by W. L. White, *One World* by Wendell L. Willkie, *Strange Fruit* by Lillian Smith, *I Chose Freedom* by Victor Kravchenko, *Gentleman's Agreement* by Laura Z. Hobson, *Kingsblood Royal* by Sinclair Lewis, *The Wall* by John Hersey, *Witness* by Whittaker Chambers, *But We Were Born Free* by Elmer Davis, *Why Johnny Can't Read* by Rudolf Flesch, *Year of Decision* by Harry S. Truman, *A Nation of Sheep* by William Lederer and *Games People Play* by Eric Berne. There are many books which have added new words and phrases to the American language: *The Virginian, Pollyanna, Over the Top, Main Street, Babbitt, Gentlemen Prefer Blondes, Back Street, Life Begins at Forty, Mr. Chips, Lost Horizon, The Hucksters, The Snake Pit, The Man in the Gray Flannel Suit* and *Lolita*. Some are known by more people because their titles are titles of songs: *The Trail of the Lonesome Pine, The Rosary, In Flanders Fields, The Sheik, Stars Fell on Alabama, My Sister and I, The Last Time I Saw Paris.*

Of interest to publishers is the number of titles on the annual lists that each firm has issued. The leaders are Doubleday (with predecessor firms), 119; Harper & Row, 88; Houghton Mifflin, Little, Brown and Simon &

6

Schuster with 51 each; Scribner and Macmillan with 45 each. With the exception of Simon & Schuster all these houses, or the firms from which they were descended, were founded in the nineteenth century. The authors who have had the most titles on the seventy annual lists are Mary Roberts Rinehart with eleven; Sinclair Lewis with ten; Zane Grey and Booth Tarkington with nine each; and Louis Bromfield, Winston Churchill (the American novelist), George Barr McCutcheon, Gene Stratton Porter, Frank Yerby, Edna Ferber, Daphne du Maurier, and John Steinbeck with eight each. In the first twenty years, 1896-1914, the authors who appeared most frequently were George Barr McCutcheon, with eight titles; Winston Churchill with seven, and Mary Johnston and Sir Gilbert Parker with five each. In the period 1915-1934, Zane Grey led with nine titles. He was followed by Warwick Deeping, Sinclair Lewis, Mary Roberts Rinehart, and Booth Tarkington, with seven each, and by Coningsby Dawson, Eleanor H. Porter, Gene Stratton Porter, and H. G. Wells with five each. In the years 1935-1955, the authors having most titles on the lists were Frank Yerby with eight; Daphne du Maurier, John P. Marquand and John Steinbeck with six each; and Thomas B. Costain, A. J. Cronin, Lloyd C. Douglas, John Gunther, James Hilton, and Frances Parkinson Keyes with five each. During the past decade the only authors to have four books each on the yearly lists were John O'Hara and Charles M. Schulz, who combines cartoons with captions. The authors whose books have covered the longest span on all the lists are: Ellen Glasgow, whose first best seller appeared on the 1904 list and her last on the 1935 list; Edna Ferber, 1924 and 1958; Mary Roberts Rinehart, 1909 and 1936; Frances Hodgson Burnett, 1896 and 1922; Anne Morrow Lindbergh, 1935 and 1962; Mary Ellen Chase, 1934 and 1960; John Steinbeck, 1937 and 1962; and William Shirer, 1941 and 1961.

As I have said, literary criticism does not enter into this book; it is a guide to the past and present, and, for those looking toward future best sellers, a starting-point for speculation. It is wise to bear in mind Samuel Butler's statement: "There are some things which it is madness not to try to know but where it is almost as much madness to try to know. Sometimes publishers hoping to buy the Holy Ghost with a price, fee a man to read for them and advise them. This is but as the vain tossing of insomnia. God will not have any human being know what will sell."

What best sellers of today will become the classics of tomorrow? Malcolm Cowley pointed out, in an article in the *New Republic* (Dec. 22, 1947), "Classics and Best Sellers," the distinction between a classic (a book admired by intelligent readers through several generations) and a best seller (a book purchased by many readers in one generation). The terms, he says, "are not mutually exclusive—a best seller may become a classic in time, as happened with Dickens' novels." In order to try to

7

find out how many of the books on the early lists, especially the lists of the twenties and thirties, were at all familiar to today's young generation, I read the titles and authors' names to several college students. Only the most obvious authors were known to most of them, and extremely few titles. Most of them had read *Arrowsmith* and were interested in reading other Sinclair Lewis novels. They had read older classics like *War and Peace* and *Don Quixote,* but few were familiar with the books of Hemingway, Steinbeck, O'Neill, Faulkner, Maugham, Dreiser, Edith Wharton or Willa Cather.

To relate the material, the facts and figures of this present book up to 1950, to their historical and sociological background, I heartily recommend the reading of James D. Hart's *The Popular Book* (Oxford University Press, 1950). For a final word on the whole business of best sellers I quote from his concluding paragraphs. "If a student of taste wants to know the thoughts and feelings of the majority who lived during Franklin Pierce's administration, he will find more positive value in Maria Cummins's *The Lamplighter* or T. S. Arthur's *Ten Nights in a Bar-Room* than he will in Thoreau's *Walden*—all books published in 1854. The mores and manners prevailing in the year of the Teapot Dome scandal can better be extrapolated from Gertrude Atherton's *Black Oxen* than from Wallace Stevens's *Harmonium.* The book that time judges to be great is occasionally also the book popular in its own period; but, by and large, the longer-lived work reflects the demands of the moment only in the most general sense. Usually the book that is popular pleases the reader because it is shaped by the same forces that mold his non-reading hours, so that its dispositions and convictions, its language and subject, re-create the sense of the present, to die away as soon as that present becomes the past. Books of that sort generally are unreadable for succeeding ages; but like other fragments of the past, they help form the present. The volumes themselves may gather dust on library shelves, but they have left lasting impression on the American mind, etched deeply into a national consciousness."

Best Sellers 1895 - 1965

COMBINED

HARDBOUND

PAPERBOUND

BEST SELLERS

1895-1965

THIS OVERALL LIST of best sellers includes books published in the United States from 1895 through 1965 which have, over seventy years, sold one million copies or more. Many of them have appeared in several different editions and in both hardbound and paperbound format. Most of them are also included in one or the other of the two lists following this combined list, that is, a list of hardbound best sellers and a list of paperbound best sellers. A few titles appear on this list which are neither on the hardbound or paperbound lists. The reason is that their combined sale in both bindings is over one million but not large enough in each binding to qualify them for the separate lists. Many have been sold by book clubs, on newsstands, and by mail as well as through bookstores. New Bible translations are not included but some new dictionaries other than Webster dictionaries have been included. Pamphlets have not been included nor encyclopedias, hymnals, prayer books, manuals, textbooks, and certain other "non-books," such as picture and game books.

Publishers' names are not given because most of these titles have been published by at least two firms and sometimes by five or six or even more. The date of original publication in this country follows the author's name. "F" indicates fiction, "J", children's books. Many of the titles listed as juvenile fiction were originally published as adult books, but changing taste has now placed them in the category of juvenile or, at least, young adult reading.

Six hundred and thirty-three titles make up this list of books which have sold over 1,000,000 copies in the years since 1895. In the original (1945) edition of the present book the comparable list was a record of books which had sold 500,000 copies or more in the years from 1895 through 1945. There were 143 titles on that list. The enormous increase in both number of best-selling books and in sales is due not only to the accelerated rate in the number of new titles issued in the years since 1945 but in much greater part to the increase in the production and distribution of paperbound books in the 1950's and 1960's and to the big jump in book club sales in the years immediately after World War II.

This revolution in the make-up of the combined best seller list has

11

resulted in the elimination of most of the popular books that were published in the years up to 1930, those that sold between 500,000 and one million. Some of the most popular authors of the early part of this century, like the American novelist Winston Churchill, whose historical tales were the best sellers of almost every year from 1901 through 1915, and Harold Bell Wright, and Gene Stratton Porter, whose names predominated on the earlier list, have all but disappeared from this one. On the other hand the paperback editions are responsible for the inclusion of many prestigious authors who never had extremely large sales of their works in hardbound format. Paperbacks are responsible as well not only for the appearance of some books of literary quality, and for the many books of information and reference, but for books essentially for entertainment—suspense stories and sensational fiction.

On the following list there are eleven books which have sold over six million copies; only the first three on the list of ten years ago had reached that figure. Ten on this list have sold between five and six million—only two on the last list. Fifteen have sold between four and five million in comparison with four by 1955. Forty-four titles have sold between three and four million. A comparable figure ten years ago was fifteen titles.

Tagged for sixty years as America's best seller (except for the Bible) was the religious novel *In His Steps*. Now it has been superseded by Dr. Spock's book on baby and child care, by reference books, and by the notorious *Peyton Place,* which is the leading fiction title. More than half the titles among the first ten on the present list were among the first ten in 1955, although their positions have shifted.

The Pocket Book of Baby and Child Care (The Common Sense Book of Baby and Child Care), by Dr. Benjamin Spock. 1946	19,076,822
Better Homes and Gardens Cook Book. 1930	11,325,299
Pocket Atlas. 1917	11,000,000
F Peyton Place, by Grace Metalious. 1956	9,919,785
F In His Steps, by Charles Monroe Sheldon. 1897	(est) 8,065,398
F God's Little Acre, by Erskine Caldwell. 1933	8,061,812
Betty Crocker's New Picture Cookbook. 1950	(est) 7,000,000
F Gone with the Wind, by Margaret Mitchell. 1937	6,978,211
How to Win Friends and Influence People, by Dale Carnegie. 1937	6,578,314
F Lady Chatterley's Lover, by D. H. Lawrence. 1932	6,326,470
101 Famous Poems, comp. by R. J. Cook. 1916	(est) 6,000,000

English-Spanish, Spanish-English Dictionary, comp. by Carlos Castillo and Otto F. Bond. 1948   5,899,000

F The Carpetbaggers, by Harold Robbins. 1961   5,563,841

Profiles in Courage, by John F. Kennedy. 1956   5,490,651

F Exodus, by Leon Uris. 1958   5,473,710

Roget's Pocket Thesaurus. 1923   5,416,857

F I, the Jury, by Mickey Spillane. 1947   5,390,105

F To Kill a Mockingbird, by Harper Lee. 1960   5,363,909

F The Big Kill, by Mickey Spillane. 1951   5,089,472

Modern World Atlas. 1922   5,000,000

J The Wonderful Wizard of Oz, by L. Frank Baum. 1900   (est) 5,000,000

F The Catcher in the Rye, by J. D. Salinger. 1951   4,988,225

F My Gun Is Quick, by Mickey Spillane. 1950   4,916,074

F One Lonely Night, by Mickey Spillane. 1951   4,873,563

F The Long Wait, by Mickey Spillane. 1951   4,835,966

F Kiss Me, Deadly, by Mickey Spillane. 1952   4,828,044

F Tragic Ground, by Erskine Caldwell. 1944   4,810,418

30 Days to a More Powerful Vocabulary, by Wilfred J. Funk and Norman Lewis. 1942   4,712,588

F Vengeance Is Mine, by Mickey Spillane. 1950   4,637,734

The Pocket Cook Book, by Elizabeth Woody. 1942   4,466,200

F Return to Peyton Place, by Grace Metalious. 1959   4,400,000

F Never Love a Stranger, by Harold Robbins. 1948   4,375,620

F Thunderball, by Ian Fleming. 1965   4,186,935

F 1984, by George Orwell. 1949   4,171,838

F The Ugly American, by William J. Lederer and Eugene L. Burdick. 1958   4,007,158

A Message to Garcia, by Elbert Hubbard. 1898   (est) 4,000,000

F Hawaii, by James A. Michener. 1959   3,913,341

F Journeyman, by Erskine Caldwell. 1935   3,910,155

The Greatest Story Ever Told, by Fulton Oursler. 1949   3,858,948

Kids Say the Darndest Things! by Art Linkletter. 1957   3,821,608

The Radio Amateur's Handbook. 1926   3,800,000

The Boston Cooking School Cook Book, by Fannie Farmer. 1896   3,768,144

Diary of a Young Girl, by Anne Frank. 1952   3,662,089

F From Here to Eternity, by James Jones. 1951   3,646,004

F Goldfinger, by Ian Fleming. 1959   3,642,411

F Lolita, by Vladimir Nabokov. 1958   3,633,467

F Trouble in July, by Erskine Caldwell. 1940   3,593,268

F Lost Horizon, by James Hilton. 1935	3,581,210
F Butterfield 8, by John O'Hara. 1935	3,577,729
The American Woman's Cook Book, ed. by Ruth Berolzheimer. 1939	3,549,276
F Duel in the Sun, by Niven Busch. 1944	3,501,866
F Georgia Boy, by Erskine Caldwell. 1943	3,501,281
Four Days, by American Heritage and U.P.I. 1964	3,500,000
F The Case of the Lucky Legs, by Erle Stanley Gardner. 1934	3,499,948
F Tobacco Road, by Erskine Caldwell. 1932	3,475,947
F Pocket Book of Short Stories, ed. by M. E. Speare. 1941	3,445,000
F The Razor's Edge, by W. Somerset Maugham. 1944	3,430,505
Larousse French-English, English-French Dictionary. 1961	3,426,000
F The Winthrop Woman, by Anya Seton, 1958	3,389,940
F The Robe, by Lloyd C. Douglas. 1942	3,316,791
F You Only Live Twice, by Ian Fleming. 1964	3,283,000
F From Russia with Love, by Ian Fleming. 1957	3,262,193
F Mutiny on the Bounty, by Charles Nordhoff and James Norman Hall. 1932	3,220,246
F The Good Earth, by Pearl S. Buck. 1931	3,216,600
F House in the Uplands, by Erskine Caldwell. 1946	3,208,361
F The Case of the Sulky Girl, by Erle Stanley Gardner. 1933	3,190,334
F The Chinese Room, by Vivian Connell. 1942	3,171,512
F The Vixens, by Frank Yerby. 1947	3,170,056
F The Royal Box, by Frances Parkinson Keyes. 1954	3,156,000
F 79 Park Ave., by Harold Robbins. 1955	3,157,592
F On Her Majesty's Secret Service, by Ian Fleming. 1963	3,142,184
F A Tree Grows in Brooklyn, by Betty Smith. 1943	3,130,306
F Anatomy of a Murder, by Robert Traver. 1958	3,100,000
F Doctor No, by Ian Fleming. 1958	3,087,532
F Doctor Zhivago, by Boris Pasternak. 1958	3,079,790
Love without Fear, by Eustace Chesser. 1947	3,075,123
The Conscience of a Conservative, by Barry Goldwater. 1960	3,007,000
The Dell Crossword Dictionary, ed. by Kathleen Rafferty. 1950	3,000,000
F The Red Badge of Courage, by Stephen Crane. 1896	(est) 3,000,000
The Story of the Bible, by Jesse Lyman Hurlbut. 1904	3,000,000
F Magnificent Obsession, by Lloyd C. Douglas. 1929.	2,974,030
F The Cardinal, by Henry Morton Robinson. 1950	2,950,807
F Casino Royale, by Ian Fleming. 1953	2,940,221
F Forever Amber, by Kathleen Winsor. 1944	2,925,268
Folk Medicine, by D. C. Jarvis, M.D. 1958	2,911,111

Columbia Viking Desk Encyclopedia. 1953	2,833,993
F The Sure Hand of God, by Erskine Caldwell. 1947	2,830,061
F The Case of the Curious Bride, by Erle Stanley Gardner. 1934	2,825,368
F Rebecca, by Daphne du Maurier. 1938	2,820,313
F Live and Let Die, by Ian Fleming. 1954	2,816,772
F The Naked and the Dead, by Norman Mailer. 1948	2,816,662
The New Joy of Cooking, by Irma S. Rombauer and Marion Rombauer Becker. 1931	2,816,028
F Tales of the South Pacific, by James Michener. 1947	2,814,394
F See Here, Private Hargrove, by Marion Hargrove. 1942	2,786,223
F All Quiet on the Western Front, by Erich Maria Remarque. 1929	2,778,577
F Kitty, by Rosamond Marshall. 1943	2,273,841
F Moonraker, by Ian Fleming. 1955	2,763,486
F The Best of Everything, by Rona Jaffe. 1959	2,760,000
The Service Cook Book, by Ida Bailey Allen. 1933	2,750,000
F The Group, by Mary McCarthy. 1963	2,739,427
The Pocket Book of Verse, ed. by M. E. Speare. 1940	2,719,500
F Around the World with Auntie Mame, by Patrick Dennis. 1958	2,716,816
F The Foxes of Harrow, by Frank Yerby, 1946	2,702,597
F The Spy Who Loved Me, by Ian Fleming. 1962	2,700,261
F On the Beach, by Nevil Shute. 1957	2,680,597
F Brave New World, by Aldous Huxley. 1932	2,672,065
F Not As a Stranger, by Morton Thompson. 1954	2,667,977
Please Don't Eat the Daisies, by Jean Kerr. 1957	2,655,208
F Mandingo, by Kyle Onstott. 1957	2,635,250
Better Homes and Gardens Baby Book. 1943	2,634,472
The Prophet, by Kahlil Gibran. 1923	2,632,358
F The Green Berets, by Robin Moore. 1965	2,625,000
F Diamonds Are Forever, by Ian Fleming. 1956	2,621,842
F Battle Cry, by Leon Uris. 1953	2,611,000
F Of Human Bondage, by W. Somerset Maugham. 1915	2,609,236
F Tropic of Cancer, by Henry Miller. 1961	2,600,000
F The Case of the Haunted Husband, by Erle Stanley Gardner. 1941	2,595,125
F The Case of the Baited Hook, by Erle Stanley Gardner. 1940	2,585,397
F Topper, by Thorne Smith. 1926	2,560,806
F The Case of the Rolling Bones, by Erle Stanley Gardner. 1939	2,530,964
F The Case of the Velvet Claws, by Erle Stanley Gardner. 1933	2,527,756
More Dennis the Menace, by Hank Ketcham. 1953	2,527,459

F The Chapman Report, by Irving Wallace. 1960		2,524,649
F For Your Eyes Only, by Ian Fleming. 1960		2,521,250
The Power of Positive Thinking, by Norman Vincent Peale. 1952		2,505,000
F The Case of the Stuttering Bishop, by Erle Stanley Gardner. 1936		2,499,660
F The Case of the Substitute Face, by Erle Stanley Gardner. 1938		2,472,710
How To Stop Worrying and Start Living, by Dale Carnegie. 1948		2,471,140
F The Case of the Counterfeit Eye, by Erle Stanley Gardner. 1935		2,469,306
F The Case of the Dangerous Dowager, by Erle Stanley Gardner. 1937		2,461,874
Dennis the Menace: Household Hurricane, by Hank Ketcham. 1957.		2,437,336
F This Very Earth, by Erskine Caldwell. 1948		2,435,928
F No Time for Sergeants, by Mac Hyman. 1954		2,433,154
F So Well Remembered, by James Hilton. 1945		2,414,460
F Women's Barracks, by Tereska Torres. 1950		2,409,163
F The Case of the Caretaker's Cat, by Erle Stanley Gardner. 1935		2,403,403
F The Case of the Black-Eyed Blonde, by Erle Stanley Gardner. 1944		2,403,269
Betty Crocker's Good and Easy Cookbook. 1954		2,400,000
I'll Cry Tomorrow, by Lillian Roth, Mike Connolly, and Gerold Frank. 1954		2,400,000
F The Agony and the Ecstasy, by Irving Stone. 1961		2,370,720
F The Glorious Pool, by Thorne Smith. 1934		2,358,945
The Nun's Story, by Kathryn Hulme. 1956		2,341,531
J Facts of Life and Love for Teen-Agers (Love and the Facts of Life), by Evelyn Willis Duvall and Sylvanus Duvall. 1950		2,340,000
F The Silver Chalice, by Thomas B. Costain. 1948		2,336,004
F Cannery Row, by John Steinbeck. 1945		2,330,000
F Strange Fruit, by Lillian Smith. 1944		2,318,230
F B.F.'s Daughter, by John P. Marquand. 1946		2,316,989
F The Case of the Half-Wakened Wife, by Erle Stanley Gardner. 1945		2,312,378
F The Case of the Silent Partner, by Erle Stanley Gardner. 1940		2,311,904
F The Pearl, by John Steinbeck. 1947		2,310,000
The Rise and Fall of the Third Reich, by William Shirer. 1960		2,299,778
A House Is Not a Home, by Polly Adler. 1953		2,286,000

16

The Greatest Book Ever Written, by Fulton Oursler. 1951   2,282,322

F This is Murder, by Erle Stanley Gardner. 1935   2,266,268

F The Case of the Sleepwalker's Niece, by Erle Stanley Gardner.
1936   2,262,024

F Advise and Consent, by Allen Drury. 1959   2,253,982

F Pavilion of Women, by Pearl S. Buck. 1946   2,353,453

Dennis the Menace Rides Again, by Hank Ketcham. 1955   2,251,960

F Mr. Roberts, by Thomas Heggen. 1946   2,246,396

F The Case of the Cautious Coquette, by Erle Stanley Gardner.
1949   2,244,552

Kon-Tiki, by Thor Heyerdahl. 1950   2,237,449

Hiroshima, by John Hersey. 1946   2,230,000

F Pocket Book of Erskine Caldwell Stories, ed. by Henry Seidel
Canby. 1947   2,229,000

F The Passionate Witch, by Thorne Smith. 1941   2,219,645

F Pride's Castle, by Frank Yerby. 1949   2,214,669

F The Amboy Dukes, by Irving Shulman. 1947   2,213,167

Masters of Deceit, by J. Edgar Hoover. 1958   2,192,133

F The Case of the Lame Canary, by Erle Stanley Gardner. 1934   2,184,145

The Outline of History, by H. G. Wells. 1921   2,183,109

F Leave Her To Heaven, by Ben Ames Williams. 1944   2,160,481

Radio Amateur's License Manual. 1930   2,153,000

F National Velvet, by Enid Bagnold. 1935   2,152,210

F Where Love Has Gone, by Harold Robbins. 1962   2,149,000

RCAF Exercise Book. 1962   2,147,000

F The Black Rose, by Thomas B. Costain. 1945   2,146,812

F The Case of the Careless Kitten, by Erle Stanley Gardner.
1942   2,136,177

F Rally Round the Flag, Boys! by Max Shulman. 1957   2,134,289

F Prince of Foxes, by Samuel Shellabarger. 1947   2,133,810

F The Case of the Golddigger's Purse, by Erle Stanley Gardner.
1945   2,121,708

F The Clue of the Forgotten Murder, by Erle Stanley Gardner.
1935   2,111,873

F The Young Lions, by Irwin Shaw. 1948   2,106,804

Wanted: Dennis the Menace, by Hank Ketcham. 1961   2,105,951

The Song of Our Syrian Guest, by William Allen Knight. 1903   2,102,522

F The Grapes of Wrath, by John Steinbeck. 1939   2,100,908

J Freckles, by Gene Stratton Porter. 1904   2,089,523

F Nevada, by Zane Grey. 1928   2,087,837

F The Caine Mutiny, by Herman Wouk. 1954	2,087,173
F Sanctuary, by William Faulkner. 1931	2,080,985
The Pocket Dictionary, by W. J. Pelo. 1941	2,075,000
F Seven Days in May, by Fletcher Knebel and Charles W. Bailey, II. 1962	2,073,434
Harlow, by Irving Shulman. 1964	2,068,000
Expectant Motherhood, by Nicholson J. Eastman. 1940	2,063,775
F Another Country, by James Baldwin. 1962	2,054,928
J The Girl of the Limberlost, by Gene Stratton Porter. 1909	2,053,892
Bible Readings for the Home Circle. 1914	2,051,488
English Through Pictures, by I. A. Richards and C. M. Gibson (The Pocket Book of Basic English). 1945	2,050,000
Black Like Me, by John H. Griffin. 1961	2,033,679
F The Case of the Crooked Candle, by Erle Stanley Gardner. 1944	2,029,248
The Hidden Persuaders, by Vance Packard. 1957	2,024,107
J The Little Engine That Could, by Watty Piper. 1929	2,011,251
F The Bramble Bush, by Charles Mergendahl. 1958	2,007,000
F The Case of the Borrowed Brunette, by Erle Stanley Gardner. 1946	2,006,808
F Bridge Over the River Kwai, by Pierre Boulle. 1954	2,007,000
F The Revolt of Mamie Stover, by William Bradford Huie. 1951	2,005,000
How To Prepare Your Income Tax, by David Joseph. 1941	2,000,000
My First World Atlas. 1959	2,000,000
Streams in the Desert, Vol. 1, by Mrs. Charles E. Cowman. 1931	2,000,000
F The Tight White Collar, by Grace Metallious. 1960	2,000,000
Dennis the Menace: Baby Sitter's Guide, by Hank Ketcham. 1954	1,983,000
F Desiree, by Annemarie Selinko. 1953	1,968,799
F The Case of the Empty Tin, by Erle Stanley Gardner. 1941	1,968,297
F East of Eden, by John Steinbeck. 1952	1,956,000
F The Case of the Buried Clock, by Erle Stanley Gardner. 1943	1,941,769
F Shane, by Jack Schaefer. 1954	1,933,949
Dennis the Menace vs. Everybody, by Hank Ketcham. 1956	1,932,000
F The Spy Who Came in from the Cold, by John Le Carré. 1964	1,930,000
F A Stone for Danny Fisher, by Harold Robbins. 1952	1,929,391
F The Deep, by Mickey Spillane. 1961	1,928,513
F The House of Flesh, by Bruno Fischer. 1950	1,926,110
F The Wayward Bus, by John Steinbeck. 1947	1,920,000

18

Standard Bartender's Guide, by P. G. Duffy and James A. Beard. 1955	1,919,214
The Story of Philosophy, by Will Durant. 1926	1,918,865
Comparative World Atlas. 1948	1,900,000
Langenscheidt German-English, English-German Dictionary. 1960	1,894,000
F A Rage to Live, by John O'Hara. 1949	1,888,785
F A Woman of Rome, by Alberto Moravia. 1949	1,186,465
Travels with Charley, by John Steinbeck. 1964	1,874,961
Dennis the Menace—Teacher's Threat, by Hank Ketcham. 1959	1,863,625
F The Girl Hunters, by Mickey Spillane. 1962	1,863,260
F The Case of the Lonely Heiress, by Erle Stanley Gardner. 1948	1,862,387
F From the Terrace, by John O'Hara. 1958	1,853,917
An Analysis of the Kinsey Report (About the Kinsey Report), ed. by Donald P. Geddes and Enid Currie. 1954	1,843,756
F A Farewell to Arms, by Ernest Hemingway. 1940	1,842,000
F Murder Up My Sleeve, by Erle Stanley Gardner. 1937	1,836,815
Thorndike-Barnhart Handy Pocket Dictionary, ed. by Clarence L. Barnhart. 1951	1,834,704
In This Corner—Dennis the Menace, by Hank Ketcham. 1958	1,830,060
F The Case of the Shoplifter's Shoe, by Erle Stanley Gardner. 1938	1,829,364
Peace with God, by Billy Graham. 1954	1,827,493
F The Bridge of San Luis Rey, by Thornton Wilder. 1928	(est) 1,826,348
F The Caretakers, by Dariel Telfer. 1959	1,820,308
The Making of the President, 1960, by Theodore H. White. 1961	1,819,000
F The Bishop's Jaegers, by Thorne Smith. 1932	1,818,649
F The Blackboard Jungle, by Evan Hunter. 1954	1,816,000
F Random Harvest, by James Hilton. 1941	1,805,277
F The New Adventures of Ellery Queen, by Ellery Queen. 1940	1,805,000
F Floodtide, by Frank Yerby. 1950	1,801,097
F The Call of the Wild, by Jack London. 1917	1,794,020
F The World of Suzie Wong, by Richard Mason. 1957	1,793,366
F The Case of the Turning Tide, by Erle Stanley Gardner. 1941	1,783,923
Better Homes and Gardens Garden Book. 1951	1,778,831
F The Case of the Lazy Lover, by Erle Stanley Gardner. 1947	1,777,027
One World, by Wendell L. Willkie. 1943	1,758,760
F The D.A. Calls It Murder, by Erle Stanley Gardner. 1937	1,755,011
F Jailbait, by William Bernard. 1949	1,755,000
F Don't Go Near the Water, by William Brinkley. 1956	1,754,975

F Knock on Any Door, by Willard Motley. 1947		1,751,498
Egermeier's Bible Story Book, by Elsie E. Egermeier. 1923		1,750,000
F Dinner at Antoine's, by Frances Parkinson Keyes. 1948		1,748,000
F The Damned, by John D. MacDonald. 1952		1,747,908
F This Side of Innocence, by Taylor Caldwell. 1946		1,740,930
F A Place Called Estherville, by Erskine Caldwell. 1949		1,738,597
F The Virginian, by Owen Wister. 1902		1,736,299
You Are What You Eat, by Victor H. Lindlahr. 1940		1,730,000
F The Case of the Demure Defendant, by Erle Stanley Gardner. 1956		1,728,151
F Studs Lonigan (Young Lonigan), by James T. Farrell. 1932		1,725,939
F The Fountainhead, by Ayn Rand. 1943		1,724,658
F Marjorie Morningstar, by Herman Wouk. 1955		1,720,328
F Strange Woman, by Ben Ames Williams. 1941		1,715,993
The American Everyday Dictionary, ed. by Jess Stein. 1953		1,710,000
F Duchess Hotspur, by Rosamond Marshall. 1946		1,706,019
F The Case of the Negligent Nymph, by Erle Stanley Gardner. 1950		1,703,816
F Impatient Virgin, by Donald Henderson Clarke. 1931		1,702,500
Family Reference Atlas. 1956		1,700,000
F The Case of the Dubious Bridegroom, by Erle Stanley Gardner. 1949		1,696,589
F The Case of the Vagabond Virgin, by Erle Stanley Gardner. 1948		1,692,921
F The Case of the Howling Dog, by Erle Stanley Gardner. 1934		1,691,878
F Spring Fire, by Vin Packer. 1952		1,690,126
F The Ninth Wave, by Eugene Burdick. 1956		1,686,367
J Seventeen, by Booth Tarkington. 1916		1,682,891
F The Murder of Roger Ackroyd, by Agatha Christie. 1926		1,676,588
F The Case of the One-Eyed Witness, by Erle Stanley Gardner. 1950		1,671,968
The Cross and the Switchblade, by David Wilkerson with John and Elizabeth Sherrill. 1963		1,661,578
F Candy, by Terry Southern and Mason Hoffenberg. 1964	(est)	1,660,000
F Mother, by Kathleen Norris. 1911		1,653,742
Word Power Made Easy, by Norman Lewis. 1949		1,652,235
F The Golden Hawk, by Frank Yerby. 1948		1,651,713
Better Homes and Gardens Handyman's Book. 1951		1,642,905
The Egg and I, by Betty MacDonald. 1945		1,640,314
F The Incredible Journey, by Sheila Burnford. 1961		1,640,000

F A Woman in the House, by Erskine Caldwell. 1949   1,631,630

The Settlement Cook Book, by Mrs. Simon Kander. 1930   1,626,135

F Bonjour Tristesse, by Françoise Sagan. 1955   1,625,000

F Atlas Shrugged, by Ayn Rand. 1957   1,620,464

The Longest Day, by Cornelius Ryan. 1960   1,617,462

F A Swell Looking Girl, by Erskine Caldwell. 1950   1,616,783

F Lust for Life, by Irving Stone. 1934   1,612,339

Report of the Warren Commission on the Assassination of President Kennedy. 1964   1,611,700

F The Harvester, by Gene Stratton Porter. 1911   1,611,007

F The Devil's Advocate, by Morris L. West. 1959   1,609,011

The Sea Around Us, by Rachel Carson. 1951   1,601,079

F Auntie Mame, by Patrick Dennis. 1955   1,600,000

F The Song of Bernadette, by Franz Werfel. 1942   1,594,000

The Day Christ Died, by Jim Bishop. 1957   1,591,489

O Ye Jigs & Juleps, by Virginia Cary Hudson. 1962   1,589,451

J The Cat in the Hat, by Dr. Seuss. 1957   1,588,972

J Laddie, by Gene Stratton Porter. 1913   1,586,529

The Microbe Hunters, by Paul De Kruif. 1926   1,586,260

F Scaramouche, by Rafael Sabatini. 1921   1,584,793

F The Case of the Perjured Parrot, by Erle Stanley Gardner. 1939   1,584,135

F Mildred Pierce, by James M. Cain. 1941   1,583,612

A Nation of Sheep, by William J. Lederer. 1961   1,583,561

F The Dream Merchants, by Harold Robbins. 1949   1,582,738

F Find This Woman, by Richard S. Prather. 1951   1,581,685

F The D.A. Draws a Circle, by Erle Stanley Gardner. 1939   1,578,234

F Jamaica Inn, by Daphne du Maurier. 1936   1,578,169

F The Case of the Drowsy Mosquito, by Erle Stanley Gardner. 1943   1,575,396

Only in America, by Harry Golden. 1958   1,575,304

F The Bridges at Toko Ri, by James Michener. 1953   1,573,479

F The Case of the Smoky Chimney, by Erle Stanley Gardner. 1943   1,571,570

Heloise's Housekeeping Hints, by Heloise Cruse. 1962   1,568,601

Child Behavior, by F. L. Ilg and L. B. Ames. 1955   1,563,117

Mine Enemy Grows Older, by Alexander King. 1958   1,560,980

F Giant, by Edna Ferber. 1954   1,558,878

F Sayonara, by James Michener. 1954   1,558,175

F Serenade, by James A. Cain. 1934   1,550,223

Federal Aviation Regulations and Flight Standards for Pilots, by Aeronautical Staff of Aero Publishers. 1947   (est) 1,550,000

F Yankee Pasha, by Edison Marshall. 1947	1,550,000
F The Saracen Blade, by Frank Yerby. 1949	1,548,471
Pocket Book of Boners. 1941	1,547,000
F Catch-22, by Joseph Heller. 1961	1,546,000
F Duke, by Hal Ellson. 1949	1,544,166
F Pocket Book of Modern American Short Stories, ed. by Philip Van Doren Stern. 1943	1,543,000
F Strip for Murder, by Richard S. Prather. 1955	1,540,572
The Status Seekers, by Vance Packard. 1959	1,539,524
F Christmas Holiday, by W. Somerset Maugham. 1939	1,536,793
F The Bigger They Come, by A. A. Fair. 1939	1,536,764
F The Wild Palms, by William Faulkner. 1939	1,534,371
F Bodies in Bedlam, by Richard S. Prather. 1951	1,531,786
Power Golf, by Ben Hogan. 1948	1,529,095
Calories Don't Count, by Dr. Herman Taller. 1961	1,525,000
Thorndike Barnhart Dictionary. 1951	1,525,000
The Marriage Art, by John E. Eichenlaub. 1961	1,520,000
My Life in Court, by Louis Nizer. 1962	1,516,156
F Ship of Fools, by Katherine Anne Porter. 1962	1,515,880
F Cry Tough! by Irving Shulman. 1949	1,515,825
In Tune with the Infinite, by Ralph Waldo Trine. 1897	1,507,502
Pocket Book of Cartoons, ed. by Bennett Cerf. 1943	1,507,000
Amy Vanderbilt's Complete Book of Etiquette, by Amy Vanderbilt. 1952	1,500,000
F Fail-Safe, by Eugene Burdick and Harvey Wheeler. 1962	1,500,000
Scholastic World Atlas. 1960	1,500,000
The Specialist, by Chic Sale. 1929	1,500,000
F Way of a Wanton, by Richard S. Prather. 1952	1,496,118
F Poor No More, by Robert Ruark. 1959	1,493,167
Dear Sir, by Juliet Lowell. 1944	1,488,097
F Everybody Had a Gun, by Richard S. Prather. 1951	1,480,130
Ann Pillsbury's Baking Book. 1950	1,480,000
F The Case of the Backward Mule, by Erle Stanley Gardner. 1946	1,479,047
F The Prize, by Irving Wallace. 1962	1,473,496
F The D.A. Holds a Candle, by Erle Stanley Gardner. 1938	1,469,432
F The Case of the Hesitant Hostess, by Erle Stanley Gardner. 1953	1,469,428
F The Case of the Fiery Fingers, by Erle Stanley Gardner. 1951	1,468,250
F Darling, It's Death, by Richard S. Prather. 1952	1,467,635
F Too Many Crooks (Ride a High Horse), by Richard S. Prather. 1953	1,464,357

F The King's General, by Daphne du Maurier. 1946   1,462,045

Believe It or Not, ed. by Robert L. Ripley. 1941   1,457,000

F The Case of the Fan-Dancer's Horse, by Erle Stanley Gardner.
1947   1,455,452

F Mrs. Miniver, by Jan Struther. 1940   1,455,110

J The Golden Dictionary, by Ellen Wales Walpole. 1944   1,450,000

Pocket History of the United States, by Allan Nevins and
Henry Steele Commager. 1960   1,436,000

F The Postman Always Rings Twice, by James M. Cain. 1934 1,436,000

F The Case of the Moth-Eaten Mink, by Erle Stanley Gardner.
1952   1,434,203

The Mad Reader, by E. C. Publications. 1954   1,433,477

F Lord Johnnie, by Leslie Turner White. 1949   1,432,000

F Written on the Wind, by Robert Wilder. 1946   1,430,000

F Green Dolphin Street, by Elizabeth Goudge. 1944   1,425,000

Pocket Book of War Humor, ed. by Bennett Cerf. 1943   1,422,000

F The Winter of Our Discontent, by John Steinbeck. 1961   1,421,157

F The River Road, by Frances Parkinson Keyes. 1946   1,421,000

F The D.A. Goes to Trial, by Erle Stanley Gardner. 1940   1,415,572

F Annie Jordan, by Mary Brinker Post. 1948   1,415,551

F Calamity Town, by Ellery Queen. 1942   1,412,000

F Bedelia, by Vera Caspery. 1945   1,409,790

F Peony, by Pearl S. Buck. 1948   1,406,700

F Lydia Bailey, by Kenneth Roberts. 1947   1,405,936

Dennis the Menace, by Hank Ketcham. 1952   1,400,000

F The Thin Man, by Dashiell Hammett. 1934   1,398,445

F Always Leave 'Em Dying, by Richard S. Prather. 1954   1,396,015

F The Man in the Gray Flannel Suit, by Sloan Wilson. 1955 1,396,000

F The Keys of the Kingdom, by A. J. Cronin. 1941   1,390,895

Sex and the Single Girl, by Helen Gurley Brown. 1962   1,388,320

F Farewell, My Lovely, by Raymond Chandler. 1940   1,388,220

F The Case of the Vanishing Beauty, by Richard S. Prather.
1950   1,383,440

F Mr. Adam, by Pat Frank. 1946   1,381,956

Nature Atlas, by E. L. Jordan. 1952   1,378,500

F Cocotte, by Theodore Pratt. 1951   1,377,373

F The Red Pony, by John Steinbeck. 1959   1,375,000

J Rebecca of Sunnybrook Farm, by Kate Douglas Wiggin. 1904 1,373,288

F The Case of the Drowning Duck, by Erle Stanley Gardner.
1942.   1,369,660

F Louis Beretti, by Donald Henderson Clarke. 1931   1,366,600

F The Golden Fury, by Marian Castle. 1949	1,363,909
F The Wailing Frail, by Richard S. Prather. 1956	1,362,139
F Destry Rides Again, by Max Brand. 1930	1,357,000
F The Dutch Shoe Mystery, by Ellery Queen. 1931	1,356,863
The Art of Loving, by Erich Fromm. 1956	1,354,347
Meat and Poultry Cook Book (Martha Logan's Meat Cook Book), by Thora Campbell and Beth Bailey McLean. 1942	1,354,000
F The Big Fisherman, by Lloyd C. Douglas. 1929	1,351,993
F By Love Possessed, by James Gould Cozzens. 1957	1,351,254
F The Tormented, by Theodore Pratt. 1950	1,350,620
F Joy Street, by Frances Parkinson Keyes. 1950	1,349,000
F The Night Life of the Gods, by Thorne Smith. 1931	1,338,950
F Hill Girl, by Charles Williams. 1951	1,336,425
F 13 French Street, by Gil Brewer. 1952	1,333,417
F Andersonville, by MacKinlay Kantor. 1955	1,327,895
F The Spirit of the Border, by Zane Grey. 1906	1,325,000
F The Citadel, by A. J. Cronin. 1937	1,322,402
F And Then There Were None, by Agatha Christie. 1940	1,320,000
F Never Come Morning, by Nelson Algren. 1942	1,319,610
F Rampart Street, by Everett and Olga Webber. 1948	1,318,000
F The D.A. Cooks a Goose, by Erle Stanley Gardner. 1942	1,317,137
F The Case of the Angry Mourner, by Erle Stanley Gardner. 1951	1,316,228
Point Count Bidding, by Charles H. Goren. 1949	1,314,077
F Easy to Kill, by Agatha Christie. 1939	1,312,700
F The Chinese Orange Mystery, by Ellery Queen. 1934	1,311,484
F Fires of Spring, by James Michener. 1949	1,310,000
F Light of Western Stars, by Zane Grey. 1914	1,308,883
I Never Left Home, by Bob Hope. 1944	1,308,014
F The Great Impersonation, by E. Phillips Oppenheim. 1920	1,303,028
F Ourselves to Know, by John O'Hara. 1960	1,300,201
Historical Atlas. 1949	1,300,000
Your Dream Home, by Hubbard Cobb. 1950	1,300,000
J The Real Mother Goose. 1915	1,296,140
F The Siamese Twin Mystery, by Ellery Queen. 1933	1,291,961
Cartoon Laffs, by True Magazine. 1952	1,290,453
F Bloody Sunrise, by Mickey Spillane. 1965	1,290,291
F Never Leave Me, by Harold Robbins. 1954	1,286,463
F The Trail of the Lonesome Pine, by John Fox, Jr. 1908	1,285,000
Mad Strikes Back, by E. C. Publications. 1955	1,282,414
F A Walk on the Wild Side, by Nelson Algren. 1956	1,280,000
F The Border Legion, by Zane Grey. 1916	1,279,518

24

F Came a Cavalier, by Frances Parkinson Keyes. 1947	1,279,000
F Damon Runyon Favorites. 1935	1,279,000
F The Case of the Sun-Bather's Diary, by Erle Stanley Gardner. 1955	1,278,951
F The Case of the Glamorous Ghost, by Erle Stanley Gardner. 1955	1,275,953
F The D.A. Breaks a Seal, by Erle Stanley Gardner. 1946	1,272,563
Fundamentals of Contract Bridge, by Charles Goren. 1950	1,269,007
F What Makes Sammy Run, by Budd Schulberg. 1965	1,266,957
F The Turquoise, by Anya Seton. 1946	1,266,206
F Day of Guns, by Mickey Spillane. 1964	1,265,336
Wise Garden Encyclopedia, by E. L. D. Seymour. 1936	1,265,000
F Franny and Zooey, by J. D. Salinger. 1961	1,262,676
My Flag Is Down, by James Maresca. 1948	1,261,000
F Before the Sun Goes Down, by Elizabeth M. Howard. 1946	1,260,725
F The D.A. Calls a Turn, by Erle Stanley Gardner. 1944	1,259,390
F The Cautious Amorist, by Norman Lindsay. 1932	1,253,793
Aircraft Spotters Handbook, by L. C. Gushman. 1943	1,250,000
Five Acres and Independence, by M. G. Kains. 1935	1,250,000
Modern Encyclopedia, by A. H. McDonnald. 1933	1,250,000
F Steamboat Gothic, by Frances Parkinson Keyes. 1952	1,247,000
F Peril at End House, by Agatha Christie. 1932.	1,246,693
Perma Crossword Puzzle and Word Game Dictionary, by Frank Newman. 1950	1,244,400
F The Crisis, by Winston Churchill. 1901	1,243,307
F The U.P. Trail, by Zane Grey. 1918	1,241,743
F Adventures of Ellery Queen, by Ellery Queen. 1934	1,241,550
F Topper Takes a Trip, by Thorne Smith. 1932	1,237,767
F Cats Prowl at Night, by A. A. Fair. 1958	1,239,916
Daily Strength for Daily Needs by Mary W. Tileston. 1901	1,237,060
F The Four of Hearts, by Ellery Queen. 1938	1,235,000
Washington Confidential, by Jack Lait and Lee Mortimer. 1951	1,235,000
F Singing Guns, by Max Brand. 1938	1,229,000
F I Have Gloria Kirby, by Richard Himmell. 1951	1,226,720
F The Egyptian Cross Mystery, by Ellery Queen. 1932	1,225,498
F Gentleman's Agreement, by Laura Z. Hobson. 1947	1,221,986
F The Snake, by Mickey Spillane. 1964	1,220,874
Think and Grow Rich, by Napoleon Hill. 1937	1,217,322
F The Riders of the Purple Sage, by Zane Grey. 1912	1,216,938
F Cassidy's Girl, by David Goodis. 1951	1,212,426

F Bugles in the Afternoon, by Ernest Haycox. 1944	1,211,394
F The Case of the Runaway Corpse, by Erle Stanley Gardner. 1954	1,210,994
F Golden Sleep, by Vivian Connell. 1948	1,210,900
F Halfway House, by Ellery Queen. 1936	1,209,029
F Mistress Glory, by Susan Morley. 1948	1,203,889
F Best of Damon Runyon, ed. by E. C. Bentley. 1938	1,200,190
American History Atlas. 1951	1,200,000
F David Harum, by Edward Noyes Westcott. 1900	1,200,000
F Elmer Gantry, by Sinclair Lewis. 1927	1,200,000
F Midsummer Passions. 1948	1,200,000
The New Century Dictionary of the English Language. 1927	1,200,000
Sex Habits of American Women, by Fritz Wittels, M.D. 1951	1,200,000
F The Shepherd of the Hills, by Harold Bell Wright. 1907	1,200,000
Simplified Auction Bridge, by Robert F. Foster. 1926	1,200,000
F Michael O'Halloran, by Gene Stratton Porter. 1915	1,194,440
F The Sheik, by E. M. Hull. 1921	1,194,000
Shorter Bartlett's Familiar Quotations. 1953	1,193,650
Cartoon Fun from True, by True Magazine. 1954	1,193,492
F Love Is Eternal, by Irving Stone. 1954	1,193,330
F My Cousin Rachel, by Daphne du Maurier. 1952	1,193,230
May This House Be Safe From Tigers, by Alexander King. 1960	1,191,374
Story of Bible World, by N. B. Keyes. 1957	1,190,086
Inside Mad, by E. C. Publications. 1955	1,188,395
F The Spanish Cape Mystery, by Ellery Queen. 1935	1,183,560
F Jeeves, by P. G. Wodehouse. 1924	1,183,063
F Shannon's Way, by A. J. Cronin. 1948	1,177,618
F Little Sister, by Lee Roberts. 1952	1,177,060
F The Sun Also Rises, by Ernest Hemingway. 1928	1,175,323
Household Encyclopedia, by Sylvia K. Mager. 1960	1,173,500
F The Big Sky, by A. B. Guthrie, Jr. 1947	1,170,042
F Something of Value, by Robert Ruark. 1955	1,168,181
Modern Home Medical Advisor, ed. by Morris Fishbein. 1935	1,165,499
Six Minutes a Day to Perfect Spelling, by Harry Shefter. 1954	1,163,900
F The Street, by Ann Petry. 1946	1,153,749
Practice for the Army Tests, by David Turner. 1942	1,152,000
F Judge Me Not, by John D. MacDonald. 1951	1,151,029
Modern Home Physician, by Victor Robinson, M.D. 1934	1,150,000
J Cat in Hat Comes Back, by Dr. Seuss. 1958	1,148,669

F Drum, by Kyle Onstott. 1962	1,148,260
F Give 'Em the Axe, by A. A. Fair. 1944	1,146,449
F The French Powder Mystery, by Ellery Queen. 1930	1,143,675
F The Tragedy of X, by Barnaby Ross (Ellery Queen). 1932	1,142,000
F The Shoes of the Fisherman, by Morris West. 1963	1,139,572
F Sangaree, by Frank G. Slaughter. 1948	1,138,891
F The Case of the Green-Eyed Sister, by Erle Stanley Gardner. 1953	1,137,563
F Charlie Chan Carries On, by Earl Derr Biggers. 1930	1,136,917
F Owls Don't Blink, by A. A. Fair. 1942	1,132,856
F The Brass Cupcake, by John D. MacDonald. 1950	1,131,270
F Three's a Shroud, by Richard S. Prather. 1957	1,131,018
F Some Came Running (abridged), by James Jones. 1958	1,128,840
F The Interns, by Richard Frede. 1960	1,126,365
F Spill the Jackpot, by A. A. Fair. 1941	1,123,136
Pocket Book of Ogden Nash. 1955	1,121,000
French Through Pictures, by I. A. Richards, M. H. Ilsley and C. Gibson. 1959	1,120,000
F Take a Murder, Darling, by Richard S. Prather. 1958	1,119,134
F No Adam in Eden, by Grace Metalious. 1963	1,118,800
Death of a Salesman, by Arthur Miller. 1949	1,117,418
P.T. 109—JFK in World War II, by Robert J. Donovan. 1961	1,115,657
F Bad Girl, by Vina Delmar. 1928	1,111,520
F Tomboy, by Hal Ellson. 1950	1,110,000
F Boys and Girls Together, by William Goldman. 1964	1,108,000
F Wildfire, by Zane Grey. 1917	1,107,754
Peace of Mind, by Joshua L. Liebman. 1946	1,107,064
The Fifty Minute Hour, by Robert Lindner. 1950	1,104,600
Appleton's English-Spanish, Spanish-English Dictionary, by Arturo Cuyas. 1903	1,100,000
Atlas of Bible Lands. 1949	1,100,000
F Fifty Great Short Stories, ed. by Milton Crane. 1952	1,100,000
F The Little Shepherd of Kingdom Come, by John Fox, Jr. 1903	1,100,000
Look Younger, Live Longer, by Gayelord Hauser. 1951	1,100,000
F The Other Room, by Worth T. Hedden. 1947	1,100,000
Rand McNally Dollar World Atlas. 1949	1,100,000
Your Own Book of Campcraft, by Catherine T. Hammett. 1950	1,099,270
F The Rosary, by Florence Barclay. 1910	1,099,000
F The Maltese Falcon, by Dashiell Hammett. 1930	1,098,001
The Sexual Side of Marriage, by Max J. Exner, M.D. 1932	1,097,716

27

F A Portrait of the Artist as a Young Man, by James Joyce. 1916   1,095,155
Complete Home Handyman's Guide, by Hubbard Cobb. 1948   1,095,000
F Fools Die on Friday, by A. A. Fair. 1947   1,094,941
F The Case of the Terrified Typist, by Erle Stanley Gardner. 1956   1,090,383
F Rawhide Range, by Ernest Haycox. 1952   1,090,000
F Rainbow Trail, by Zane Grey. 1915   1,089,767
F The Case of the Screaming Woman, by Erle Stanley Gardner. 1957   1,088,744
F Mystery of the Blue Train, by Agatha Christie. 1941   1,087,000
F Dagger of Flesh, by Richard S. Prather. 1961   1,083,623
Sunset Western Garden Book, by Editors of Sunset Magazine. 1933   1,081,906
God Is My Co-Pilot, by General Robert L. Scott. 1943   1,081,810
F Turn On the Heat, by A. A. Fair. 1940   1,079,655
F Armageddon, by Leon Uris. 1964   1,079,000
Crusade in Europe, by Dwight E. Eisenhower. 1948   1,076,380
The Greek Way, by Edith Hamilton. 1930   1,077,453
F The Saint Goes West, by Leslie Charteris. 1942   1,070,392
F Bedrooms Have Windows, by A. A. Fair. 1949   1,068,363
F Crows Can't Count, by A. A. Fair, 1946   1,068,139
F Hungry Hill, by Daphne du Maurier. 1943   1,068,004
The Pocket Entertainer, ed. by Shirley Cunningham. 1942   1,068,000
F Strangers When We Meet, by Evan Hunter. 1958   1,063,000
J Pollyanna, by Eleanor H. Porter. 1913   1,059,000
A Man Called Peter, by Catherine Marshall. 1951   1,058,890
F Spoonhandle, by Ruth Moore. 1946   1,057,837
F Ramrod, by Luke Short. 1943   1,056,992
F Nine Coaches Waiting, by Mary Stewart. 1959   1,056,196
Utterly Mad, by E. C. Publications. 1956   1,055,923
F The Beach House, by Stephen Longstreet. 1952   1,055,000
Anthology of Robert Frost's Poems, ed. by Louis Untermeyer. 1949   1,054,910
Immortal Poems of the English Language, ed. by Oscar Williams. 1952   1,054,500
New Pocket Thesaurus in Dictionary Form (abridged) by Norman Lewis. 1961   1,053,700
Strength for Service to God and Country, by Norman F. Nygaard. 1942   1,050,000
F The Case of the Daring Decoy, by Erle Stanley Gardner. 1957   1,049,006
F Lusty Wind for Carolina, by Inglis Fletcher. 1944   1,048,247

F The Case of the Long-Legged Models, by Erle Stanley Gardner. 1958 — 1,047,991

F Some Women Won't Wait, by A. A. Fair. 1953 — 1,045,981

F My Friend Flicka, by Mary O'Hara. 1941 — 1,045,000

F Pitcairn's Island, by Charles Nordhoff and James Norman Hall. 1934 — 1,040,000

F The Dragon's Teeth, by Ellery Queen. 1939 — 1,039,000

F Lie Down Killer, by Richard F. Prather. 1961 — 1,034,716

F Tarzan of the Apes, by Edgar Rice Burroughs. 1914 — 1,033,525

Their Finest Hour, by Sir Winston Churchill. 1949 — 1,032,681

F The Deer Park, by Norman Mailer. 1955 — 1,031,180

F The $100 Misunderstanding, by Robert Gover. 1962 — 1,028,109

F The Case of the Fugitive Nurse, by Erle Stanley Gardner. 1954 — 1,028,000

Better Homes and Gardens Barbecue Book. 1956 — 1,027,505

F Scrambled Yeggs, by Richard S. Prather. 1958 — 1,026,322

F High Towers, by Thomas B. Costain. 1949 — 1,021,233

F I Can Get It For You Wholesale, by Jerome Weidman. 1962 — 1,018,942

All the Ship's At Sea, by William J. Lederer. 1950 — 1,018,000

F Spencer Brade, M.D., by Frank Slaughter. 1942 — 1,017,351

F Have Gat—Will Travel, by Richard S. Prather. 1957 — 1,016,784

Gardening: A Complete Guide, by Montague Free. 1947 — 1,011,000

F Harrison High, by John Farris. 1959 — 1,010,000

F Gold Comes in Bricks, by A. A. Fair. 1940 — 1,010,437

Nobody Knows My Name, by James Baldwin. 1961 — 1,010,000

F The Sun Is My Undoing, by Marguerite Steen. 1941 — 1,010,000

F Louisville Saturday, by Margaret Long. 1950 — 1,009,606

F Bats Fly at Dusk, by A. A. Fair. 1942 — 1,008,937

F Scarlet Sister Mary, by Julia Peterkin. 1928 — 1,007,997

F Beware the Curves, by A. A. Fair. 1956 — 1,007,136

Great Controversy, by Ellen G. White. 1926 — 1,005,381

Rascal, by Sterling North. 1963 — 1,005,374

F Fast Company, by Marco Page. 1938 — 1,005,000

J Winnie-the-Pooh, by A. A. Milne. 1926 — 1,005,000

I Kid You Not, by Jack Paar. 1960 — 1,002,754

Pocket Book of Crossword Puzzles, by Margaret Petherbridge. 1943 — 1,001,000

Happiness Is a Warm Puppy, by Charles M. Schulz. 1962 — 1,000,054

F Anthony Adverse, by Hervey Allen. 1933 — 1,000,000

Brave Men, by Ernie Pyle. 1944 — 1,000,000

Etiquette, by Emily Post. 1922 — 1,000,000

The Fire Next Time, by James Baldwin. 1963		1,000,000
A Heap O'Livin', by Edgar Guest. 1916		1,000,000
J Little Black Sambo, by Helen Bannerman. 1899	(est)	1,000,000
F The Moneyman, by Thomas B. Costain. 1947		1,000,000
J Pollyanna Grows Up, by Eleanor H. Porter. 1915		1,000,000
F Short Story Masterpieces, ed. by Robert Penn Warren and Albert Erskine. 1958		1,000,000
The Simple Life, by Charles Wagner. 1901		1,000,000
F Stiletto, by Harold Robbins. 1960		1,000,000
Twixt Twelve and Twenty, by Pat Boone. 1957		1,000,000
F The Web of Days, by Edna L. Lee. 1947		1,000,000
Will Rogers, by Patrick J. O'Brien. 1935		1,000,000
F Youngblood Hawke, by Herman Wouk. 1962		1,000,000

BEST SELLERS

1895-1965

HARDBOUND

These are the books, published in the past seventy years, which, in their hardcover editions, have sold 750,000 copies or more. Seventy-two new titles have been added to the list that was published ten years ago in the previous edition of this volume. There are three new books which have sold over two million; five have moved up into that range. There are ten new titles in the group of one million or more.

It is quite remarkable that there are so many additions. The big sales, in the millions, of hardbound books, especially novels, occurred during the period of World War II and the few years following, when paper restrictions were on and the book clubs, because their paper quotas did not have to be extended over many titles as did those of the trade publishers, were able to market millions of books. These were also the years of other wartime restrictions and before television. People stayed home to read!

Sales through the Literary Guild and the Dollar Book Club raised high the sales figures of many popular novelists such as Frank Yerby and Frances Parkinson Keyes. The Book-of-the-Month Club, founded in 1926, had acquired 50,000 members by 1930 and about 75,000 by 1935. In 1946 its membership was almost 900,000. That was its peak, each year since being marked by a decline.

Among the books which have gone over the 750,000-mark in the past ten years are many well-established older books, some new ones, very few of them fiction. Outstanding novel added to the list was *Dr. Zhivago*. There were several children's books that climbed up, two of them published many years ago, a number of them published since 1955. A book of poetry which has been adding to its sales over the years to attain bestseller status was *The Prophet*. By far the largest number of new hardcover best sellers was in the reference book field.

These titles are arranged by order of sales. The names of the original publishers and the dates of original publication in the United States are included. If the original publisher has gone out of business but the book is still in print, the name of the present publisher is given. If the book is

31

out of print, the name of the original publisher is stated, whether or not the firm is still in existence.

Better Homes and Gardens Cook Book. 1930 Meredith	11,325,299
Betty Crocker's New Picture Cookbook. 1950 McGraw-Hill	(est) 7,000,000
F Gone with the Wind, by Margaret Mitchell. 1937 Macmillan	5,170,004
The American Woman's Cook Book, ed. by Ruth Berolzheimer. 1939 Doubleday	3,549,276
F The Winthrop Woman, by Anya Seton. 1958 Houghton Mifflin	3,347,901
The Boston Cooking School Cook Book, by Fannie Farmer. 1896 Little, Brown	3,300,744
The Story of the Bible by Jesse Lyman Hurlbut. 1904 Winston	3,000,000
J The Wonderful Wizard of Oz, by L. Frank Baum. 1900 Bobbs-Merrill	2,834,049
The New Joy of Cooking, by Irma S. Rombauer and Marion Becker Rombauer. 1931 Bobbs-Merrill	2,816,028
F The Robe, by Lloyd C. Douglas. 1942 Houghton Mifflin	2,724,688
Better Homes and Gardens Baby Book. 1943 Meredith	2,634,472
The Prophet, by Kahlil Gibran. 1923 Knopf	2,632,358
Columbia Viking Desk Encyclopedia. 1953 Viking	2,565,899
The Power of Positive Thinking, by Norman Vincent Peale. 1952 Prentice-Hall	2,505,000
F A Tree Grows in Brooklyn, by Betty Smith. 1943 Harper	2,487,740
Betty Crocker's Good and Easy Cookbook. 1954 Simon & Schuster	2,400,000
F The Silver Chalice, by Thomas B. Costain. 1948 Doubleday	2,236,004
F The Black Rose, by Thomas B. Costain. 1945 Doubleday	2,146,812
The Song of Our Syrian Guest, by William Allen Knight. 1903 United Church Press	2,102,522
J Freckles, by Gene Stratton Porter. 1904 Doubleday	2,089,523
The Outline of History, by H. G. Wells. 1921 Macmillan	2,070,170
Expectant Motherhood. Nicholson J. Eastman. 1940 Little, Brown	2,063,775
J The Girl of the Limberlost, by Gene Stratton Porter. 1909 Doubleday	2,053,892
F Leave Her to Heaven, by Ben Ames Williams. 1944 Houghton Mifflin	2,031,210
J The Little Engine That Could, by Watty Piper. 1929 Platt & Munk	2,011,251
F In His Steps, by Charles Monroe Sheldon. 1897 Grosset & Dunlap et. al.	(est) 2,000,000

F The Razor's Edge, by W. Somerset Maugham. 1944 Doubleday   1,920,505
F The Call of the Wild, by Jack London. 1917 Macmillan   1,794,020
30 Days to a More Powerful Vocabulary, by Wilfred J. Funk and Norman Lewis. 1922 Funk & Wagnalls   1,789,161
Better Homes and Gardens Garden Book. 1951 Meredith   1,778,831
Egermeier's Bible Story Book, by Elsie E. Egermeier. 1923 Warner Press   1,750,000
F Dinner at Antoine's, by Frances Parkinson Keyes. 1948 Messner   1,748,000
The American Everyday Dictionary, ed. by Jess Stein. 1953 Random House   1,710,000
Family Reference Atlas. 1956 Hammond   1,700,000
F Not As a Stranger, by Morton Thompson. 1954 Scribner   1,700,000
F The Caine Mutiny, by Herman Wouk. 1952 Doubleday   1,696,989
F The Foxes of Harrow, by Frank Yerby. 1946 Dial Press   1,671,697
F Forever Amber, by Kathleen Winsor. 1944 Macmillan   1,652,837
F The Golden Hawk, by Frank Yerby. 1948 Dial Press   1,648,064
Better Homes and Gardens Handyman's Book. 1951 Meredith   1,642,905
F The Virginian, by Owen Wister. 1902 Macmillan   1,636,299
How To Win Friends and Influence People, by Dale Carnegie. 1937 Simon & Schuster   1,627,511
The Settlement Cook Book, by Mrs. Simon Kander. 1930 Simon & Schuster   1,626,135
F The Harvester, by Gene Stratton Porter. 1911 Doubleday   1,611,007
J The Cat in the Hat, by Dr. Seuss. 1957 Random House   1,588,972
J Laddie, by Gene Stratton Porter. 1913 Doubleday   1,586,529
The Greatest Story Ever Told, by Fulton Oursler. 1949 Doubleday   1,553,988
F Mother, by Kathleen Norris. 1911 Doubleday   1,553,742
F The Vixens, by Frank Yerby. 1947 Dial Press   1,524,123
In Tune with the Infinite, by Ralph Waldo Trine. 1897 Bobbs-Merrill   1,507,502
Amy Vanderbilt's Complete Book of Etiquette, by Amy Vanderbilt. 1952 Doubleday   1,500,000
The Specialist, by Chic Sale. 1929. Specialist Publishing Co.   1,500,000
F All Quiet on the Western Front, by Erich Maria Remarque. 1929 Little, Brown   1,453,351
F Strange Woman, by Ben Ames Williams. 1941 Houghton Mifflin   1,443,524
F Green Dolphin Street, by Elizabeth Goudge. 1944 Coward-McCann   1,425,000
F Lydia Bailey, by Kenneth Roberts. 1947 Doubleday   1,405,936
Nature Atlas, by E. L. Jordan. 1952 Hammond   1,378,500
F The King's General, by Daphne du Maurier. 1946 Doubleday   1,362,045

J	Rebecca of Sunnybrook Farm, by Kate Douglas Wiggin. 1904 Houghton Mifflin	1,357,714
F	Joy Street, by Frances Parkinson Keyes. 1950 Messner	1,349,000
F	Annie Jordan, by Mary Brinker Post. 1948 Doubleday	1,315,551
	Your Dream Home, by Hubbard Cobb. 1950 W. H. Wise	1,300,000
J	The Real Mother Goose. 1915 Rand McNally	1,296,140
F	The Trail of the Lonesome Pine, by John Fox, Jr. 1908 Scribner	1,285,000
F	The Keys of the Kingdom, by A. J. Cronin. 1941 Little, Brown	1,284,198
F	Came a Cavalier, by Frances Parkinson Keyes. 1947 Messner	1,279,000
F	This Side of Innocence, by Taylor Caldwell. 1946 Scribner	1,276,000
	Wise Garden Encyclopedia, by E. L. D. Seymour. 1936 W. H. Wise	1,265,000
F	Before the Sun Goes Down, by Elizabeth M. Howard. 1946 Doubleday	1,260,725
F	Desiree, by Annemarie Selinko. 1953 Morrow	1,251,709
	Modern Encyclopedia, by A. H. McDonnald. 1933 W. H. Wise	1,250,000
F	Steamboat Gothic, by Frances Parkinson Keyes. 1952 Messner	1,247,000
F	Mutiny on the Bounty, by Charles Nordhoff and James Norman Hall. 1932 Little, Brown	1,246,694
F	The Crisis, by Winston Churchill. 1901 Macmillan	1,243,307
	The Greatest Book Ever Written, by Fulton Oursler. 1951 Doubleday	1,237,887
	The Egg and I, by Betty MacDonald. 1945 Lippincott	1,228,737
F	Gentleman's Agreement, by Laura Z. Hobson. 1947 Simon & Schuster	1,221,986
F	The Riders of the Purple Sage, by Zane Grey. 1912 Harper	1,215,938
	Daily Strength for Daily Needs, by Mary W. Tileston. 1901 Little, Brown and Revell	1,212,060
F	David Harum, by Edward Noyes Westcott. 1900 Appleton	1,200,000
	Story of Bible World, by N. B. Keyes. 1957 Hammond	1,190,086
	The New Century Dictionary of the English Language. 1927 Appleton-Century	1,200,000
F	The Shepherd of the Hills, by Harold Bell Wright. 1907 Appleton	1,200,000
F	Rebecca, by Daphne du Maurier. 1938 Doubleday	1,194,587
F	Michael O'Halloran, by Gene Stratton Porter. 1915 Doubleday	1,194,440
F	The Sheik, by E. M. Hull. 1921 Dodd, Mead	1,194,000
F	The River Road, by Frances Parkinson Keyes. 1946 Messner	1,168,000
	Modern Home Medical Advisor, ed. by Morris Fishbein. 1935 Doubleday	1,165,499

F The Royal Box, by Frances Parkinson Keyes. 1954 Messner   1,156,000

F Shannon's Way, by A. J. Cronin. 1948 Little, Brown   1,155,018

Modern Home Physician, by Victor Robinson, M.D. 1934
W. H. Wise   1,150,000

J The Cat in the Hat Comes Back, by Dr. Seuss. 1958 Random
House   1,148,669

F The Good Earth, by Pearl S. Buck. 1931 John Day   1,115,500

F Light of Western Stars, by Zane Grey. 1914 Harper   1,112,697

F Wildfire, by Zane Grey. 1917 Harper   1,107,754

Kids Say the Darndest Things, by Art Linkletter. 1957 Prentice-Hall   1,107,318

Peace of Mind, by Joshua L. Liebman. 1946 Simon & Schuster   1,107,064

Appleton's English-Spanish, Spanish-English Dictionary, by
Arturo Cuyas. 1903 Appleton-Century   1,100,000

Rand McNally Dollar World Atlas. 1949 Rand, McNally   1,100,000

F The Little Shepherd of Kingdom Come, by John Fox, Jr. 1903
Scribner   1,100,000

F The Rosary, by Florence Barclay. 1910 Putnam   1,099,000

Complete Home Handyman's Guide, by Hubbard Cobb. 1948
W. H. Wise   1,095,000

F Love Is Eternal, by Irving Stone. 1954 Doubleday   1,093,330

F My Cousin Rachel, by Daphne du Maurier. 1952 Doubleday   1,093,230

How To Stop Worrying and Start Living, by Dale Carnegie.
1948 Simon & Schuster   1,090,000

F So Well Remembered, by James Hilton. 1945 Little, Brown   1,083,409

Crusade in Europe, by Dwight D. Eisenhower. 1948 Doubleday   1,076,380

F Pride's Castle, by Frank Yerby. 1949 Dial Press   1,073,679

F Hungry Hill, by Daphne du Maurier. 1943 Doubleday   1,068,004

J Pollyanna, by Eleanor H. Porter. 1913 Page   1,059,000

Strength for Service to God and Country, by Norman F.
Nygaard. 1942 Abingdon Press   1,050,000

F Lusty Wind for Carolina, by Inglis Fletcher. 1944 Bobbs-Merrill   1,048,247

Five Acres and Independence, by M. G. Kains. 1935 Greenberg   1,044,000

F Doctor Zhivago, by Boris Pasternak. 1958 Pantheon Books   1,042,520

Their Finest Hour, by Sir Winston Churchill. 1949 Houghton
Mifflin   1,032,681

Better Homes and Gardens Barbecue Book. 1956 Meredith   1,027,505

Calories Don't Count. Dr. Herman Taller. 1961. Simon &
Schuster   1,025,000

Kon-Tiki, by Thor Heyerdahl. 1950 Rand McNally 1,022,949
F High Towers, by Thomas B. Costain. 1949 Doubleday 1,021,233
F Topper, by Thorne Smith. 1926 Doubleday 1,018,806
F B. F.'s Daughter, by John P. Marquand. 1946 Little, Brown 1,013,977
The Day Christ Died, by Jim Bishop. 1957 Harper 1,012,677
F The Sun Is My Undoing, by Marguerite Steen. 1941 Viking 1,010,000
F Scarlet Sister Mary, by Julia Peterkin. 1928 Bobbs-Merrill 1,007,997
Great Controversy, by Ellen G. White. 1926 Review & Herald 1,005,381
J Winnie-the-Pooh, by A. A. Milne. 1926 Dutton 1,005,000
Happiness Is a Warm Puppy, by Charles M. Schulz. 1962 Determined Productions 1,000,054
F Anthony Adverse, by Hervey Allen. 1933 Rinehart 1,000,000
Brave Men, by Ernie Pyle. 1944 Holt 1,000,000
Etiquette, by Emily Post. 1922 Funk & Wagnalls (est) 1,000,000
A Heap o' Livin', by Edgar Guest. 1916 Reilly & Lee (est) 1,000,000
J Little Black Sambo, by Helen Bannerman. 1899 Lippincott (est) 1,000,000
A Message to Garcia, by Elbert Hubbard. 1898 Roycroft (est) 1,000,000
101 Famous Poems, comp. by R. J. Cook. 1916 Regnery (est) 1,000,000
J Pollyanna Grows Up, by Eleanor H. Porter. 1915 Page 1,000,000
The Simple Life, by Charles Wagner. 1901 Doubleday 1,000,000
F The Song of Bernadette, by Franz Werfel. 1942 Viking 1,000,000
F The Web of Days, by Edna L. Lee. 1947 Appleton-Century 1,000,000
Will Rogers, by Patrick J. O'Brien. 1935 Winston 1,000,000
F Yankee Pasha, by Edison Marshall. 1947 Farrar, Straus 1,000,000
A Man Called Peter, by Catherine Marshall. 1951 McGraw-Hill 998,890
F Floodtide, by Frank Yerby. 1950 Dial Press 993,726
The Story of the Other Wise Man, by Henry Van Dyke. 1895 Harper (est) 989,088
The Culbertson Summary, by Ely Culbertson. 1935 Winston 983,628
F The Golden Fury, by Marian Castle. 1949 Morrow 969,499
Here Is Your War, by Ernie Pyle. 1943 Holt 967,000
J Better Homes and Gardens Story Book. 1951 Meredith 964,770
F Lone Star Ranger, by Zane Grey. 1915 Harper 960,482
History of the World War, by Richard J. Beamish and F. A. March. Winston 960,000
Better Homes and Gardens Flower Arranging. 1957 Meredith 959,551
Grand Alliance, by Sir Winston Churchill. 1950 Houghton Mifflin 956,579
F My Friend Flicka, by Mary O'Hara. 1941 Lippincott 955,000

F The Prince of Foxes, by Samuel Shellabarger. 1947 Little, Brown   954,021

F Pavilion of Women, by Pearl S. Buck. 1946 John Day   953,500

Land Birds East of the Rockies, by Chester A. Reed. 1906 Doubleday   953,173

F Desert Gold, by Zane Grey. 1913 Harper   950,632

J One Fish, Two Fish, Red Fish, Blue Fish, by Dr. Seuss. 1960 Random House   947,971

Hinge of Fate, by Sir Winston Churchill. 1950 Houghton Mifflin   930,616

F The Calling of Dan Matthews, by Harold Bell Wright. 1916 Appleton   925,000

F The Great Impersonation, by E. Phillips Oppenheim. 1920 Little, Brown   912,782

Triumph and Tragedy, by Sir Winston Churchill. 1953 Houghton Mifflin   907,413

Profiles in Courage, by John F. Kennedy. 1956 Harper   904,324

F The Winning of Barbara Worth, by Harold Bell Wright. 1911 Appleton   900,000

F The Mysterious Rider, by Zane Grey. 1921 Harper   898,031

F The Cleft Rock, by Alice Tisdale Hobart. 1948 Bobbs-Merrill   887,200

F Rainbow Trail, by Zane Grey. 1915 Harper   885,563

F Pilgrim's Inn, by Elizabeth Goudge. 1944 Coward-McCann   885,000

Closing the Ring, by Sir Winston Churchill. 1951 Houghton Mifflin   883,957

F Thunderhead, by Mary O'Hara. 1943 Lippincott   880,000

F The Chain, by Paul Wellman. 1949 Doubleday   878,813

The Story of Philosophy, by Will Durant. 1926 Simon & Schuster   874,975

Abundant Living, by E. Stanley Jones. 1942 Abingdon Press   873,534

F Heritage of the Desert, by Zane Grey. 1910 Harper   873,400

F Scaramouche, by Rafael Sabatini. 1921 Houghton Mifflin   862,901

F The Big Fisherman, by Lloyd C. Douglas. 1948 Houghton Mifflin   862,764

F The Moneyman, by Thomas B. Costain. 1947 Doubleday   855,944

F Green Light, by Lloyd C. Dougles. 1935 Houghton Mifflin   854,828

F Bride of Fortune, by Harnett Kane. 1948 Doubleday   853,672

Better Homes and Gardens Sewing Book. 1961. Meredith   852,222

J My First Book About Jesus, by Mary Alice Jones. 1953 Rand, McNally   850,000

The Gathering Storm, by Sir Winston Churchill. 1948 Houghton Mifflin   849,094

F The Private Life of Helen of Troy, by John Erskine. 1925 Bobbs-
Merrill   844,000

F To the Last Man, by Zane Grey. 1922 Harper   842,946

F The Parasites, by Daphne du Maurier. 1950 Doubleday   841,715

J Green Eggs and Ham, by Dr. Seuss. 1960 Random House   839,887

They Were Expendable, by W. L. White. 1942 Harcourt,
Brace   830,851

Better Homes and Gardens Salad Book. 1958 Meredith   827,953

F The Chinese Parrot, by Earl Derr Biggers. 1940 Bobbs-Merrill   812,383

Pictorial History World War II. 1944 W. H. Wise   811,000

J Just So Stories, by Rudyard Kipling. 1902 Doubleday   810,788

Amateur Builder's Handbook, by Hubbard Cobb. 1950 W. H.
Wise   810,000

J Penrod, by Booth Tarkington. 1914 Doubleday   808,916

F For Whom the Bell Tolls, by Ernest Hemingway. 1940 Scribner   805,400

F Impatient Virgin, by Donald Henderson Clarke. 1931 Vanguard
Press   802,500

F The Circular Staircase, by Mary Roberts Rinehart. 1908 Rinehart   800,000

Classics World Atlas. 1951 Hammond   800,000

Diet and Health, by Lulu Hunt Peters. 1922 Reilly & Lee   800,000

J When We Were Very Young, by A. A. Milne. 1924 Dutton   800,000

The Royal Road to Romance, by Richard Halliburton. 1925
Bobbs-Merrill   795,000

Better Homes and Gardens Meat Cook Book. 1959 Meredith   791,122

F The Peacock Sheds His Tail, by Alice Tisdale Hobart. 1945   (est) 791,000

F The Miracle of the Bells, by Russell Janney. 1946 Prentice-
Hall   (est) 790,000

F Parris Mitchell of Kings Row, by Katherine Bellamann, 1948
Simon & Schuster   788,634

Better Homes and Gardens Decorating Book. 1956 Meredith   784,686

J A Friend Is Someone Who Likes You, by Joan Walsh Anglund.
1958 Harcourt, Brace   784,265

Illustrated World Atlas. 1956 Hammond   780,000

F Richard Carvel, by Winston Churchill. 1899 Macmillan   780,000

F The Border Legion, by Zane Grey. 1916 Harper   779,854

F The View from Pompey's Head, by Hamilton Basso. 1954
Doubleday   774,533

F The Man of the Forest, by Zane Grey. 1920 Harper   774,500

F The Case of the Cautious Coquette, by Erle Stanley Gardner.
1949 Morrow   770,552

The Gold Cook Book, by Louis P. De Gouy. 1947 Chilton   769,000
The Book of Etiquette, by Lillian Eichler. 1922 Doubleday   756,432
John Brown's Body, by Stephen Vincent Benét. 1928 Holt,
Rinehart & Winston   755,630
F The U.P. Trail, by Zane Grey. 1918 Harper   751,926
F Eben Holden, by Irving Bacheller. 1900 Lothrop, Lee &
Shepard   750,000
Our Hearts Were Young and Gay, by Cornelia Otis Skinner
and Emily Kimbrough. 1942 Dodd, Mead   (est) 750,000
F The Re-Creation of Brian Kent, by Harold Bell Wright. 1919
Appleton   750,000
F Tarzan of the Apes, by Edgar Rice Burroughs. 1914 McClurg   750,000

BEST SELLERS

1895-1965

PAPERBACK

This third list of best sellers includes books which have sold at least one million copies in paperbound editions, whether reprints or originals. Names of the paperback publishers are given, but not those of the publishers of the hardbound editions, if the books are reprints. When the title was issued only by the publisher of the paperback, this is indicated by "(orig.)" after the publisher's name.

This list has more than doubled, almost tripled, since its first publication in *Sixty Years of Best Sellers*. Ten years ago the paperback boom was getting into full swing. The price of most novels and detective stories was still 25 cents. By 1965 very few novels were priced at 35 cents, more at 50 and 60 cents, and higher. As in the case of the hardbound best sellers there was a big increase in the number of paperback reference books. Many of these are priced at $2, $3, and more.

Unlike hardcover best sellers, which showed little increase in the number of new best-selling novels, these paperbacks have brought many good novelists, both old and new, into the million-copy range. Among them are J. D. Salinger, Harper Lee, Henry Miller, Aldous Huxley, Mary McCarthy, Sinclair Lewis, Thornton Wilder, and James Baldwin.

Pocket Book of Baby and Child Care, by Benjamin Spock.
Pocket Books   18,601,822

Pocket Atlas. Hammond (orig)   11,000,000

F Peyton Place, by Grace Metalious. Pocket Books   9,317,483

F God's Little Acre, by Erskine Caldwell. New American Library   8,040,212

F Lady Chatterley's Lover, by D. H. Lawrence. New American
Library and Pocket Books   6,314,580

F In His Steps, by Charles Monroe Sheldon. Advance Publish-
ing Co. (orig)   (est) 6,000,000

F I, the Jury, by Mickey Spillane. New American Library   5,383,105

English-Spanish, Spanish-English Dictionary, comp. by Carlos Castillo and Otto F. Bond. Pocket Books — 5,892,000

F The Carpetbaggers, by Harold Robbins. Pocket Books — 5,442,000

Roget's Pocket Thesaurus. Pocket Books — 5,416,857

F To Kill a Mockingbird, by Harper Lee. Popular Library — 5,100,000

F The Big Kill, by Mickey Spillane. New American Library — 5,081,472

F Exodus, by Leon Uris. Bantam — 5,000,000

Modern World Atlas. Hammond (orig.) — 5,000,000

101 Famous Poems, comp. by R. J. Cook. Regnery — 5,000,000

How To Win Friends and Influence People, by Dale Carnegie. Pocket Books — 4,950,803

F My Gun Is Quick, by Mickey Spillane. New American Library — 4,911,074

F One Lonely Night, by Mickey Spillane. New American Library — 4,868,563

F The Long Wait, by Mickey Spillane. New American Library — 4,824,966

F Tragic Ground, by Erskine Caldwell. New American Library — 4,770,265

F Kiss Me, Deadly, by Mickey Spillane. New American Library — 4,747,044

F Vengeance Is Mine, by Mickey Spillane. New American Library — 4,633,234

F The Catcher in the Rye, by J. D. Salinger. New American Library and Bantam — 4,566,499

The Pocket Cook Book, by Elizabeth Woody. Pocket Books (orig) — 4,466,200

F Return to Peyton Place, by Grace Metalious. Dell — 4,400,000

F Thunderball, by Ian Fleming. New American Library — 4,186,935

F 1984, by George Orwell. New American Library — 4,082,257

F Journeyman, by Erskine Caldwell. New American Library — 3,909,655

F Never Love a Stranger, by Harold Robbins. Pocket Books and Bantam — 3,770,440

The Radio Amateur's Handbook. American Radio Relay League — (est.) 3,724,000

F Goldfinger, by Ian Fleming. New American Library — 3,632,411

F The Ugly American, by William J. Lederer and Eugene L. Burdick. Crest — 3,612,382

F Trouble in July, by Erskine Caldwell. New American Library — 3,578,018

The Diary of a Young Girl, by Anne Frank. Pocket Books — 3,538,648

F Butterfield 8, by John O'Hara. Bantam and Avon — 3,500,000

F Hawaii, by James A. Michener. Bantam — 3,500,000

F Tobacco Road, by Erskine Caldwell. New American Library — 3,469,851

F Pocket Book of Short Stories, ed. by M. E. Speare. Pocket Books (orig) — 3,445,000

Larousse French-English, English-French Dictionary. Pocket Books — 3,426,000

41

F Lolita, by Vladimir Nabokov. Crest 3,400,000
F Duel in the Sun, by Niven Busch. Popular Library 3,300,000
F From Russia with Love, by Ian Fleming. New American
Library 3,252,193
F You Only Live Twice, by Ian Fleming. New American Library 3,204,605
F A House in the Uplands, by Erskine Caldwell. New American
Library 3,186,195
F From Here to Eternity, by James Jones. New American Library 3,164,904
F On Her Majesty's Secret Service, by Ian Fleming. New American Library 3,142,184
F 79 Park Ave., by Harold Robbins. Pocket Books 3,122,000
F The Chinese Room, by Vivian Connell. Bantam 3,100,000
F Doctor No, by Ian Fleming. New American Library 3,072,532
F Georgia Boy, by Erskine Caldwell. New American Library and
Avon 3,011,281
Love Without Fear, by Eustace Chesser. New American Library 3,005,123
F Anatomy of a Murder, by Robert Traver. Dell 3,000,000
The Dell Crossword Dictionary, ed. by Kathleen Rafferty.
Dell (orig) 3,000,000
Four Days, by American Heritage and U.P.I. U.P.I. 3,000,000
A Message to Garcia, by Elbert Hubbard. Roycroft (orig) (est.) 3,000,000
F The Case of the Sulky Girl, by Erle Stanley Gardner. Pocket
Books 2,936,000
F Casino Royale, by Ian Fleming. New American Library 2,930,221
30 Days to a More Powerful Vocabulary, by Wilfred J. Funk
and Norman Lewis. Pocket Books 2,923,427
F Lost Horizon, by James Hilton. Pocket Books 2,867,000
F Live and Let Die, by Ian Fleming. New American Library 2,806,772
F The Sure Hand of God, by Erskine Caldwell. New American
Library 2,802,095
F Moonraker, by Ian Fleming. New American Library 2,753,486
The Service Cook Book, by Ida Bailey Allen. Service, Inc.
(orig) 2,750,000
The Pocket Book of Verse, ed. by M. E. Speare. Pocket Books
(orig) 2,719,500
F Tales of the South Pacific, by James Michener. Pocket Books 2,717,000
Kids Say the Darndest Things! by Art Linkletter. Pocket
Books 2,714,290
F The Spy Who Loved Me, by Ian Fleming. New American
Library 2,700,261
F The Best of Everything, by Rona Jaffe. Dell and Pocket Books 2,695,000
F Mandingo, by Kyle Onstott. Crest 2,630,250

42

F The Case of the Lucky Legs, by Erle Stanley Gardner. Pocket Books   2,621,000

F Diamonds Are Forever, by Ian Fleming. New American Library   2,616,842

F The Case of the Curious Bride, by Erle Stanley Gardner. Pocket Books   2,578,000

F On the Beach, by Nevil Shute. New American Library   2,568,455

F For Your Eyes Only, by Ian Fleming. New American Library   2,521,250

F The Case of the Haunted Husband, by Erle Stanley Gardner. Pocket Books   2,507,540

F Battle Cry, by Leon Uris. Bantam   2,500,000

F Brave New World, by Aldous Huxley. Bantam   2,500,000

The Conscience of a Conservative, by Barry Goldwater. Macfadden-Bartell   2,500,000

F Tropic of Cancer, by Henry Miller.   2,500,000

F The Case of the Rolling Bones, by Erle Stanley Gardner. Pocket Books   2,462,000

F The Case of the Baited Hook, by Erle Stanley Gardner. Pocket Books   2,448,000

F The Chapman Report, by Irving Wallace. New American Library   2,447,649

F The Naked and the Dead, by Norman Mailer. New American Library   2,443,662

Folk Medicine, by D. C. Jarvis, M.D. Crest   2,423,111

F This Very Earth, by Erskine Caldwell. New American Library   2,412,276

F Women's Barracks, by Tereska Torres. Gold Medal (orig)   2,409,163

F The Case of the Substitute Face, by Erle Stanley Gardner. Pocket Books   2,402,000

Dennis the Menace: Household Hurricane, by Hank Ketcham. Pocket Books   2,383,000

Please Don't Eat the Daisies, by Jean Kerr. Crest   2,376,220

F Magnificent Obsession, by Lloyd C. Douglas. Pocket Books   2,335,123

F The Case of the Velvet Claws, by Erle Stanley Gardner. Pocket Books   2,333,000

F The Case of the Counterfeit Eye, by Erle Stanley Gardner. Pocket Books   2,311,541

F The Group, by Mary McCarthy. New American Library   2,307,765

The Greatest Story Ever Told, by Fulton Oursler. Pocket Books   2,304,960

F Cannery Row, by John Steinbeck. Bantam   2,300,000

F The Pearl, by John Steinbeck. Bantam   2,300,000

F The Case of the Stuttering Bishop, by Erle Stanley Gardner. Pocket Books   2,287,000

43

F The Case of the Caretaker's Cat, by Erle Stanley Gardner. Pocket Books	2,260,000
See Here, Private Hargrove, by Marion Hargrove. Pocket Books	2,260,000
Facts of Life and Love for Teenagers, by Evelyn Millis Duvall and Sylvanus Duvall. Popular Library	2,250,000
F Pocket Book of Erskine Caldwell Stories, ed. by Henry Seidel Canby. Pocket Books	2,229,000
F No Time for Sergeants, by Mac Hyman. New American Library	2,221,502
F Singing Guns, by Max Brand. Pocket Books	2,219,000
F The Glorious Pool, by Thorne Smith. Pocket Books	2,216,000
F The Case of the Silent Partner, by Erle Stanley Gardner. Pocket Books	2,211,000
F The Amboy Dukes, by Irving Shulman. Avon	2,200,000
A House Is Not a Home, by Polly Adler. Popular Library	2,200,000
I'll Cry Tomorrow, by Lillian Roth. Popular Library	2,200,000
Dennis the Menace Rides Again, by Hank Ketcham. Pocket Books	2,177,000
Radio Amateur's License Manual. American Radio Relay League (orig.)	2,153,000
RCAF Exercise Book. Pocket Books	2,147,000
F The Red Badge of Courage, by Stephen Crane. Pocket Books	2,147,000
F Mr. Roberts, by Thomas Heggen. Pocket Books	2,131,000
J The Wonderful Wizard of Oz, by L. Frank Baum. 1900 Bobbs-Merrill	2,130,395
F The Good Earth, by Pearl S. Buck. Pocket Books	2,101,100
F The Passionate Witch, by Thorne Smith. Pocket Books	2,099,000
F Where Love Has Gone, by Harold Robbins. Pocket Books	2,093,000
F The Clue of the Forgotten Murder, by Erle Stanley Gardner. Pocket Books	2,082,000
The Pocket Dictionary, by W. J. Pelo. Pocket Books	2,075,000
F Sanctuary, by William Faulkner. New American Library	2,074,985
F The Case of the Dangerous Dowager, by Erle Stanley Gardner. Pocket Books	2,066,000
F The Case of the Sleepwalker's Niece, by Erle Stanley Gardner. Pocket Books	2,066,000
Wanted: Dennis the Menace, by Hank Ketcham. Pocket Books	2,052,000
English Through Pictures (The Pocket Book of Basic English), by I. A. Richards and C. M. Gibson. Pocket Books (orig.)	2,050,000
F The Case of the Half-Wakened Wife, by Erle Stanley Gardner. Pocket Books	2,047,000
F The Case of the Lame Canary, by Erle Stanley Gardner. Pocket Books	2,038,000

44

F Doctor Zhivago, by Boris Pasternak. New American Library   2,037,270
F The Case of the Careless Kitten, by Erle Stanley Gardner.
Pocket Books   2,024,000
F This Is Murder, by Erle Stanley Gardner. Pocket Books   2,001,000
F Another Country, by James Baldwin. Dell   2,000,000
Black Like Me, by John H. Griffin. New American Library   2,000,000
F The Bramble Bush, by Charles Mergendahl. Bantam   2,000,000
F Bridge Over the River Kwai, by Pierre Boulle. Bantam   2,000,000
Harlow, by Irving Shulman. Dell   2,000,000
Hiroshima, by John Hersey. Bantam   2,000,000
How To Prepare Your Income Tax, by David Joseph. Double-
day (orig)   2,000,000
My First World Atlas. Hammond (orig)   2,000,000
F Rally Round the Flag, Boys! by Max Shulman. Bantam   2,000,000
F The Revolt of Mamie Stover, by William Bradford Huie. New
American Library   2,000,000
Streams in the Desert, Vol. 1, by Mrs. Charles E. Cowman
Zondervan   2,000,000
F The Tight White Collar, by Grace Metalious. Dell   2,000,000
F The Good Earth, by Pearl S. Buck. Pocket Books   1,990,000
The Nun's Story, by Kathryn Hulme. Pocket Books   1,980,000
Dennis the Menace: Baby Sitter's Guide, by Hank Ketcham.
Pocket Books   1,973,000
F The Young Lions, by Irwin Shaw. New American Library   1,961,003
F The Case of the Empty Tin, by Erle Stanley Gardner. Pocket
Books   1,928,000
F The House of Flesh, by Bruno Fischer. Gold Medal (orig)   1,926,110
Standard Bartender's Guide, by Patrick Gavin Duffy and
James A. Beard. Pocket Books   1,919,210
Dennis the Menace vs. Everybody, by Hank Ketcham. Pocket
Books   1,917,000
F A Stone for Danny Fisher, by Harold Robbins. Pocket Books   1,910,000
F The Deep, by Mickey Spillane. New American Library   1,903,495
Comparative World Atlas. Hammond (orig)   1,900,000
The Hidden Persuaders, by Vance Packard. Pocket Books   1,896,584
Langenscheidt German-English, English-German Dictionary.
Pocket Books   1,894,000
F Shane, by Jack Schaefer. Bantam   1,875,000
Dennis the Menace—Teacher's Threat, by Hank Ketcham.
Crest   1,853,625
F The Case of the Gold-Digger's Purse, by Erle Stanley Gardner.   1,852,000

F The Girl Hunters, by Mickey Spillane. New American Library	1,848,119
An Analysis of the Kinsey Report (About the Kinsey Report), ed. by Donald P. Geddes and Enid Currie. New American Library	1,840,756
F The Case of the Buried Clock, by Erle Stanley Gardner. Pocket Books	1,837,664
F The Agony and the Ecstasy, by Irving Stone. New American Library	1,824,002
In This Corner—Dennis the Menace, by Hank Ketcham. Crest	1,820,060
F East of Eden, by John Steinbeck. Bantam	1,816,000
F Gone with the Wind, by Margaret Mitchell. Pocket Books	1,808,207
F Advise and Consent, by Allen Drury. Pocket Books	1,807,264
F The Blackboard Jungle, by Evan Hunter. Pocket Books	1,796,000
F The Caretakers, by Dariel Telfer. New American Library	1,795,308
F The Case of the Borrowed Brunette, by Erle Stanley Gardner. Pocket Books	1,793,000
F Of Human Bondage, by W. Somerset Maugham. Pocket Books	1,790,000
F The Case of the Black-Eyed Blonde, by Erle Stanley Gardner. Pocket Books	1,779,000
F Mutiny on the Bounty, by Charles Nordhoff and James Norman Hall. Pocket Books	1,764,957
Masters of Deceit, by J. Edgar Hoover. Pocket Books	1,751,133
F From the Terrace, by John O'Hara. Bantam	1,750,000
F Jailbait, by William Bernard. Popular Library	1,750,000
F A Rage to Live, by John O'Hara. Bantam	1,750,000
F The Damned, by John D. MacDonald. Gold Medal (orig)	1,747,908
You Are What You Eat, by Victor H. Lindlahr. Journal of Lifetime Living (orig.)	1,730,000
F The Case of the Turning Tide, by Erle Stanley Gardner. Pocket Books	1,727,000
F The World of Suzie Wong, by Richard Mason. New American Library	1,724,260
F A Place Called Estherville, by Erskine Caldwell. New American Library	1,721,616
F The Case of the Lonely Heiress, by Erle Stanley Gardner. Pocket Books	1,712,573
F The Fountainhead, by Ayn Rand. New American Library	1,710,749
F Studs Lonigan (Young Lonigan), by James T. Farrell. New American Library	1,701,003
F The Spy Who Came in From the Cold, by John Le Carré. Dell	1,700,000
F Strange Fruit, by Lillian Smith. New American Library	1,697,407

46

F Spring Fire, by Vin Packer. Gold Medal (orig)   1,690,126
The Rise and Fall of the Third Reich, by William L. Shirer.
Crest   1,677,778
F Nevada, by Zane Grey. Bantam   1,659,990
F The Case of the Shoplifter's Shoe, by Erle Stanley Gardner.
Pocket Books   1,650,900
F The Bishop's Jaegers, by Thorne Smith. Pocket Books   1,650,000
F The Case of the Crooked Candle, by Erle Stanley Gardner.
Pocket Books   1,647,847
F The Vixens, by Frank Yerby. Pocket Books   1,645,933
F Murder Up My Sleeve, by Erle Stanley Gardner. Pocket Books   1,634,000
F The Case of the Lazy Lover, by Erle Stanley Gardner. Pocket
Books   1,632,000
F Kitty, by Rosamond Marshall. Pocket Books and New American
Library   1,630,175
F Rebecca, by Daphne du Maurier. Pocket Books   1,625,726
F A Woman in the House, by Erskine Caldwell. New American
Library   1,623,630
F A Swell Looking Girl, by Erskine Caldwell. New American
Library (orig)   1,604,783
F The Incredible Journey, by Shelia Burnford. Bantam   1,600,000
F Find This Woman, by Richard S. Prather. Gold Medal (orig)   1,581,685
F Duchess Hotspur, by Rosamond Marshall. New American Lib-
rary and Pyramid   1,580,441
The Cross and the Switchblade, by David Wilkerson et al.
1963 Pyramid and Revell   1,571,578
F The Dream Merchants, by Harold Robbins. Pocket Books   1,552,000
F The Case of the Vagabond Virgin, by Erle Stanley Gardner.
Pocket Books   1,548,000
Pocket Book of Boners. Pocket Books (orig)   1,547,000
F Lust for Life, by Irving Stone. Pocket Books   1,545,816
F Pocket Book of Modern American Short Stories, ed Philip Van
Doren Stern. Pocket Books (orig)   1,543,000
F Topper, by Thorne Smith. Pocket Books   1,542,000
F Strip for Murder, by Richard S. Prather. Gold Medal (orig)   1,540,572
F Duke, by Hal Ellson. Popular Library   1,540,000
F Bodies in Bedlam, by Richard S. Prather. Gold Medal (orig)   1,531,786
F Atlas Shrugged, by Ayn Rand. New American Library   1,526,507
F The Bridge of San Luis Rey, by Thornton Wilder. Pocket Books   1,526,348
Thorndike Barnhart Dictionary. Bantam   1,525,000
F Serenade, by James M. Cain. New American Library   1,524,223

F Marjorie Morningstar, by Herman Wouk. New American Library   1,514,191

F The Case of the Dubious Bridegroom, by Erle Stanley Gardner. Pocket Books   1,512,806

One World, by Wendell L. Willkie. Simon & Schuster (orig)   1,512,647

The Longest Day, by Cornelius Ryan. Crest   1,512,462

F The Case of the Howling Dog, by Erle Stanley Gardner. Pocket Books   1,510,000

F The Razor's Edge, by W. Somerset Maugham. Pocket Books   1,510,000

Pocket Book of Cartoons, ed. by Bennett Cerf. Pocket Books (orig)   1,507,000

F The Wild Palms, by William Faulkner. New American Library   1,503,600

F Knock on Any Door, by Willard Motley. New American Library   1,501,498

F Bonjour Tristesse, by Françoise Sagan. Dell   1,500,000

F The Bridges at Toko Ri, by James Michener. Bantam   1,500,000

F Candy, by Terry Southern and Mason Hoffenberg. Dell   1,500,000

The Marriage Art, by John E. Eichenlaub. Dell   1,500,000

Child Behavior, by F. L. Ilg and L. B. Ames. Dell   1,500,000

F The Ninth Wave, by Eugene Burdick. Dell   1,500,000

F Catch-22, by Joseph Heller. Dell   1,500,000

F Sayonara, by James Michener. Bantam   1,500,000

Scholastic World Atlas. Hammond (orig)   1,500,000

F Seven Days in May, by Fletcher Knebel and Charles W. Bailey II. Bantam   1,500,000

F Way of a Wanton, by Richard S. Prather. Gold Medal (orig)   1,496,118

F Everybody Had a Gun, by Richard S. Prather. Gold Medal (orig)   1,480,130

The Microbe Hunters, by Paul de Kruif. Pocket Books   1,475,960

F The Bigger They Come, by A. A. Fair. Pocket Books   1,475,000

F The Case of the Cautious Coquette, by Erle Stanley Gardner. Pocket Books   1,474,000

Ann Pillsbury's Baking Book. Barnes (orig)   1,470,000

F Darling, It's Death, by Richard S. Prather. Gold Medal (orig)   1,467,635

F The Case of the Smoking Chimney, by Erle Stanley Gardner. Pocket Books   1,466,000

F Too Many Crooks (Ride a High Horse), by Richard S. Prather. Gold Medal (orig)   1,464,357

Heloise's Housekeeping Hints. Pocket Books   1,461,360

Believe It or Not, ed. by Robert L. Ripley. Pocket Books   1,457,000

F Poor No More, by Robert Ruark. Crest   1,453,167

The Sea Around Us, by Rachel Carson. New American Library   1,450,000

F The Case of the One-Eyed Witness, by Erle Stanley Gardner. Pocket Books   1,437,000

F The D.A. Calls It Murder, by Erle Stanley Gardner. Pocket Books   1,436,000

Pocket History of the United States, by Allan Nevins and Henry Steele Commager. Pocket Books (orig)   1,436,000

F National Velvet, by Enid Bagnold.   1,434,626

The Mad Reader, by E. C. Publications. Ballantine (orig)   1,433,477

Pocket Book of War Humor, ed. by Bennett Cerf. Pocket Books (orig)   1,422,000

F The Case of the Perjured Parrot, by Erle Stanley Gardner. Pocket Books   1,418,000

F The Postman Always Rings Twice, by James M. Cain. Pocket Books   1,410,000

F The Case of the Negligent Nymph, by Erle Stanley Gardner. Pocket Books   1,408,000

Mine Enemy Grows Older, by Alexander King. New American Library   1,405,980

F Cry Tough! by Irving Shulman. Avon   1,400,000

Report of the Warren Commission on the Assassination of President Kennedy. Bantam   1,400,000

F Fail-Safe, by Eugene Burdick and Harvey Wheeler. Dell   (est) 1,400,000

F The Wayward Bus, by John Steinbeck. Bantam   1,400,000

F Written on the Wind, by Robert Wilder. Bantam   1,400,000

F Pavilion of Women, by Pearl S. Buck. Pocket Books   1,399,953

F The Cardinal, by Henry Morton Robinson. Pocket Books   1,398,000

F Always Leave 'Em Dying, by Richard S. Prather. Gold Medal (orig)   1,396,015

F The Prize, by Irving Wallace. New American Library   1,393,496

F The Case of the Drowsy Mosquito, by Erle Stanley Gardner. Pocket Books   1,385,000

F The D.A. Holds a Candle, by Erle Stanley Gardner. Pocket Books   1,385,000

F Farewell, My Lovely, by Raymond Chandler. Pocket Books   1,384,340

F The Case of the Vanishing Beauty, by Richard S. Prather. Gold Medal (orig)   1,383,440

Power Golf, by Ben Hogan. Pocket Books   1,383,095

How To Stop Worrying and Start Living, by Dale Carnegie. Pocket Books   1,381,140

F Stranger in Paris (Christmas Holiday), by W. Somerset Maugham. Bantam   1,381,000

F Cocotte, by Theodore Pratt. Gold Medal (orig)   1,377,373

Word Power Made Easy, by Norman Lewis. Pocket Books   1,375,000

F The Red Pony, by John Steinbeck. Bantam   1,365,000

F The Thin Man, by Dashiell Hammett. Pocket Books   1,363,000

F The Wailing Frail, by Richard S. Prather. Gold Medal (orig)   1,362,139

F New Adventures of Ellery Queen, by Ellery Queen. Pocket Books   1,357,000

Meat and Poultry Cook Book, by Thora Campbell and Beth Bailey McLean (Martha Logans' Meat Cook Book). Pocket Books (orig)   1,354,000

F The Tormented, by Theodore Pratt. Gold Medal (orig)   1,350,620

F Auntie Mame, by Patrick Dennis. Popular Library   1,350,000

F Destry Rides Again, by Max Brand. Pocket Books   1,347,000

F The Case of the Backward Mule, by Erle Stanley Gardner. Pocket Books   1,346,000

F The Dutch Shoe Mystery, by Ellery Queen. Pocket Books   1,344,000

Only in America, by Harry Golden. Pocket Books   1,343,000

F Giant, by Edna Ferber. Pocket Books   1,342,000

F Hill Girl, by Charles Williams. Gold Medal (orig)   1,336,425

F Around the World with Auntie Mame, by Patrick Dennis. New American Library   1,334,390

F 13 French Street, by Gil Brewer. Gold Medal (orig)   1,333,417

F So Well Remembered, by James Hilton. Pocket Books   1,330,991

F All Quiet on the Western Front, by Erich Maria Remarque. Crest   1,325,226

F The Spirit of the Border, by Zane Grey. Pocket Books   1,325,000

F The D.A. Draws a Circle, by Erle Stanley Gardner. Pocket Books   1,321,000

The Making of the President, 1960, by Theodore H. White. Pocket Books   1,319,000

Point Count Bidding, by Charles H. Goren. Simon & Schuster (orig)   1,314,077

F And Then There Were None, by Agatha Christie. Pocket Books   1,310,000

F Easy to Kill, by Agatha Christie. Pocket Books   1,307,700

F The Case of the Drowning Duck, by Erle Stanley Gardner. Pocket Books   1,303,711

F B.F.'s Daughter, by John P. Marquand. Bantam   1,303,012

A Nation of Sheep, by William J. Lederer. Crest   1,302,192

F The Chinese Orange Mystery, by Ellery Queen. Pocket Books   1,302,034

F The D.A. Goes to Trial, by Erle Stanley Gardner. Pocket Books   1,301,000

F Fires of Spring, by James Michener. Bantam   1,300,000

Historical Atlas. Hammond (orig)   1,300,000

F Rampart Street, by Everett and Olga Webber. Pocket Books   1,300,000

F	This Side of Innocence, by Taylor Caldwell. Popular Library	1,300,000
	Travels with Charley, by John Steinbeck. Bantam	1,300,000
	My Life in Court, by Louis Nizer. Pyramid	1,297,746
F	The Man in the Gray Flannel Suit, by Sloan Wilson. Pocket Books	1,296,000
F	The Siamese Twin Mystery, by Ellery Queen.	1,291,961
	Cartoon Laffs, by True Magazine. Gold Medal (orig)	1,290,433
F	Bloody Sunrise, by Mickey Spillane. New American Library	1,283,291
	Mad Strikes Back, by E. C. Publications. Ballantine (orig)	1,282,414
F	Damon Runyon Favorites, by Damon Runyon. Pocket Books	1,279,000
F	Forever Amber, by Kathleen Winsor. New American Library	1,272,431
F	Mr. Adam, by Pat Frank. Pocket Books	1,269,000
F	The Case of the Fan-Dancer's Horse, by Erle Stanley Gardner. Pocket Books	1,268,000
F	Mildred Pierce, by James M. Cain. New American Library	1,259,521
F	The Case of the Hesitant Hostess, by Erle Stanley Gardner. Pocket Books	1,258,000
F	Day of Guns, by Mickey Spillane. New American Library	1,256,671
	My Flag Is Down, by James Maresca. Bantam	1,251,000
	Aircraft Spotters Handbook, by L. C. Gushman. Wise (orig)	1,250,000
F	Never Leave Me, by Harold Robbins. Avon	1,250,000
F	Ourselves To Know, by John O'Hara. Bantam	1,250,000
F	A Walk on the Wild Side, by Nelson Algren. Crest	1,250,000
	Perma Crossword Puzzle and Word Game Dictionary, by Frank Newman. Pocket Books	1,244,000
F	The Case of the Fiery Fingers, by Erle Stanley Gardner. Pocket Books	1,242,000
F	Peril at End House, by Agatha Christie. Pocket Books	1,241,693
F	The Adventures of Ellery Queen, by Ellery Queen. Pocket Books	1,238,000
	Sex and the Single Girl, by Helen Gurley Brown. Pocket Books	1,233,320
F	Jamaica Inn, by Daphne du Maurier. Pocket Books	1,233,000
F	I Have Gloria Kirby, by Richard Himmell. Gold Medal (orig)	1,226,720
F	The Four of Hearts, by Ellery Queen. Pocket Books	1,226,135
F	The Case of the Moth-Eaten Mink, by Erle Stanley Gardner. Pocket Books	1,223,690
	Kon-Tiki, by Thor Heyerdahl. Pocket Books	1,214,500
F	The Night Life of the Gods, by Thorne Smith. Pocket Books and Pyramid	1,214,336
F	The Egyptian Cross Mystery, by Ellery Queen. Pocket Books	1,213,748
F	Mrs. Miniver, by Jan Struther.	1,213,498

F The Snake, by Mickey Spillane. New American Library 1,213,325
F Cassidy's Girl, by David Goodis. Gold Medal (orig) 1,212,426
American History Atlas. Hammond (orig) 1,200,000
Dennis the Menace, by Hank Ketcham. Avon (est) 1,200,000
F Midsummer Passions. Avon (orig) 1,200,000
Sex Habits of American Women, by Fritz Wittels, M.D. Avon (orig) 1,200,000
F What Makes Sammy Run, by Budd Shulberg. Bantam 1,200,000
F The Cautious Amorist, by Norman Lindsay. Bantam 1,198,000
F Halfway House, by Ellery Queen. Pocket Books 1,196,889
F Best of Damon Runyon, ed. by E. C. Bentley. Pocket Books 1,195,000
Shorter Bartlett's Familiar Quotations. Pocket Books 1,193,650
Cartoon Fun from True, by True Magazine. Gold Medal (orig) 1,193,492
F Cats Prowl at Night, by A. A. Fair. Pocket Books 1,191,581
Fundamentals of Contract Bridge, by Charles Goren. Pocket Books 1,190,492
F Mistress Glory, by Susan Morley. New American Library 1,189,427
F Golden Sleep, by Vivian Connell. New American Library 1,189,365
Inside Mad, by E. C. Publications. Ballantine (orig) 1,188,395
F The D.A. Calls a Turn, by Erle Stanley Gardner. Pocket Books 1,186,000
F Prince of Foxes, by Samuel Shellabarger. Bantam 1,179,789
F Little Sister, by Lee Roberts. Gold Medal (orig) 1,177,060
F The Murder of Roger Ackroyd, by Agatha Christie. Pocket Books 1,176,558
F The Spanish Cape Mystery, by Ellery Queen. Pocket Books 1,174,000
Household Encyclopedia, by Sylvia K. Mager. Pocket Books (orig) 1,173,500
F Topper Takes a Trip, by Thorne Smith. Pocket Books 1,169,000
Six Minutes a Day to Perfect Spelling, by Harry Shefter. Pocket Books (orig) 1,163,900
F A Woman of Rome, by Alberto Moravia. New American Library 1,161,465
Peace with God, by Billy Graham. Pocket Books 1,152,040
F The Case of the Demure Defendant, by Erle Stanley Gardner. Pocket Books 1,152,000
Practice for the Army Tests, by David Turner. Arco (orig) 1,152,000
F Judge Me Not, by John D. MacDonald. Gold Medal (orig) 1,151,029
F Drum, by Kyle Onstott. Crest 1,143,260
F The Golden Hawk, by Frank Yerby. Pocket Books 1,143,000
F Pride's Castle, by Frank Yerby. Pocket Books 1,140,990
The Art of Loving, by Erich Fromm. Bantam 1,134,670

52

F Andersonville, by MacKinlay Kantor. New American Library 1,133,967
F The French Powder Mystery, by Ellery Queen. Pocket Books 1,133,878
F The Big Sky, by A. B. Guthrie, Jr. Pocket Books 1,131,660
F The Brass Cupcake, by John D. MacDonald. Gold Medal (orig) 1,131,270
F Three's a Shroud, by Richard S. Prather. Gold Medal (orig) 1,131,018
F Some Came Running (abridged), by James Jones. New American Library 1,128,840
F The D.A. Breaks a Seal, by Erle Stanley Gardner. Pocket Books 1,128,000
The Status Seekers, by Vance Packard. Pocket Books 1,126,378
I Never Left Home, by Bob Hope. Simon & Schuster (orig) 1,121,088
Pocket Book of Ogden Nash. Pocket Books 1,121,000
F French Through Pictures, by I. A. Richards, M. H. Ilsley, and Christine Gibson. Pocket Books (orig) 1,120,000
F Take a Murder, Darling, by Richard S. Prather. Gold Medal (orig) 1,119,134
F By Love Possessed, by James Gould Cozzens. Crest 1,116,369
F No Adam in Eden, by Grace Metalious. Pocket Books 1,113,800
F The Sun Also Rises, by Ernest Hemingway. Bantam 1,107,000
P.T. 109—JFK in World War II, by Robert J. Donovan. Crest 1,105,657
F The Case of the Angry Mourner, by Erle Stanley Gardner. Pocket Books 1,103,000
F Don't Go Near the Water, by William Brinkley. New American Library 1,100,655
Atlas of Bible Lands. Hammond (orig) 1,100,000
F Boys and Girls Together, by William Goldman. Bantam 1,100,000
F Fifty Great Short Stories, ed. by Milton Crane. Bantam 1,100,000
The Fifty Minute Hour, by Robert Lindner. Bantam 1,100,000
F The Interns, by Richard Frede. Bantam 1,100,000
More Dennis the Menace, by Hank Ketcham. Avon 1,100,000
Your Own Book of Campcraft, by Catherine T. Hammett. Pocket Books 1,099,270
F A Portrait of the Artist As a Young Man, by James Joyce. Viking Press 1,095,155
F The D.A. Cooks a Goose, by Erle Stanley Gardner. Pocket Books 1,094,277
F Rawhide Range, by Ernest Haycox. Popular Library (orig) 1,090,000
F The Maltese Falcon, by Dashiell Hammett. Pocket Books 1,085,800
Death of a Salesman, by Arthur Miller. Viking Press 1,084,617
F Dagger of Flesh, by Richard S. Prather. Gold Medal (orig) 1,083,623

Sunset Western Garden Book, by Editors of Sunset Magazine. Lane (orig) 1,081,906

F Mystery of the Blue Train, by Agatha Christie. Pocket Books 1,077,000

F The Case of the Sun-Bather's Diary, by Erle Stanley Gardner. Pocket Books 1,075,000

F The Case of the Glamorous Ghost, by Erle Stanley Gardner. Pocket Books 1,071,000

The Pocket Entertainer, ed. by Shirley Cunningham. Pocket Books (orig) 1,068,000

F Bugles in the Afternoon, by Ernest Haycox. Bantam 1,067,900

Think and Grow Rich, by Napoleon Hill. Crest 1,067,322

F The Other Room, by Worth T. Hedden. Bantam 1,065,000

F Random Harvest, by James Hilton. Pocket Books 1,058,350

Utterly Mad, by E. C. Publications. Ballantine (orig) 1,055,923

F Ship of Fools, by Katherine Anne Porter. New American Library 1,055,678

Immortal Poems of the English Language, ed. by Oscar Williams. Pocket Books 1,054,500

New Pocket Thesaurus in Dictionary Form (abridged), by Norman Lewis. Pocket Books 1,053,700

F Something of Value, by Robert Ruark. Pocket Books 1,052,990

F Turn on the Heat, by A. A. Fair. Pocket Books 1,052,051

God Is My Co-Pilot, by General Robert L. Scott. Ballantine 1,051,810

F The Beach House, by Stephen Longstreet. Popular Library 1,050,000

F Ramrod, by Luke Short. Popular Library 1,050,000

The Sexual Side of Marriage, by Max J. Exner, M.D. Pocket Books 1,050,000

The Greatest Book Ever Written, by Fulton Oursler. Pocket Books 1,044,415

The Story of Philosophy, by Will Durant. Pocket Books 1,043,890

F The Street, by Ann Petry. New American Library 1,042,505

Thorndike-Barnhart Handy Pocket Dictionary, ed. by Clarence L. Barnhart. Pocket Books 1,037,750

Anthology of Robert Frost's Poems, ed. by Louis Untermeyer. Pocket Books 1,037,150

May This House Be Safe from Tigers, by Alexander King. New American Library 1,035,374

F Lie Down Killer, by Richard S. Prather. Gold Medal 1,034,716

F Fools Die on Friday, by A. A. Fair. Pocket Books 1,032,601

F A Farewell to Arms, by Ernest Hemingway. Bantam 1,031,000

F The Foxes of Harrow, by Frank Yerby. Pocket Books 1,030,900

F Scrambled Yeggs, by Richard S. Prather. Gold Medal (orig) 1,026,322

F Nine Coaches Waiting, by Mary Stewart. Crest		1,026,196
F Strangers When We Meet, by Evan Hunter. Pocket Books		1,023,000
F The Deer Park, by Norman Mailer. New American Library		1,021,180
F The Case of the Fugitive Nurse, by Erle Stanley Gardner. Pocket Books		1,018,000
F Owls Don't Blink, by A. A. Fair. Pocket Books		1,018,000
F Have Gat—Will Travel, by Richard S. Prather. Gold Medal (orig)		1,016,784
F Jeeves, by P. G. Wodehouse. Pocket Books		1,012,000
F Never Come Morning, by Nelson Algren. Avon		1,010,000
F Pitcairn's Island, by Charles Nordhoff and James Norman Hall. Pocket Books		1,010,000
F All the Ships at Sea, by William J. Lederer. Pocket Books		1,008,600
F Spencer Brade, M.D., by Frank Slaughter. Pocket Books		1,008,130
Gardening: A Complete Guide, by Montague Free. Pocket Books		1,006,000
F Spill the Jackpot, by A. A. Fair. Pocket Books		1,002,570
F The Case of the Runaway Corpse, by Erle Stanley Gardner. Pocket Books		1,001,000
Pocket Book of Crossword Puzzles, by Margaret Petherbridge. Pocket Books		1,001,000
F Elmer Gantry, by Sinclair Lewis. Dell		1,000,000
F Fast Company, by Marco Page. Pocket Books		1,000,000
F Franny and Zooey, by J. D. Salinger. Bantam		1,000,000
F Harrison High, by John Farris. Dell		1,000,000
F I Can Get It for You Wholesale, by Jerome Weidman. Avon		1,000,000
F Louisville Saturday, by Margaret Long. Bantam		1,000,000
F Nobody Knows My Name, by James Baldwin. Dell		1,000,000
F Short Story Masterpieces, ed. by Robert Penn Warren and Albert Erskine. Dell		1,000,000
F Stiletto, by Harold Robbins. Dell (orig)		1,000,000
F Tomboy, by Hal Ellson. Bantam		1,000,000
Washington Confidential, by Jack Lait and Lee Mortimer. Dell		1,000,000

Best Seller Subjects

BEST SELLER SUBJECTS

THIS SECTION presents a picture of the best sellers in the categories people ask most questions about, such as the best-selling religious books after the Bible and the best-selling cookbooks. Aside from books of general interest, the majority of the best sellers in the preceding lists fall easily into specific classifications: children's books, cookbooks, crime and suspense stories (by far the largest group), novelty and game books, poetry and drama (the smallest group), reference books, books on religious themes, both nonfiction and fiction, and westerns.

COOKBOOKS

Probably more questions are asked in the field of best sellers about the Bible, next about cookbooks. All sorts of people and business organizations ask what the best-selling cookbooks are and how many copies of cookbooks are published and sold. Next to the Bible and books on religious subjects, cookbooks have been the most consistent sellers in nonfiction since 1895. It is apparent from a study of the best seller lists that only the need for advice on feeding the spirit surpasses the need for advice—and books—on feeding the body.

Paradoxically, cookbooks are seldom seen on the bookstore reports that appear weekly, monthly, and annually in newspapers and magazines. When a new, especially salable, and well-publicized cookbook is brought out or when a new edition of a standard cookbook is published, it does appear on these lists for a short time. Booksellers are really not averse to listing standard books that sell year in and year out on their reports, but what periodicals would find news value in listing such repetitive lists, dominated by the Bible, dictionaries, cookbooks, and other bookstore staples?

Figures on the number of new cookbooks published annually have been compiled by the *Publishers' Weekly* only since 1952. They comprise one of the smallest categories. In 1965 only 160 cookbooks were among the 28,595 new books and new editions published in the United States. Though small in number of titles, they are among the most important stock items for bookstores and among the most popular for the general public. The number of new cookbooks and new editions remains fairly steady: 141 in 1962; 162 in 1963; 206 in 1964; and 160 in 1965.

Cookbooks vary from basic, comprehensive volumes to guides to

59

every conceivable specialty. There are national and American regional cookbooks, collections of the favorite recipes of well-known persons, books on various techniques such as barbecuing or using an electric mixer, and books for people on all kinds of diets. Many of the new cookbooks and new editions have resulted from the many new cooking and packaging methods, that is, frozen food and other prepared dishes that save the home cook's time and effort. Time saving is emphasized in many modern cookbooks. On the other hand, gourmet meals have also been a strong feature in recent years. There are many new cookbooks every year offering directions for preparing exotic dishes; there are also cookbooks based on the indigenous cookery of nearly every country in the Orient, South America, and Europe.

The leading best seller among cookbooks, the *Better Homes and Gardens Cook Book,* is also one of the top best sellers in all fields. It ranks second in the overall list of best sellers during the past 70 years, first in the list of best sellers available only in hardcover editions. It is remarkable that, considering the comparatively small output of cookbooks in comparison with other types of nonfiction, there are five cookbooks among the first 50 on the all-time list. The top ten on the following cookbook best seller list are mostly the standard encyclopedic type that are reissued from time to time in new editions which incorporate new culinary methods. They include such long-established favorites as "Fannie Farmer" and *The Joy of Cooking,* as well as *Better Homes and Gardens Cook Book,* and vary from some quite expensive deluxe volumes to paperbacks selling at under $1. A number of these books have been originated by women's magazines and food product companies.

Out-of-print cookbooks and diet books, which, in some cases, are obsolete, have been omitted from the following list. About 12 new titles have been added since the last revision.

Better Homes and Gardens Cook Book. 1930 Meredith   11,325,299

Betty Crocker's New Picture Cookbook. 1950 McGraw-Hill (est)7,000,000

The Pocket Cook Book, by Elizabeth Woody. 1942 Pocket Books   4,466,200

The Boston Cooking School Cook Book, by Fannie Farmer. 1896
    Little, Brown   3,768,144

The American Woman's Cook Book, ed. by Ruth Berolzheimer.
    1939 Doubleday   3,549,276

The New Joy of Cooking, by Irma S. Rombauer and Marion
    Rombauer Becker. 1931 Bobbs-Merrill   2,816,028

Betty Crocker's Good and Easy Cookbook. 1954 Simon & Schuster   2,400,000

The Settlement Cook Book, by Mrs. Simon Kander. 1930 Simon
    & Schuster   1,626,135

Ann Pillsbury's Baking Book. 1950 Barnes	1,480,000
Meat and Poultry Cook Book, by J. Campbell and B. B. McLean. 1942 Pocket Books	1,354,000
Better Homes and Gardens Barbecue Book. 1956. Meredith	1,027,505
Better Homes and Gardens Salad Book. 1958	827,953
Better Homes and Gardens Meat Cook Book. 1959 Meredith	791,122
The Gold Cook Book, by Louis P. De Gouy. 1947 Greenberg	769,000
The General Foods Kitchen Cookbook. 1959 Random House	725,860
Sunset Barbecue Cook Book, by editors of Sunset Magazine. 1938 Lane	620,666
Better Homes and Gardens Holiday Cook Book. 1959 Meredith	595,334
Better Homes and Gardens Junior Cook Book. 1955 Meredith	552,334
Encyclopedia of Cookery. 1948 W. H. Wise	550,000
Better Homes and Gardens Casserole Cook Book. 1961 Meredith	539,264
Better Homes and Gardens Dessert Cook Book. 1960 Meredith	533,817
Let's Eat Right to Keep Fit, by Adelle Davis. 1954 Harcourt, Brace	502,058

CRIME AND SUSPENSE

CRIME, suspense, detection, mystery, espionage compose by far the largest special subject group among best sellers. Many of these multiple million sellers are close to the tops of both the paperback and overall combined lists. However, their numbers among the hardbound best sellers are comparatively few.

The books by Mickey Spillane, Erle Stanley Gardner and Ian Fleming dominate, Mickey Spillane in single-title sales and Gardner in number of million-copy sellers. Ian Fleming is the notable addition to the big suspense sellers since the previous edition of this book. About 75 titles have been added to the crime and suspense section: 35 by Gardner; ten by Fleming; five by Spillane; and 13 by Richard Prather, whose novels of violence have become increasingly popular during recent years. There are more Agatha Christie titles on the list too, since more of her work has been published in paperback format.

There are 151 books which have sold a million or more copies on this list, and 91 of them are by Erle Stanley Gardner, both Perry Mason cases and the books he writes under the pen name, A. A. Fair, which exploit the detective adventures of Bertha Cool and Donald Lam. Next in numerical representation is Ellery Queen. Mickey Spillane leads in sales of individual titles. There are only 12 of his books on this list, but seven of them are the first seven on the list, each selling more than four and one-half million copies. The original dates of publication for all these titles are given; the original publishers' names are given, and the names of the reprint publishers as well because, in most cases, these titles have become big best sellers in their paperback editions. The dates range from 1908 when Mary Roberts Rinehart's *The Circular Staircase* was first published up to *The Spy Who Came in From the Cold,* by John Le Carré and *You Only Live Twice* by Ian Fleming in 1964. In the past decade the production of all the books roughly classified as mysteries, both entirely new books and new editions, which, in most cases, means paperback reprints, has increased by more than 300 titles. There were 448 in 1956 increasing gradually to 785 published in 1965.

All books are included in this "crime and suspense" section which may be considered novels of crime, suspense, espionage, mystery, detection, psychological mysteries, gangster tales, romantic mysteries, and stories of violent action. Times have changed since the publication in 1840 of Edgar Allan Poe's *Murders in the Rue Morgue,* generally considered the first detective story. One of the early American best-selling detective stories was *The Leavenworth Case* by Anna Katharine Green. It was published in 1878 and sold more than half a million copies. Louis Vance, Meredith Nicholson, Sir Arthur Conan Doyle (his Sherlock Holmes is probably the best-known detective in history), and Mary Roberts Rinehart were authors who appeared regularly on all the annual best seller lists after the turn of the twentieth century. In the late 1920's S. S. Van Dine created Philo Vance, a new type of detective for the period. Through the '20's and '30's Agatha Christie was considered the favorite of the most literate detective story fans. Many of her books appear on this list of crime stories, among them the one that made her famous, *The Murder of Roger Ackroyd.* Dashiell Hammett's *The Thin Man* came along in 1934, introducing a new sort of writing in detective fiction. This story, of swift action and terse phrasing, was the starting point of a new school, in which Hammett was followed by Raymond Chandler and, more recently, Ross MacDonald. This school was also to give birth to an offshoot, the sex-and-guts detective of the '50's and '60's personified by Mickey Spillane's Mike Hammer and Richard Prather's Shell Scott.

In an article in the *Saturday Review* called "A Cosmic View of the Private Eye," John Paterson wrote in praise of the hardboiled detective as evolved by Hammett and Chandler, of the change from "the 'transcendant' detective of an older, safely established order to one in a bewildering world of disintegrated values . . . He is, in the final analysis, the apotheosis of the everyman of good will who, alienated by the values of his time, seeks desperately and mournfully to live without shame, to live without compromise to his integrity." This article was written before the advent of the phenomenon of the 1960's, James Bond, Agent 007. Though Bond's activities are deplored by many, there have been articles and books published which seriously appraise Fleming's writing and its popularity in relation to our modern society.

Though changing times bring changing trends in mystery and suspense, readers are still loyal to their old favorite sleuths and writers. Films and television have increased the popularity of such books. In number of copies sold, Erle Stanley Gardner must still be judged the favorite in this field over more than thirty years. His first Perry Mason story, *The Case of the Velvet Claws* was published in 1933. Since then he has produced about 100 books, including a few volumes of nonfiction. In real life, his Court of Last Resort is a functioning bureau for persons who have exhausted traditional methods to prove themselves not guilty of offenses against the law. Ellery Queen, pseudonym of two writers, Frederic Dannay and Manfred B. Lee, is another author who has produced a tremendous number of mystery titles since their first, *The Roman Hat Mystery,* of 1929.

The list of writers of mystery and action stories whose popularity has persisted over many years is long. To name but a few, there are Brett Halliday, most of whose stories feature the Miami detective, Mike Shayne, whose total paperback sales are 35 million; Agatha Christie, with paperback sales of 25 million; Richard Prather with paperback sales of 25 million; and, going back further than any, Mary Roberts Rinehart, only recently published in quantity in paperback, who has reached a 15 million total in that format alone.

In the 1960's espionage became the most popular theme in the suspense field. Paperback editions and movies made from James Bond stories made 007 probably the most highly publicized spy-detective ever. The James Bond craze became almost a cult. Unfortunately, Ian Fleming, his creator, died in 1964. There will be more James Bond movies, but the last full-length James Bond novel, *The Man with the Golden Gun,* was published in hardbound form in 1965. One can only speculate as to whether this English writer would have outdistanced his closest American rivals in ultimate sales.

In 1964, for the first time in best seller history, a suspense story headed the year's best-selling fiction. The famous *The Spy Who Came in From the Cold* by John Le Carré made no use of 007 gadgets; instead it deliberately took the glamor out of the spy business. Other writers followed the Le Carré pattern, many even produced spoofs on the ubiquitous spy stories; others comically celebrated the anti-hero. Whatever views were taken, the 1960's definitely proved spying and counter-spying the most popular themes in the field of escape reading.

The private eye stories innovated by Hammett and Chandler, followed by writers like Graham Greene, Eric Ambler, and Ross MacDonald also continued to find big audiences. Nor has the romantic school, pioneered by Mary Roberts Rinehart, fallen by the wayside. The "had I but known"

63

group in glamorous modern dress has been successfully represented by such best-selling authors as Mary Stewart and Helen MacInnes.

Daphne du Maurier's *Rebecca* was the twentieth century prototype (*Jane Eyre* in the nineteenth) for what became another paperback craze of the 1960's—for Gothica. Hundreds of titles appeared, on the cover of each a terrified young girl with a sinister looking castle in the background. Though as a group, they have reached very large sales, no single title has, as yet attained the million-copy rating.

Neither has science fiction approached the tremendous sale of suspense stories. Some of the best sellers, though laid in the future in worlds somewhat different from our own, like George Orwell's *1984* and Aldous Huxley's *Brave New World* cannot accurately be classified under this heading. Best sellers such as *Fail-Safe* by Eugene Burdick and Harvey Wheeler and *On the Beach* by Nevil Shute, which are based upon new scientific inventions, more nearly approach the category. Just as the science fiction of Jules Verne became later reality, it is safe to predict that novels dealing with new techniques, both scientific and political, will no longer be considered unbelievably fantastic. The distinction between science fiction and the traditional suspense story is rapidly becoming less rigid.

I, the Jury, by Mickey Spillane. 1962 Dutton, New American
Library 5,390,105

The Big Kill, by Mickey Spillane. 1951 Dutton, New American
Library 5,089,472

My Gun Is Quick, by Mickey Spillane. 1950 Dutton, New American Library 4,916,074

One Lonely Night, by Mickey Spillane. 1951 Dutton, New American Library 4,873,563

The Long Wait, by Mickey Spillane. 1951 Dutton, New American
Library 4,835,966

Kiss Me, Deadly, by Mickey Spillane. 1952 Dutton, New American Library 4,828,044

Vengeance Is Mine, by Mickey Spillane. 1950 Dutton, New
American Library 4,637,734

Thunderball, by Ian Fleming. 1965 New American Library 4,186,935

Goldfinger, by Ian Fleming. 1959 Macmillan, New American
Library 3,642,411

The Case of the Lucky Legs, by Erle Stanley Gardner. 1934
Morrow, Pocket Books 3,499,948

You Only Live Twice, by Ian Fleming. 1964 New American
Library 3,283,000

From Russia with Love, by Ian Fleming. 1957 Macmillan, New American Library   3,262,193

The Case of the Sulky Girl, by Erle Stanley Gardner. 1933 Morrow, Pocket Books   3,190,334

On Her Majesty's Secret Service, by Ian Fleming. 1963 New American Library   3,142,184

Anatomy of a Murder, by Robert Traver. 1958 St. Martin's Press, Dell   3,100,000

Casino Royale, by Ian Fleming. 1953 Macmillan, New American Library   2,940,221

The Case of the Curious Bride, by Erle Stanley Gardner. 1934 Morrow, Pocket Books   2,825,368

Live and Let Die, by Ian Fleming. 1954 Macmillan, New American Library   2,816,772

Moonraker, by Ian Fleming. 1955 Macmillan, New American Library   2,763,486

The Spy Who Loved Me, by Ian Fleming. 1962 New American Library   2,700,261

Diamonds Are Forever, by Ian Fleming. 1956 Macmillan, New American Library   2,621,842

The Case of the Haunted Husband, by Erle Stanley Gardner. 1941 Morrow, Pocket Books   2,595,125

The Case of the Baited Hook, by Erle Stanley Gardner. 1940 Morrow, Pocket Books   2,585,397

The Case of the Rolling Bones, by Erle Stanley Gardner. 1939 Morrow, Pocket Books   2,530,964

The Case of the Velvet Claws, by Erle Stanley Gardner. 1933 Morrow, Pocket Books   2,527,756

For Your Eyes Only, by Ian Fleming. 1960 New American Library   2,521,250

The Case of the Stuttering Bishop, by Erle Stanley Gardner. 1936 Morrow, Pocket Books   2,499,660

The Case of the Substitute Face, by Erle Stanley Gardner. 1938 Morrow, Pocket Books   2,472,710

The Case of the Counterfeit Eye, by Erle Stanley Gardner. 1935 Morrow, Pocket Books   2,469,306

The Case of the Dangerous Dowager, by Erle Stanley Gardner. 1937 Morrow, Pocket Books   2,461,874

The Case of the Caretaker's Cat, by Erle Stanley Gardner. 1935 Morrow, Pocket Books   2,403,403

The Case of the Black-Eyed Blonde, by Erle Stanley Gardner. 1944 Morrow, Pocket Books   2,403,269

The Case of the Half-Wakened Wife, by Erle Stanley Gardner.
1945 Morrow, Pocket Books 2,312,378

The Case of the Silent Partner, by Erle Stanley Gardner. 1940
Morrow, Pocket Books 2,311,904

This Is Murder, by Erle Stanley Gardner. 1935 Morrow, Pocket
Books 2,266,268

The Case of the Sleepwalker's Niece, by Erle Stanley Gardner.
1936 Morrow, Pocket Books 2,262,024

The Case of the Cautious Coquette, by Erle Stanley Gardner.
1949 Morrow, Pocket Books 2,244,552

The Case of the Lame Canary, by Erle Stanley Gardner. 1934
Morrow, Pocket Books 2,184,145

The Case of the Careless Kitten, by Erle Stanley Gardner. 1942
Morrow, Pocket Books 2,136,177

The Case of the Golddigger's Purse, by Erle Stanley Gardner.
1945 Morrow, Pocket Books 2,121,708

The Clue of the Forgotten Murder, by Erle Stanley Gardner.
1935 Morrow, Pocket Books 2,111,873

Seven Days in May, by Fletcher Knebel and Charles S. Bailey II.
1962 Harper & Row, Bantam 2,073,434

The Case of the Crooked Candle, by Erle Stanley Gardner. 1944
Morrow, Pocket Books 2,029,248

The Case of the Borrowed Brunette, by Erle Stanley Gardner.
1946 Morrow, Pocket Books 2,006,808

The Case of the Empty Tin, by Erle Stanley Gardner. 1941
Morrow, Pocket Books 1,968,297

The Case of the Buried Clock, by Erle Stanley Gardner. 1943
Morrow, Pocket Books 1,941,769

The Spy Who Came in from the Cold, by John Le Carré. 1964
Coward-McCann, Dell 1,930,000

The Deep, by Mickey Spillane. 1961 Dutton, New American
Library 1,928,513

The House of Flesh, by Bruno Fischer. 1950 Gold Medal 1,926,110

The Girl Hunters, by Mickey Spillane. 1962 Dutton, New American Library 1,863,260

The Case of the Lonely Heiress, by Erle Stanley Gardner. 1948
Morrow, Pocket Books 1,862,387

Murder Up My Sleeve, by Erle Stanley Gardner. 1937 Morrow,
Pocket Books 1,836,815

The Case of the Shoplifter's Shoe, by Erle Stanley Gardner.
1938 Morrow, Pocket Books 1,829,364

The New Adventures of Ellery Queen, by Ellery Queen. 1940
Lippincott, Pocket Books 1,786,168

66

The Case of the Turning Tide, by Erle Stanley Gardner. 1941 Morrow, Pocket Books ... 1,783,923

The Case of the Lazy Lover, by Erle Stanley Gardner. 1947 Morrow, Pocket Books ... 1,777,027

The D.A. Calls It Murder, by Erle Stanley Gardner. 1937 Morrow, Pocket Books ... 1,755,011

The Case of the Demure Defendant, by Erle Stanley Gardner. 1956 Morrow, Pocket Books ... 1,728,151

The Case of the Negligent Nymph, by Erle Stanley Gardner. 1950 Morrow, Pocket Books ... 1,703,816

The Case of the Dubious Bridegroom, by Erle Stanley Gardner. 1949 Morrow, Pocket Books ... 1,696,589

The Case of the Vagabond Virgin, by Erle Stanley Gardner. 1948 Morrow, Pocket Books ... 1,692,921

The Case of the Howling Dog, by Erle Stanley Gardner. 1934 Morrow, Pocket Books ... 1,691,878

The Adventures of Ellery Queen, by Ellery Queen. 1934 Lippincott, Pocket Books ... 1,679,550

The Murder of Roger Ackroyd, by Agatha Christie. 1926 Dodd, Mead, Pocket Books ... 1,676,558

The Case of the One-Eyed Witness, by Erle Stanley Gardner. 1950 Morrow, Pocket Books ... 1,671,968

The Case of the Perjured Parrot, by Erle Stanley Gardner. 1939 Morrow, Pocket Books ... 1,584,135

Find This Woman, by Richard S. Prather. 1951 Gold Medal ... 1,581,685

The D.A. Draws a Circle, by Erle Stanley Gardner. 1939 Morrow, Pocket Books ... 1,578,234

The Case of the Drowsy Mosquito, by Erle Stanley Gardner. 1943 Morrow, Pocket Books ... 1,575,396

The Case of the Smoking Chimney, by Erle Stanley Gardner. 1943 Morrow, Pocket Books ... 1,571,570

Strip for Murder, by Richard S. Prather. 1955 Gold Medal ... 1,540,572

The Bigger They Come, by A.A. Fair. 1939 Morrow, Pocket Books ... 1,536,764

Bodies in Bedlam, by Richard S. Prather. 1951 Gold Medal ... 1,531,786

Fail-Safe, by Eugene Burdick and Harvey Wheeler. 1962 McGraw-Hill, Dell ... 1,500,000

Way of a Wanton, by Richard S. Prather. 1952 Gold Medal ... 1,496,118

Everybody Had a Gun, by Richard S. Prather. 1951 Gold Medal ... 1,480,130

The Case of the Backward Mule, by Erle Stanley Gardner. 1946 Morrow, Pocket Books ... 1,479,047

The D.A. Holds a Candle, by Erle Stanley Gardner. 1938 Morrow, Pocket Books ... 1,469,432

67

The Case of the Hesitant Hostess, by Erle Stanley Gardner. 1953 Morrow, Pocket Books — 1,469,428

The Case of the Fiery Fingers, by Erle Stanley Gardner. 1951 Morrow, Pocket Books — 1,468,250

Darling, It's Death, by Richard S. Prather. 1952 Gold Medal — 1,467,635

Too Many Crooks (Ride a High Horse), by Richard S. Prather. 1953 Gold Medal — 1,464,357

The Case of the Fan-Dancer's Horse, by Erle Stanley Gardner. 1947 Morrow, Pocket Books — 1,455,452

The Case of the Moth-Eaten Mink, by Erle Stanley Gardner. 1952 Morrow, Pocket Books — 1,434,203

The D.A. Goes to Trial, by Erle Stanley Gardner. 1940 Morrow, Pocket Books — 1,415,572

Calamity Town, by Ellery Queen. 1942 Pocket Books — 1,412,000

The Thin Man, by Dashiell Hammett. 1934 Knopf, Pocket Books — 1,398,445

Always Leave 'Em Dying, by Richard S. Prather. 1954 Gold Medal — 1,396,015

Farewell, My Lovely, by Raymond Chandler. 1940 Knopf, Pocket Books — 1,388,220

The Case of the Vanishing Beauty, by Richard S. Prather. 1950 Gold Medal — 1,383,440

The Case of the Drowning Duck, by Erle Stanley Gardner. 1942 Morrow, Pocket Books — 1,369,660

The Wailing Frail, by Richard S. Prather. 1956 Gold Medal — 1,362,139

The Dutch Shoe Mystery, by Ellery Queen. 1931 Lippincott, Pocket Books — 1,356,863

And Then There Were None, by Agatha Christie. 1940 Dodd, Mead, Pocket Books — 1,320,000

The D.A. Cooks a Goose, by Erle Stanley Gardner. 1942 Morrow, Pocket Books — 1,317,137

The Case of the Angry Mourner, by Erle Stanley Gardner. 1951 Morrow, Pocket Books — 1,316,228

Easy to Kill, by Agatha Christie. 1939 Dodd, Mead, Pocket Books — 1,312,700

The Chinese Orange Mystery, by Ellery Queen. 1934 Lippincott, Pocket Books — 1,311,484

The Great Impersonation, by E. Phillips Oppenheim. 1920 Little, Brown — 1,303,028

The Siamese Twin Mystery, by Ellery Queen. 1933 Lippincott, Pocket Books — 1,291,961

Bloody Sunrise, by Mickey Spillane. 1965 Dutton, New American Library — 1,290,291

The Case of the Sun-Bather's Diary, by Erle Stanley Gardner. 1955 Morrow, Pocket Books — 1,278,951

The Case of the Glamorous Ghost, by Erle Stanley Gardner. 1955 Morrow, Pocket Books   1,275,953

The D.A. Breaks a Seal, by Erle Stanley Gardner. 1946 Morrow, Pocket Books   1,272,563

Day of Guns, by Mickey Spillane. 1964 Dutton, New American Library   1,265,336

The D.A. Calls a Turn, by Erle Stanley Gardner. 1944 Morrow, Pocket Books   1,259,390

Peril at End House, by Agatha Christie. 1932 Dodd, Mead, Pocket Books   1,246,693

Cats Prowl at Night, by A. A. Fair. 1958 Morrow, Pocket Books   1,239,916

The Four of Hearts, by Ellery Queen. 1938 Lippincott, Pocket Books   1,235,000

I Have Gloria Kirby, by Richard Himmell. 1951 Gold Medal   1,226,720

The Egyptian Cross Mystery, by Ellery Queen. 1932 Lippincott, Pocket Books   1,225,498

The Snake, by Mickey Spillane. 1964 Dutton, New American Library   1,220,874

The Case of the Runaway Corpse, by Erle Stanley Gardner. 1954 Morrow, Pocket Books   1,210,994

Halfway House, by Ellery Queen. 1936 Lippincott, Pocket Books   1,209,029

The Spanish Cape Mystery, by Ellery Queen. 1935 Lippincott, Pocket Books   1,183,560

Judge Me Not, by John D. MacDonald. 1951 Gold Medal   1,151,029

Give 'Em the Ax, by A. A. Fair. 1944 Morrow, Pocket Books   1,146,449

The French Powder Mystery, by Ellery Queen. 1930 Lippincott, Pocket Books   1,143,675

The Tragedy of X, by Barnaby Ross (Ellery Queen). 1932 Viking Press, Pocket Books   1,142,000

The Case of the Green-Eyed Sister, by Erle Stanley Gardner. 1953 Morrow, Pocket Books   1,137,563

Charlie Chan Carries on, by Earl Derr Biggers. 1930 Bobbs-Merrill   1,136,917

Owls Don't Blink, by A. A. Fair. 1942 Morrow, Pocket Books   1,132,856

The Brass Cupcake, by John D. MacDonald. 1950 Gold Medal   1,131,270

Three's a Shroud, by Richard S. Prather. 1957 Gold Medal   1,131,018

Spill the Jackpot, by A. A. Fair. 1941 Morrow, Pocket Books   1,123,136

Take a Murder, Darling, by Richard S. Prather. 1958 Gold Medal   1,119,134

The Maltese Falcon, by Dashiell Hammett. 1930 Knopf, Pocket Books   1,098,001

Fools Die on Friday, by A. A. Fair. 1947 Morrow, Pocket Books   1,094,941

The Case of the Terrified Typist, by Erle Stanley Gardner. 1956 Morrow, Pocket Books   1,090,383

The Case of the Screaming Woman, by Erle Stanley Gardner.
1957 Morrow, Pocket Books 1,088,744

Mystery of the Blue Train, by Agatha Christie. 1941 Dodd, Mead,
Pocket Books 1,087,000

Dagger of Flesh, by Richard S. Prather. 1961 Gold Medal 1,083,623

Turn on the Heat, by A. A. Fair. 1940 Morrow, Pocket Books 1,079,655

The Saint Goes West, by Leslie Charteris. 1942 Doubleday, Avon 1,070,392

Bedrooms Have Windows, by A. A. Fair. 1949 Morrow, Pocket
Books 1,068,363

Crows Can't Count, by A. A. Fair. 1946 Morrow, Pocket Books 1,068,139

Nine Coaches Waiting, by Mary Stewart. 1959 Morrow, Crest 1,056,196

The Case of the Daring Decoy, by Erle Stanley Gardner. 1957
Morrow, Pocket Books 1,049,006

The Case of the Long-Legged Models, by Erle Stanley Gardner.
1958 Morrow, Pocket Books 1,047,991

Some Women Won't Wait, by A. A. Fair. 1953 Morrow, Pocket
Books 1,045,981

The Dragon's Teeth, by Ellery Queen. 1939 Lippincott, Pocket
Books 1,039,000

Lie Down Killer, by Richard S. Prather. 1961 Gold Medal 1,034,716

The Case of the Fugitive Nurse, by Erle Stanley Gardner. 1954
Morrow, Pocket Books 1,028,000

Scrambled Yeggs, by Richard S. Prather. 1958 Gold Medal 1,026,322

Have Gat—Will Travel, by Richard S. Prather. 1957 Gold Medal 1,016,784

Gold Comes in Bricks, by A. A. Fair. 1940 Morrow, Pocket Books 1,010,437

Bats Fly at Dusk, by A. A. Fair. 1942 Morrow, Pocket Books 1,008,937

Beware the Curves, by A. A. Fair. 1956 Morrow, Pocket Books 1,007,136

Fast Company, by Marco Page. 1938 Dodd, Mead, Pocket Books
(est) 1,005,000

Stiletto, by Harold Robbins. 1960 Dell 1,000,000

JUVENILE BOOKS

STATISTICS on best sellers in the children's book field are more difficult to assemble accurately and consistently than in any other. The following list is an attempt to record the individual titles, published in the United States since 1895, that have sold a half million copies or more.

There are many of the oldest favorites and classics on the list of early best sellers, those published before 1895 in this country. As these books have gone out of copyright they have been issued by various publishers, perhaps newly illustrated or in re-edited or condensed versions. It becomes impossible to collect exact statistics for all these scattered versions, even for some published after 1895. Many of the original publishers have gone out of existence. When there have been many publishers and many versions of the same story, it is an impossible task to assemble all the sales records, hence the absence on the list of some favorites published since 1895. Modern versions of older favorites are not included in the list unless a specific volume, perhaps with its own illustrator, has accurate sales records, like *The Real Mother Goose*.

Juvenile fiction has the disconcerting habit of changing its audience. Some of these best sellers like *Freckles* and *Penrod* started their careers as adult fiction. Others were launched as children's books and have since added an adult audience, like the A. A. Milne books. Milne's *Winnie-the-Pooh*, in Latin as *Winnie Ille Pu,* was one of the ten best sellers in 1961, presumably in the adult field. Younger readers have become more sophisticated over the years. Many trade publishers note in their catalogs that certain titles are suitable for Young Adults. A definite attempt has been made to include adult books in reading lists for young people.

For the very young readers and pre-readers, the field is easily defined. But some books or toy-books, sold in large quantities in stores specializing in low-priced merchandise, in supermarkets and on newsstands, are impractical to assess in terms of quantities sold of individual titles. They include comic books, coloring books, cut-out books, puzzle books ad infinitum. During the 1955 Davy Crockett craze, Grosset & Dunlap sold about two million copies of three Davy Crockett books, including one million of *The Picture Story of Davy Crockett* and 600,000 of *The Davy Crockett Coloring Book.*

Series books sell in great quantities to generation after generation of youngsters. Some of the older series, the many volumes of which have sold many millions, are the *Frank Merriwell* books, by Burt L. Standish, which flourished in the 1920's, the *Childhood of Famous Americans* books, the Thornton Burgess *Animal Books* and *Bedtime Story Book* series, the *Doctor Dolittle* books by Hugh Lofting, the *Oz* books by L. Frank Baum, the *Raggedy Ann* books, and the *Little Colonel* books by Annie Fellows Johnston. The *Nancy Drew, Bobbsey Twins, Tom Swift* and *Uncle Wiggily* series have been devoured by several generations of young readers. The first *Elsie Dinsmore* book, by Martha Finley, was published in 1868, and the first of the *Five Little Peppers* series, by Margaret Sidney, in 1880. Highly popular newer series are Walter Farley's *Black Stallion* books, H. A. Rey's *Curious George* books, the *Little Golden Books* and *Giant Golden Books, True Books, Colby Books, Messner Biographies, Landmark Books, Allabout Books,* and Watts *First Books.* There are many standard books for young people which sell year after year in the religious field and other areas. They include the *Boy Scouts Handbook,* first published in 1910, and the *Girl Scouts Handbook,* first published in 1916, both of which have gone through many revisions.

Although production of new children's books has apparently doubled, title for title, in the past decade, a corresponding percentage of individual titles has not achieved the half-million sales of the best seller children's books list. In general, children's books which have sold several million copies in the hardbound trade field are the older books, most of them published in the first quarter of this century. About 30 titles have been added to this group in the past decade.

The Wonderful Wizard of Oz, by L. Frank Baum. 1900 Bobbs-Merrill	(est) 5,000,000
Facts of Life and Love for Teen-Agers, by Evelyn Willis Duvall and Sylvanus Duvall. 1950 Association Press	2,340,000
Freckles, by Gene Stratton Porter. 1904 Doubleday, Page	2,089,523
The Girl of the Limberlost, by Gene Stratton Porter. 1909 Doubleday, Page	2,053,892
The Little Engine That Could, by Watty Piper. 1929 Platt & Munk	2,011,251
My First World Atlas. 1959 Hammond	2,000,000
Egermeier's Bible Story Book, by Elsie E. Egermeier. 1923 Warner Press	1,750,000
Seventeen, by Booth Tarkington. 1916 Harper	(est) 1,682,891
The Cat in the Hat, by Dr. Seuss. 1957 Random House	1,588,972
Laddie, by Gene Stratton Porter. 1913 Doubleday, Page	1,586,529
The Golden Dictionary, by Ellen Wales Walpole. 1944 Golden Press	1,450,000
Rebecca of Sunnybrook Farm, by Kate Douglas Wiggin. 1904 Houghton Mifflin	1,373,288
The Real Mother Goose. 1915 Rand McNally	1,296,140
The Cat in the Hat Comes Back, by Dr. Seuss. 1958 Random House	1,148,669
Pollyanna, by Eleanor H. Porter. 1913 Page	1,059,000
Winnie-the-Pooh, by A. A. Milne. 1926 Dutton	1,005,000
Little Black Sambo, by Helen Bannerman. 1899 Lippincott	(est) 1,000,000
Pollyanna Grows Up, by Eleanor H. Porter. 1915 Page	1,000,000
Better Homes and Gardens Story Book. 1951 Meredith	964,770
One Fish, Two Fish, Red Fish, Blue Fish, by Dr. Seuss. 1960 Random House	947,971
My First Book About Jesus, by Mary Alice Jones. 1953 Rand McNally	850,000
Green Eggs and Ham, by Dr. Seuss. 1960 Random House	839,887

Lassie Come-Home, by Eric Knight. 1940 Winston	819,000
Anne of Green Gables, by L. M. Montgomery. 1908 Page	812,000
Just So Stories, by Rudyard Kipling. 1902 Doubleday	810,788
Penrod, by Booth Tarkington. 1914 Doubleday	808,916
When We Were Very Young, by A. A. Milne. 1924 Dutton	800,000
A Friend Is Someone Who Likes You, by Joan Walsh Anglund. 1958 Harcourt, Brace	784,265
Love Is a Special Way of Feeling, by Joan Walsh Anglund. 1960 Harcourt, Brace	741,318
The House at Pooh Corner, by A. A. Milne. 1928 Dutton	713,000
Now We Are Six, by A. A. Milne. 1927 Dutton	700,000
Mrs. Wiggs of the Cabbage Patch, by Alice Hegan Rice. 1903 Appleton	665,000
Album of Horses, by Marguerite Henry. 1951 Rand McNally	640,000
Yertle the Turtle, by Dr. Seuss. 1958 Random House	637,045
I Believe, a Christian Faith for Youth, by Nevin C. Harner. 1950 United Church Press	633,933
Hop on Pop, by Dr. Seuss. 1963 Random House	625,803
Dr. Seuss's ABC, by Dr. Seuss. 1963 Random House	605,477
Just David, by Eleanor H. Porter. 1916 Houghton Mifflin	604,957
The Cat in the Hat Beginner Book Dictionary, by P. D. Eastman. 1964 Random Rouse	593,506
The Rainbow Dictionary, by Wendell Wright. 1947 World	593,393
Charlotte's Web, by E. B. White. 1952. Harper	552,666
The Golden Encyclopedia, by Dorothy Bennett. 1946 Golden Press	548,000
The Golden Egg Book, by Margaret Wise Brown. 1947 Golden Press	534,000
Better Homes and Gardens Junior Cook Book. 1955 Meredith	522,334
Big Golden Book of Poetry, by Jane Werner. 1947 Golden Press	500,000
Golden Book of Science, by Bertha Morris Parker. 1952 Golden Press	500,000
Courtis Watters Illustrated Golden Dictionary for Young Readers, by Stuart A. Courtis and Garnette Watters. 1952 Golden Press	500,000
Golden Mother Goose, by Jane Werner. 1948 Golden Press	500,000
Golden Picture Dictionary, by Lilian Moore. 1954 Golden Press	500,000
Golden Song Book, by Katharine Tyler Wessels. 1945 Golden Press	500,000
Golden Treasury of Natural History, by Bertha Morris Parker. 1952 Golden Press	500,000
Indian Crafts and Lore, by W. Ben Hunt. 1954 Golden Press	500,000
King of the Wind, by Marguerite Henry. 1948 Rand McNally	500,000

73

Misty of Chincoteague, by Marguerite Henry. 1947 Rand McNally	500,000
Tell Me About God, by Mary Alice Jones. 1943 Rand McNally	500,000
Tell Me About Jesus, by Mary Alice Jones. 1944 Rand McNally	500,000
Walt Disney's Mary Poppins, by Alice Chase. 1964 Golden Press	500,000
Walt Disney's Uncle Remus Stories, retold by Marion Palmer. 1946 Golden Press	500,000

NOVELTY BOOKS

Periodically a new fad hits the American public. It may be a dance or a song, a slang phrase or a game. Sometimes such a fad is opportunely made the basis of a book that sells for a few months or years. Sometimes a new kind of book creates the fad, as happened with the *Cross Word Puzzle Books,* which have gone on selling ever since the first one appeared in 1934 as the first publication of the new firm of Simon & Schuster. There were not nearly as many *Believe It Or Not* books. Like the cross word puzzles, they were also first a newspaper feature. Robert L. Ripley, the feature's originator, capitalized on the *Believe It Or Not* fad not only in books and newspaper syndication but in shows and exhibits. *Boners* and *Ask Me Another,* also great fads in their day, were published in many successive volumes.

In more recent years, cartoons and humor have been the prime best sellers in the novelty or so-called non-book field (as distinguished from books of reading matter rather than books of pictures with captions). Forerunners of this field were the photographic books of Clare Barnes, Jr., *White Collar Zoo* and *Campus Zoo,* which were best sellers in 1949 and 1950. Like the *Cross Word Puzzles* and others, most of the popular cartoon books of the fifties and sixties originated in the newspapers like Walt Kelly's *Pogo* books. Charles M. Schulz's *Peanuts* books have appeared in many different formats, both hardcover and paperback, selling over four million copies altogether. The Schulz books (not *Peanuts* titles), *Happiness Is a Warm Puppy* and *Security Is a Thumb and a Blanket* were leading best sellers in 1962 and 1963. *Dennis the Menace,* Hank Ketcham's first best seller, was published in 1952. Ten years ago only that first book and *More Dennis the Menace* were on this list. In the past decade though Dennis himself has not grown older, his adventures and sales have proliferated. Many new titles have been added to this list, their million-copy sales accounted for in great part by the paperback reprint editions. Other series additions to this list are the *Mad* and *True* titles reprinted from the magazines.

More Dennis the Menace, by Hank Ketcham. 1953 Holt, Rinehart & Winston	2,527,459
Dennis the Menace: Household Hurricane, by Hank Ketcham. 1957 Holt, Rinehart & Winston	2,437,336
Dennis the Menace Rides Again, by Hank Ketcham. 1955 Holt, Rinehart & Winston	2,251,960
Wanted: Dennis the Menace, by Hank Ketcham. 1961 Holt, Rinehart & Winston	2,105,951
Dennis the Menace: Baby Sitter's Guide, by Hank Ketcham. 1954 Holt, Rinehart & Winston	1,988,000
Dennis the Menace vs. Everybody, by Hank Ketcham. 1956 Holt, Rinehart & Winston	1,932,000
Dennis the Menace—Teacher's Threat, by Hank Ketcham. 1959 Holt, Rinehart & Winston	1,898,753
Pocket Book of Boners. 1943 Pocket Books	1,547,000
Pocket Book of Cartoons, ed. by Bennett Cerf. 1943 Pocket Books	1,507,000
The Specialist, by Chic Sale. 1929 Specialist Publishing Co.	1,500,000
Believe It Or Not, ed. by Robert L. Ripley. 1941 Pocket Books	1,457,000
The Mad Reader, by E. C. Publications. 1954 Ballantine	1,433,477
Pocket Book of War Humor, ed. by Bennett Cerf. 1943 Pocket Books	1,422,000
Dennis the Menace, by Hank Ketcham. 1952 Holt, Rinehart & Winston	1,400,000
Cartoon Laffs, by True Magazine. 1952 Gold Medal	1,290,433
Mad Strikes Back, by E. C. Publications. 1955 Ballantine	1,282,414
Cartoon Fun from True, by True Magazine. 1954 Gold Medal	1,193,492
Inside Mad, by E. C. Publications. 1955 Ballantine	1,188,395
Utterly Mad, by E. C. Publications. 1956 Ballantine	1,055,923
Happiness Is a Warm Puppy, by Charles M. Schulz. 1962 Determined Productions	1,000,054

PAMPHLETS AND SERIES

Pamphleteering was originally the preoccupation of the politically minded and crusaders in such causes as religious freedom. Pamphlets were, as now, fairly cheap to produce and could be sold at low prices to promulgate their authors' ideas. A pamphlet is usually considered a self-bound book of 48 pages or less, but the paging varies. Most famous American pamphleteer of the past was Thomas Paine who chose pamphlet publishing to publicize his support of the American Revolution and later the French Revolution. Although hundreds of millions of pamphlets are produced in the United States each year, they offer, in the main, practical advice rather than revolutionary ideas. Political and religious pamphleteering of course still flourishes but such writings seldom have the widespread influence that they did two centuries ago.

Universities and colleges and semi-public organizations issue many pamphlets on a great variety of subjects, scholarly, technical and topical. By far the largest pamphlet publisher in the United States over the years is the Government Printing Office. Ten years ago it had sold over one million copies each of five titles. Its latest records show thirteen titles which have sold over a million. They are *Infant Care* (13,805,244); *Your Federal Income Tax* (11,134,100); *Prenatal Care* (7,879,517); *Your Child From One to Six* (6,085,303); *Your Child From Six to Twelve* (2,737,518); *Your Social Security* (2,152,139); *Tax Guide for Small Business* (2,092,226); *Strictly for Teenagers* (1,672,750); *Postage Stamps of the United States* (1,401,099); *Breast Feeding* (1,399,395); *Septic Tank Care* (1,257,417); *About Syphilis and Gonorrhea* (1,050,300); and *The Adolescent in Your Family* (1,023,104). It is interesting to note the purchasers' interests, entirely practical, and parallel in many cases to the interest lines of the best-selling trade paperbacks. These pamphlets are realistically priced, ranging from the five cents for *Strictly for Teenagers* to the $1.25 for what one may consider the luxury item on the list, *Postage Stamps of the United States.*

There are many trade publishers who feature inexpensively priced series of informational books. Among them, to sample a few, are Meredith Press, which sold 2,627,848 copies of its 99-cent line of *Better Homes and Gardens Creative Cookbooks* in two years. Lane Publishing Company, which specializes in guides for the Far Western home owner, has many of its *Sunset Magazine* paperbound building books in six-figure quantities. C. S. Hammond & Co., producer of globes, atlases, and scholastic books, has sold five million copies of its *Words Are Important* paperback series by H. C. Hardwick. Oceana Publications specializes in law for the layman. Its *Legal Almanac Series* has sold well over one million copies.

POETRY AND DRAMA

This section is the smallest of the best seller subject lists. Five volumes of poetry and one play, selling over one-half million copies have been added in the past ten years. But even that small number is an achievement in this category. Notable additions are the poems of Robert Frost and Arthur Miller's play, *Death of a Salesman,* which achieved its sales in what is known as the quality paperback format, distributed to great extent by college bookstores.

76

Collections containing the verse of many poets have attained great sales, rather than the volumes containing the works of only one poet. Only *John Brown's Body* by Stephen Vincent Benét, *The White Cliffs* by Alice Duer Miller, and *I'm a Stranger Here Myself* by Ogden Nash have appeared on annual lists since World War I. There were many in 1917 and 1918: *Poems of Alan Seeger, Rhymes of a Red Cross Man* by Robert W. Service, *Over Here* by Edgar Guest, *Treasury of War Poetry* compiled by G. H. Clark, and *In Flanders Fields* by John McCrae. Edgar Guest and Robert W. Service were America's popular poets for years. Rudyard Kipling also reached best seller status with *The Years Between*. The only best-selling volume of poetry stemming from World War II was Alice Duer Miller's *The White Cliffs*. In the 1930's Edna St. Vincent Millay was a runner-up for an annual list as was Robert Frost in 1962 with his *In the Clearing*.

William Shakespeare is, of course, the best-selling playwright of all time in English. Not only is the scope of this book limited to books first published since 1895, but it would be an impossible task to try to determine the total volume of all the Shakespeare plays published. Recent notable Shakespeare sales are the Folger Library edition of "Hamlet," "Four Great Comedies" and "Four Great Tragedies," of which Pocket Books sold 1,333,000, 1,347,879, and 3,066,455 copies in that order. In drama record sales have been even scantier than in poetry. Before the 1930's plays in book form by Eugène Brieux, Bernard Shaw and Eugene O'Neill appeared on some annual lists, but there has been none since then. Individual modern plays have, however, achieved substantial sales, especially those issued by publishers of drama series and publishers who specialize in printing worthwhile current plays in book form. Besides *Death of a Salesman,* modern plays with good sales are, among others, *The Deputy* by Rolf Hochhuth, *Waiting for Godot* by Samuel Beckett and *Four Plays* by Eugene Ionesco.

101 Famous Poems, comp. by R. J. Cook. 1916 Regnery	(est) 6,000,000
The Pocket Book of Verse, ed. by M. E. Speare. 1940 Pocket Books	2,719,500
The Prophet, by Kahlil Gilbran. 1923 Knopf	2,632,358
Pocket Book of Ogden Nash. 1955 Pocket Books	1,121,000
Death of a Salesman, by Arthur Miller. 1949 Viking Press	1,117,418
Anthology of Robert Frost's Poems, ed. by Louis Untermeyer. 1949 Holt, Rinehart & Winston	1,054,910
Immortal Poems of the English Language, ed. by Oscar Williams. 1952 Pocket Books	1,054,500
A Heap O'Livin', by Edgar Guest. 1916 Regnery	1,000,000

John Brown's Body, by Stephen Vincent Benét. 1928 Holt, Rinehart & Winston 755,630

Best Loved Poems of the American People, ed. by Hazel Felleman. 1936 Doubleday 608,417

REFERENCE

This section comprises generally best-selling volumes of information. In the first part, most works are concerned with language and its usage. They consist mainly of dictionaries, both English and foreign language. There was a notable increase in this type of reference work of best-seller status since the previous edition of this book. Twenty-nine new titles, each selling one-half million copies or more, have been added.

People often speak of *the* Bible, *the* dictionary, and *the* encyclopedia. Actually there are many Bibles, many dictionaries, and many encyclopedias, so many editions of each that it is indeed impossible to collate figures on their sales. There are about 100 publishers of dictionaries and encyclopedias. There were many others in the past. Most of the present such publishers will not release sales figures and the records of the others are no longer available. Many of the dictionaries originated before 1895, the year in which this best seller survey begins. Noah Webster, founder of American lexicography, published his first dictionary in 1806. It was superseded by his *American Dictionary of the English Language* in 1828. The Webster work and name have been perpetuated by a number of publishers, chief among them the G. & C. Merriam Company, which, in 1844, purchased the rights to publish future editions of the Webster dictionary. Pocket Books has sold 15,110,000 copies of the *Merriam-Webster Pocket Dictionary*. Other recent versions of Webster, the Popular Library *Webster's New World Dictionary* and the *New American Webster Dictionary*, published by New American Library, have sold 4,000,000 and 3,130,625 copies respectively.

Another important branch of reference works is the almanac. The *World Almanac* has large sales every year. The *Old Farmer's Almanac* was founded in 1792 and is still going strong. A more recent almanac is the *Information Please Almanac* which, in its first year of publication, 1947, when the radio program for which it was named was at the height of popularity, sold almost 300,000 copies. It continued to sell at the rate of about 100,000 annually. One of the best-known American reference works is *Robert's Rules of Order*. First published in 1876, it is well into the millions. An important work in the field of literature, originally published in the nineteenth century, is Bartlett's *Familiar Quotations*. It has been issued under the imprint of several publishers, latest in hardbound by Little, Brown and Company, which has sold 1,168,116 copies since

1937, and in paperback, *Shorter Bartlett's Familiar Quotations,* of which Pocket Books sold 1,193,650 copies through 1965. *Roget's Thesaurus,* originally published by T. Y. Crowell Company, has also been issued by many different publishers in various versions. A. N. Marquis Company brought out the first volume of *Who's Who in America* in 1899. Since then, *Who's Who* and related works have sold their millions. Rand Mc-Nally's *Road Atlas,* revised annually since 1924, has sold 6,000,000.

Among best-selling encyclopedias are *Encyclopaedia Britannica* and its related volumes; *The Lincoln Library* and *The Standard Dictionary of Facts* (Frontier Press Company); *The World Book Encyclopedia* (Field Enterprises); *The Book of Knowledge* and *Encyclopedia Americana* (Grolier Society); *The American Educator* and *My Book House* (United Educators, Inc.); and the *Collier Encyclopedia* (Crowell-Collier). *The Columbia Encyclopedia,* first published in 1935, has sold well as a large hardcover volume, as has the *Columbia-Viking Desk Encyclopedia.* The latter has sold 2,833,993 copies.

Pocket Atlas. 1917 Hammond	11,000,000
The English-Spanish, Spanish-English Dictionary, comp. by Carlos Castillo and Otto F. Bond. 1948 (University of Chicago Press) Pocket Books	5,892,000
Roget's Pocket Thesaurus. 1923 Pocket Books	5,416,857
Modern World Atlas. 1922 Hammond	5,000,000
30 Days to a More Powerful Vocabulary, by Wilfred J. Funk and Norman Lewis. 1942 Funk & Wagnalls	4,712,588
Larousse French-English, English-French Dictionary 1961 Pocket Books	3,426,000
The Dell Crossword Dictionary, ed. by Kathleen Rafferty. 1950	3,000,000
Columbia Viking Desk Encyclopedia. 1953 Viking Press	2,833,993
The Pocket Dictionary, by W. J. Pelo. 1941 Pocket Books	2,075,000
English Through Pictures, by I. A. Richards and C. M. Gibson. 1945 Pocket Books	2,050,000
My First World Atlas. 1959 Hammond	2,000,000
The Thorndike Century Beginning Dictionary, by E. L. Thorndike. 1952 Scott, Foresman	2,000,000
The Thorndike Century Junior Dictionary, by E. L. Thorndike. 1952 Scott, Foresman	2,000,000
Comparative World Atlas. 1948 Hammond	1,900,000
Langenscheidt German-English, English-German Dictionary. 1960 Pocket Books	1,894,000
Thorndike-Barnhart Handy Pocket Dictionary, ed. by Clarence L. Barnhart. 1951 Doubleday	1,834,704

The American Everyday Dictionary, ed. by Jess Stein. 1953
Random House   1,710,000

Word Power Made Easy, by Norman Lewis. 1949 Doubleday   1,652,235

Thorndike-Barnhart Comprehensive Desk Dictionary, ed. by
Clarence L. Barnhart. 1951 Doubleday   1,612,854

Thorndike-Barnhart Dictionary. 1951 Bantam   1,525,000

Scholastic World Atlas. 1960 Hammond   1,500,000

Nature Atlas, by E. L. Jordan. 1952 Hammond   1,378,500

Historical Atlas. 1949 Hammond   1,300,000

Modern Encyclopedia, by A. H. McDonnald. 1933 W. H. Wise   1,250,000

Perma Crossword Puzzle and Word Game Dictionary, by Frank
Newman. 1950 Pocket Books   1,244,400

American History Atlas. 1951 Hammond   1,200,000

The New Century Dictionary of the English Language. 1927
Appleton-Century   1,200,000

Shorter Bartlett's Familiar Quotations. 1953 Pocket Books   1,193,650

Story of Bible World, by N. B. Keyes. 1957 Hammond   1,190,086

Six Minutes a Day to Perfect Spelling, by Harry Shefter. 1954
Pocket Books   1,163,900

French Through Pictures, by I. A. Richards, M. H. Ilsley, and
C. Gibson. 1959 Pocket Books   1,120,000

Appleton's English-Spanish, Spanish-English Dictionary, by Arturo Cuyas. 1903 Appleton   1,100,000

Atlas of Bible Lands. 1949 Hammond   1,100,000

Dollar World Atlas. 1949 Rand, McNally   1,100,000

New Pocket Thesaurus in Dictionary Form (abridged), by Norman Lewis. Pocket Books   1,053,700

Six Weeks to Words of Power, by Wilfred Funk. 1953 Funk &
Wagnalls   932,621

Classics World Atlas. 1951 Hammond   800,000

Illustrated World Atlas. 1956 Hammond   780,000

Road Atlas. 1964 Hammond   691,259

The American Vest Pocket Dictionary, ed. by Clarence L. Barnhart. 1951 Random House   655,000

The American College Dictionary, ed. by Clarence L. Barnhart.
1947 Random House   625,000

Rainbow Dictionary, by Wendell W. Wright. 1947 World   593,393

Complete World Atlas. 1950 Hammond   500,000

Goode's World Atlas. 1922 Rand, McNally   500,000

Library World Atlas. 1945 Hammond   500,000

The Columbia Encyclopedia, ed. by William Bridgwater and
Elizabeth J. Sherwood. 1935 Columbia University Press   500,000

Technical Reference Works

This list attempts to include reference works for the general book buyer such as the home owner, the automobile owner, and the radio ham, eliminating textbooks sold primarily to school and college students. With rapidly changing modern techniques, both in subjects and in methods of teaching, no twentieth century textbooks could reach the totals of such traditional best sellers as the nineteenth century *McGuffey Readers* (estimated 122,000,000) and Noah Webster's *The American Spelling Book,* the "blue-backed speller" (estimated 60,000,000).

Eight new titles have been added to the list in this edition, and out-of-print titles omitted.

The Radio Amateur's Handbook. 1926 American Radio Relay League	3,800,000
Radio Amateur's License Manual. 1930 American Radio Relay League	2,153,000
Standard Bartender's Guide, by P. G. Duffy and James A. Beard. 1955 Pocket Books	1,919,214
Federal Aviation Regulations and Flight Standards for Pilots, by Aeronautical Staff of Aero Publishers. 1947 Aero Publishers	(est.) 1,550,000
Aircraft Spotters Handbook, by L. C. Gushman. 1943 Wise	1,250,000
Practice for the Army Tests, by David Turner. 1942 Arco	1,152,000
Motor Service's New Automotive Encyclopedia. 1921 Goodheart-Wilcox	950,000
How To Become a Radio Amateur. 1930 American Radio Relay League	843,500
Amateur Builder's Handbook, by Hubbard Cobb. 1950 W. H. Wise	810,000
Learning the Radiotelegraph Code. 1942 American Radio Relay League	574,000
The A.R.R.L. Antenna Book. 1939 American Radio Relay League	526,200

Home Reference Works

Twenty-four new titles have been added to this list, which includes popular reference books primarily for the domestic scene. Four out-of-print titles have been omitted. Cookbooks, which naturally belong in this category, are treated under a separate heading because there are so many best-selling cookbooks and because they form such an important section of book merchandising in this country.

This seems the most appropriate heading under which to mention widely-distributed books of guidance, with more than domestic use. These are the *American Red Cross First Aid Text Book,* best seller of World War II years, during which many million copies were sold, and the annual income tax guides, chief among them *Your Income Tax* by J. K. Lasser, the first annual guide published in 1939 by Simon & Schuster, and, by the '60's selling half a million copies each year.

Pocket Book of Baby and Child Care, by Benjamin Spock. (The Common Sense Book of Baby and Child Care. 1946 Duell, Sloan & Pearce) Pocket Books	19,076,822
Folk Medicine, by D. C. Jarvis, M.D. 1958 Holt, Rinehart & Winston	2,911,111
Better Homes and Gardens Baby Book. 1943 Meredith	2,634,472
Expectant Motherhood, by Nicholson J. Eastman. 1940 Little, Brown	2,063,775
Better Homes and Gardens Garden Book. 1951 Meredith	1,778,831
Family Reference Atlas. 1956 Hammond	1,700,000
Better Homes and Gardens Handyman's Book. 1951 Meredith	1,642,905
Heloise's Housekeeping Hints, by Heloise Cruse. 1962 Prentice-Hall	(est) 1,568,601
Child Behavior, by F. L. Ilg & L. B. Ames. 1955 Harper	1,563,117
Calories Don't Count, by Dr. Herman Taller. 1961 Simon & Schuster	1,525,000
The Marriage Art, by John E. Eichenlaub. 1961 Lyle Stuart	1,520,000
Amy Vanderbilt's Complete Book of Etiquette, by Amy Vanderbilt. 1952 Doubleday	1,500,000
Your Dream Home, by Hubbard Cobb. 1950 W. H. Wise	1,300,000
Wise Garden Encyclopedia, by E. L. D. Seymour. 1936 W. H. Wise	1,265,000
Household Encyclopedia, by Sylvia K. Mager. 1960 Pocket Books	1,173,500
Modern Home Medical Advisor, ed. by Morris Fishbein. 1935 Doubleday	1,165,499
Modern Home Physician, by Victor Robinson, M.D. 1934 W. H. Wise	1,150,000
The Sexual Side of Marriage, by Max J. Exner, M.D. 1932 Norton	1,097,716
Complete Home Handyman's Guide, by Hubbard Cobb. 1948. W. H. Wise	1,095,000

Sunset Western Garden Book, by editors of Sunset Magazine.
1933   1,081,906
Gardening: A Complete Guide, by Montague Free. 1947 Pocket
Books   1,006,000
Etiquette, by Emily Post. 1922 Funk & Wagnalls   (est) 1,000,000
Better Homes and Gardens Flower Arranging. 1957 Meredith   959,551
Better Homes and Gardens Sewing Book. 1961 Meredith   852,222
Better Homes and Gardens Decorating Book. 1956 Meredith   784,686
The Book of Etiquette, by Lillian Eichler. 1922 Doubleday   756,432
Encyclopedia of Modern Sewing, by F. Blondin. 1946 W. H. Wise   625,000
The Complete Book of Interior Decorating, by Mary Derieux and
Isabelle Stevenson. 1949 Hawthorn   500,000
The Complete Book of Sewing, by Constance Talbot and Isabelle
Stevenson. 1949 Hawthorn   500,000

RELIGION

Although the Bible is not included in this list of religious best sellers, any discussion of such a list must start with the Bible. The general public probably asks more questions of libraries and trade specialists about the Bible than about any other book. The most familiar question is, "Is the Bible *the* best seller?" The answer is unequivocally in the affirmative. The statement is probably true as to world sales as well as to those in the United States. Since the time of its first printing by Gutenberg, the Bible has proliferated in number of copies sold. It has also been given away in quantity by such organizations as the American Bible Society, the Gideons, and missionary groups. The U. S. Government, during World War II, issued a portion of the Bible to every man and woman who entered the Armed Services. A *King James* or *Douay New Testament* was given to those of Protestant or Catholic persuasion, and a condensation of the Old Testament to those of Jewish faith, 17,000,000 volumes in all.

In this country, ever since John Eliot translated the New Testament into the language of the Massachusetts Indians in 1661, the Bible has been issued in very many different editions and translations. A great many early Bible publishers are no longer in existence. It is impossible to collect sales figures for complete Bibles, let alone the Bible issued in parts, and in many different versions, including Catholic, Jewish, Episcopal, and Protestant. At the end of 1965 there were editions of the complete Bible available from about 40 different Bible publishers. In addition, trade publishers often issue special editions of the Bible or Books of the Bible, sometimes as illustrated gift editions.

Whenever an important new edition or translation of the Bible is published, it becomes a best seller of its year and is so indicated on the *Publishers' Weekly* monthly and annual best seller lists. Otherwise the Bible is not included on those lists. For example, the *Revised Standard Version* topped the years' lists in 1952, 1953 and 1954. Nelson sold over four million copies in those years. Since then the *Revised Standard Version* has been produced by five other publishers, selling an estimated 15,000,000 copies. In 1958 *The New Testament in Modern English* translated by J. B. Phillips was a best seller. *The New English Bible: The New Testament* was the top seller in 1961, second in 1962, and with a three-year total of 2,277,303. Other new Bibles with large sales are *The Interpreters Bible* (Abingdon) and *The Amplified Bible* (Zondervan).

A larger percentage of the titles in the following list of religious books selling over half a million copies have appeared on the annual lists than titles in any other classification, although most of them were published before 1956. The decade right after World War II showed the greatest number of religious best sellers. In 1953 six out of the first ten nonfiction best sellers were books on religious themes. *Peace of Mind* appeared on three consecutive lists, 1946-1948, *A Man Called Peter* in 1952, 1953 and 1955. *The Power of Positive Thinking* was sixth in 1952, second only to the *Revised Standard Version* in 1953 and 1954, and was second again in 1955.

Ten new best sellers of religious interest have been added to this list in the past ten years, although only a few of them have shown up on the annual lists. As far as production of new religious titles goes, they have doubled in the past ten years, from 909 in 1956 to 1855 in 1965.

The Greatest Story Ever Told, by Fulton Oursler. 1949 Doubleday	3,858,948
The Story of the Bible, by Jesse Lyman Hurlbut. 1904 Winston	3,000,000
The Power of Positive Thinking, by Norman Vincent Peale. 1952 Prentice-Hall	2,505,000
The Greatest Book Ever Written, by Fulton Oursler. 1951 Doubleday	2,282,322
The Song of Our Syrian Guest, by William Allen Knight. 1903 United Church Press	2,102,522
Bible Readings for the Home Circle. 1914 Review & Herald	2,051,448
Streams in the Desert, Vol. 1, by Mrs. Charles E. Cowman. 1931 Zondervan	2,000,000
Story of Bible World, by N. B. Keyes. 1957 Hammond	1,190,086
Peace with God, by Billy Graham. 1954 Doubleday	1,827,493
Egermeier's Bible Story Book, by Elsie E. Egermeier. 1923 Warner Press	1,750,000

The Cross and the Switchblade, by David Wilkerson. 1963 Geis 1,661,578
The Day Christ Died, by Jim Bishop. 1957 Harper & Row 1,591,489
O Ye Jigs & Juleps, by Virginia Cary Hudson. 1962 Macmillan 1,589,451
In Tune with the Infinite, by Ralph Waldo Trine. 1897 Bobbs-
Merrill 1,507,502
Daily Strength for Daily Needs, by Mary W. Tileston. 1901
Little, Brown and Revell 1,237,060
Peace of Mind, by Joshua L. Liebman. 1946 Simon & Schuster 1,107,064
God Is My Co-Pilot, by General Robert L. Scott. 1943 Scribner 1,071,810
Strength for Service to God and Country, by Norman F. Nygaard.
1942 Abingdon Press 1,050,000
Great Controversy, by Ellen G. White. 1926 Review & Herald 1,005,381
Angel Unaware, by Dale Evans Rogers. 1953 Revell 800,000
The Man Nobody Knows, by Bruce Barton. 1925 Bobbs-Merrill 728,000
Seeds of Contemplation, by Thomas Merton. 1949 Harcourt,
Brace & World 710,000
I Believe, A Christian Faith for Youth, by Nevin C. Harner.
1950 United Church Press 633,933
A Guide to Confident Living, by Norman Vincent Peale. 1948
Prentice-Hall 612,000
The Sermon on the Mount, by Emmet Fox. 1934 Harper & Row 604,734
Mr. Jones, Meet the Master, by Peter Marshall. 1949 Revell 600,000
Human Destiny, by Pierre Lecomte du Noüy. 1947 McKay 560,000
Quiet Talks on Power, by S. D. Gordon. 1904 Revell 500,000
The Story of the Bible, by Hendrik W. Van Loon. 1933 Live-
right 500,000

Religious Novels

Religious novels have dominant themes closely concerned with religion in some aspect or deal with a character or characters of some religious significance. Only three novels have been added to this list during the past ten years, but one of them, *Exodus,* has sold more than five million copies. Other religious novels that have shown up on annual lists of the past ten years are *Dear and Glorious Physician, The Listener,* and *Grandmother and the Priests,* all three by Taylor Caldwell, and *The Shoes of the Fisherman* by Morris L. West.

In His Steps, by Charles Monroe Sheldon. 1897 Grosset & Dunlap
et. al. (est.) 8,065,398
Exodus, by Leon Uris. 1958 Doubleday 5,473,710
The Razor's Edge, by W. Somerset Maugham. 1944 Doubleday 3,430,505

The Robe, by Lloyd C. Douglas. 1942 Houghton Mifflin   3,316,791

Magnificent Obsession, by Lloyd C. Douglas. 1929 Houghton
Mifflin   2,974,030

The Cardinal, by Henry Morton Robinson. 1950 Simon &
Schuster   2,950,807

The Silver Chalice, by Thomas B. Costain. 1948 Doubleday   2,336,004

The Song of Bernadette, by Franz Werfel. 1943 Viking   (est.)1,594,000

The Keys of the Kingdom, by A. J. Cronin. 1941 Little, Brown 1,390,895

The Shepherd of the Hills, by Harold Bell Wright. 1907 Appleton 1,200,000

The Shoes of the Fisherman, by Morris West. 1963 Morrow   1,139,572

The Little Shepherd of Kingdom Come, by John Fox, Jr. 1903
Scribner   1,100,000

The Story of the Other Wise Man, by Henry Van Dyke. 1895
Harper   (est)989,088

The Calling of Dan Matthews, by Harold Bell Wright. 1916
Appleton   925,000

The Chain, by Paul I. Wellman. 1949 Doubleday   878,813

Green Light, by Lloyd C. Douglas. 1935 Houghton Mifflin   854,828

The Big Fisherman, by Lloyd C. Douglas. 1948 Houghton Mifflin   814,637

The Miracle of the Bells, by Russell Janney. 1946 Prentice-Hall
                                                             (est)790,000

Quo Vadis, by Henryk Sienkiewicz. 1896 Little, Brown   754,000

The Re-creation of Brian Kent, by Harold Bell Wright. 1919
Appleton   750,000

The Bishop's Mantle, by Agnes Sligh Turnbull. 1948 Macmillan   626,843

Black Rock, by Ralph Connor. 1908 Revell   600,000

The Sky Pilot, by Ralph Connor. 1899 Revell   600,000

The Apostle, by Sholem Asch. 1943 Putnam   554,000

SCIENCE

During the years from 1895 to 1966 there have been few best-selling
books on scientific subjects for the layman. Of course nonfiction was not
reported in the very early years of these best seller lists. The first best
seller in the field of science emerged in 1922 when popularization of
various cultural subjects became a publishing trend. The book was J. Arthur Thomson's *The Outline of Science*. It was followed by two books,
at two-year intervals. They were *The New Decalogue of Science* by Albert
E. Wiggam and *Why We Behave Like Human Beings* by George A. Dorsey. In 1933 appeared Hendrik Willem Van Loon's first big best seller
Van Loon's Geography, which, like many of his books, featured his own
drawings and maps in black and white and color.

In three consecutive years, 1935, 1936, and 1937, there were four best sellers in the category of science: *Rats, Lice and History* by Hans Zinsser; *Man the Unknown* by Alexis Carrel, which was the top nonfiction seller of 1936; *An American Doctor's Odyssey* by Victor Heiser; and *Mathematics for the Million* by Lancelot Hogben, one of the most long-lived of all these books, and which, over the years, has sold 222,404 copies in its original hardcover edition. There was a fourteen-year skip in scientific best sellers to 1951 when the biggest seller of them all appeared, *The Sea Around Us* by Rachel L. Carson. In 1951 and 1952 there were 272,976 copies sold through the trade. Since then, with its sales as a paperback, the book has reached 1,601,079. Over ten years ago appeared the only other title among those related to pure science on these lists, *The Family of Man* by Edward Steichen, which sold 15,000 copies in cloth in 1955 and 364,000 in paper. Another title, one which has never appeared on the annual lists, but which has reached the half-million mark since its publication by Lippincott in 1939, is *You and Heredity* by Amram Scheinfeld.

WESTERNS

It is the paperbacks that have, in recent years, built up the greatest sales in western fiction. A number of the titles on the following list are paperback "originals," not reprints of hardcover books. The introduction of the first twenty-five cent paperbacks began the era of the really big sale in westerns. Despite the popularity of television westerns, which, in general, help the sale of western fiction, title production has been falling off rather sharply through the past decade—from 282 titles in 1956 to a low of 158 in 1964, then a rise to 234 in 1965. Zane Grey is still the author of the greatest number of best-selling titles in the field. There are ten of his books among the top twenty-five. Many of his books have appeared on the annual lists in the early years of this century, when he was at the peak of his writing career. In fact, *The U.P. Trail* was 1918's fiction leader. Total sales of all Zane Grey books are over 40 million. Besides the Zane Grey titles the only book on this list which has appeared on an annual list is Owen Wister's *The Virginian,* top of fiction on the 1902 list and fifth in 1903. Sixty-five years old, the book has been a stage play, has had four movie versions, and, only recently, was the title of a television series.

Nevada, by Zane Grey. 1928 Harper	2,087,837
Shane, by Jack Schaefer. 1954 Houghton, Mifflin	1,933,949
The Virginian, by Owen Wister. 1902 Macmillan	1,736,299
Destry Rides Again, by Max Brand. 1930 Dodd, Mead	1,357,000
The Spirit of the Border, by Zane Grey. 1906 Pocket Books	1,325,000

Light of Western Stars, by Zane Grey. 1914 Harper — 1,308,883
The Border Legion, by Zane Grey. 1916 Harper — 1,279,518
The U.P. Trail, by Zane Grey. 1918 Harper — 1,241,743
Singing Guns, by Max Brand. 1938 Dodd, Mead — 1,229,000
The Riders of the Purple Sage, by Zane Grey. 1912 Harper — 1,216,938
Bugles in the Afternoon, by Ernest Haycox. 1944 Little, Brown — 1,211,394
Wildfire, by Zane Grey. 1917 Harper — 1,107,754
Rawhide Range, by Ernest Haycox. 1952 Popular Library — 1,090,000
Rainbow Trail, by Zane Grey. 1915 Harper — 1,089,767
Ramrod, by Luke Short. 1943 Macmillan — 1,056,992
Lone Star Ranger, by Zane Grey. 1915 Harper — 960,482
Desert Gold, by Zane Grey. 1913 Harper — 950,632
The Winning of Barbara Worth, by Harold Bell Wright. 1911 Appleton — 900,000
The Mysterious Rider, by Zane Grey. 1921 Harper — 898,031
Heritage of the Desert, by Zane Grey. 1910 Harper — 873,400
To the Last Man, by Zane Grey. 1922 Harper — 842,946
The Man of the Forest, by Zane Grey. 1920 Harper — 774,500
Fightin' Fool, by Max Brand. 1939 Dodd, Mead — 605,000
Desert of Wheat, by Zane Grey. 1919 Harper — 602,000
Gone to Texas, by John W. Thomason, Jr. 1936 Scribner — 550,000

Best Sellers By Years

1895 - 1966

1895

Fiction

1. Beside the Bonnie Brier Bush, by *Ian Maclaren*. Dodd, Mead
2. Trilby, by *George du Maurier*. Harper
3. Adventures of Captain Horn, by *Frank R. Stockton*. Scribner
4. The Manxman, by *Hall Caine*. Appleton
5. Princess Aline, by *Richard Harding Davis*. Harper
6. Days of Auld Lang Syne, by *Ian Maclaren*. Dodd, Mead
7. The Master, by *Israel Zangwill*. Harper
8. The Prisoner of Zenda, by *Anthony Hope*. Holt
9. Regeneration, by *Max Nordau*. Appleton
10. My Lady Nobody, by *Maarten Maartens*. Harper

THE YEAR in which the first American best seller lists were published was in the era of bicycles (which were to stage a return nearly fifty years later during the gas rationing days of World War II) and the Gibson girl, with her pompadour hair-do. Rural free delivery was established in that year, an event that was to have a notable effect upon merchandising of every kind, including the marketing of books. Romantic novels like *The Prisoner of Zenda* by Anthony Hope and Richard Harding Davis' *Princess Aline,* which was illustrated by Charles Dana Gibson, suited the mood of the period, though the homely *Beside the Bonnie Brier Bush* of Ian Maclaren and the exotic *Trilby* were the top best sellers. Best remembered of the first ten are these two, both of them tremendously successful in play form. Only two of the books on this first list were written by Americans. The other eight titles, by British and European authors, would have been unprotected by copyright in this country five years earlier, and several publishers or printers could have issued them without any legal arrangement with the rightful publishers. The passage of the international copyright law in 1891 resulted in orderly publication—a fact which helped to make possible the compiling of best seller lists.

1896

Fiction

1. Tom Grogan, by *F. Hopkinson Smith*. Houghton Mifflin
2. A Lady of Quality, by *Frances Hodgson Burnett*. Scribner
3. The Seats of the Mighty, by *Gilbert Parker*. Appleton
4. A Singular Life, by *Elizabeth Stuart Phelps Ward*. Houghton Mifflin
5. The Damnation of Theron Ware, by *Harold Frederic*. Stone & Kimball
6. A House-Boat on the Styx, by *John Kendrick Bangs*. Harper
7. Kate Carnegie, by *Ian Maclaren*. Dodd, Mead
8. The Red Badge of Courage, by *Stephen Crane*. Appleton
9. Sentimental Tommy, by *J. M. Barrie*. Scribner
10. Beside the Bonnie Brier Bush, by *Ian Maclaren*. Dodd, Mead

GOLD WAS DISCOVERED in the Klondike. Bryan ran for President. Books on bimetallism and the gold standard were the most widely-read nonfiction. The best-known of them, *Coin's Financial School*, enjoyed a revival. In Boston the *Aeronautical Annual* was, strangely enough, a best seller. 1896 was the year in which the first movies were shown—introducing a new medium of entertainment that was to have noticeable effect upon the business of publishing. The popularity of the historical novel, America's favorite reading all through the 1890's and the early 20th century and revived again and again, was marked by the sales of such books as *A Lady of Quality* and *The Seats of the Mighty*. *Tom Grogan*, heading the 1896 list, is the first appearance on these lists of its author, that long-time favorite, F. Hopkinson Smith. The success of *A Singular Life* and *The Damnation of Theron Ware* illustrates the continuance of interest in religious novels from the previous decade, when *Robert Elsmere*, by Mrs. Humphry Ward, and *John Ward, Preacher*, by Margaret Deland, were high favorites. The list shows an increase in the number of books by American authors. Books by six of these authors—F. Hopkinson Smith, Frances Hodgson Burnett, Gilbert Parker, Harold Frederic, John Kendrick Bangs, and Stephen Crane—have been in demand by collectors of American first editions over the years.

1897

Fiction

1. Quo Vadis, by *Henryk Sienkiewicz*. Little, Brown
2. The Choir Invisible, by *James Lane Allen*. Macmillan
3. Soldiers of Fortune, by *Richard Harding Davis*. Scribner
4. On the Face of the Waters, by *Flora Annie Steel*. Macmillan
5. Phroso, by *Anthony Hope*. Stokes
6. The Christian, by *Hall Caine*. Appleton
7. Margaret Ogilvy, by *J. M. Barrie*. Scribner
8. Sentimental Tommy, by *J. M. Barrie*. Scribner
9. The Pursuit of the House-Boat, by *John Kendrick Bangs*. Harper
10. The Honorable Peter Stirling, by *Paul Leicester Ford*. Holt

ALTHOUGH the sophisticated "400" ruled New York society and decreed conventions, the great novel of the day was that famous story of the early Christians, *Quo Vadis*. This year marked the appearance of Little, Brown & Company as a publisher of best sellers. James McIntyre of that firm showed genius in reaching large markets, especially difficult at that period with a book with a Latin title, the author of which had a long Polish name. The semi-religious novels of Hall Caine were coming into prominence too. This year also saw the first appearance among best sellers of Paul Leicester Ford, whose books, together with those of Winston Churchill (the American novelist), Charles Major, Mary Johnston, and others, were the record makers of their day in the field of historical fiction. *The Honorable Peter Stirling* had an interesting publishing history. Its publisher, Henry Holt & Company, was chiefly known for scholarly volumes and textbooks, although in 1895 it had taken a successful fling in trade publishing with *The Prisoner of Zenda*. *Peter Stirling*, issued in a small first printing, did not reach large sales until one San Francisco bookseller announced that the chief character was modeled upon President Cleveland. Word-of-mouth advertising brought the sales of the book eventually to 228,000 copies.

1898

Fiction

1. Caleb West, by *F. Hopkinson Smith.* Houghton Mifflin
2. Hugh Wynne, by *S. Weir Mitchell.* Century
3. Penelope's Progress, by *Kate Douglas Wiggin.* Houghton Mifflin
4. Helbeck of Bannisdale, by *Mrs. Humphry Ward.* Macmillan
5. Quo Vadis, by *Henryk Sienkiewicz.* Little, Brown
6. The Pride of Jennico, by *Agnes and Egerton Castle.* Macmillan
7. The Day's Work, by *Rudyard Kipling.* Doubleday, McClure
8. Shrewsbury, by *Stanley Weyman.* Longmans, Green
9. Simon Dale, by *Anthony Hope.* Stokes
10. { The Adventures of François, by *S. Weir Mitchell.* Century
{ The Battle of the Strong, by *Gilbert Parker.* Houghton Mifflin

"REMEMBER THE MAINE!" was the slogan that swept the nation following that battleship's destruction by an explosion in Havana Harbor. It was "Remember Pearl Harbor!" forty-three years later. Spain declared war on the United States on April 24. The Spanish fleet was destroyed in Manila Bay on May 1. The Philippines (temporarily captured by the Japanese forty-four years later) were annexed by the United States and the peace treaty with Spain was signed on December 10. "The end of the war came at an opportune time for autumn business," says a book trade letter of the period. Several authors were included on the best seller list for the first time—Rudyard Kipling, whose books created a furor, Kate Douglas Wiggin, and S. Weir Mitchell. The sale of Mitchell's *Hugh Wynne* was not handicapped by the book's being published in two volumes, nor was that of *Helbeck of Bannisdale*, by Mrs. Humphry Ward, also a two-volume novel. Though Mark Twain was writing at this period, his books never appeared on bookstore best seller lists, for most of them were issued by subscription companies whose house-to-house sales were not recorded in best seller reports from bookstores.

1899

Fiction

1. David Harum, by *Edward Noyes Westcott*. Appleton.
2. When Knighthood Was in Flower, by *Charles Major*. Bowen-Merrill
3. Richard Carvel, by *Winston Churchill*. Macmillan
4. The Day's Work, by *Rudyard Kipling*. Doubleday, McClure
5. Red Rock, by *Thomas Nelson Page*. Scribner
6. Aylwin, by *Theodore Watts-Dunton*. Dodd, Mead
7. Janice Meredith, by *Paul Leicester Ford*. Dodd, Mead
8. Mr. Dooley in Peace and War, by *Finley Peter Dunne*. Small, Maynard
9. No. 5 John Street, by *Richard Whiteing*. Century
10. The Market Place, by *Harold Frederic*. Stokes

AN INTERNATIONAL PEACE CONFERENCE sponsored by the Russian government met at The Hague. Aguinaldo staged an insurrection in the Philippines. The Boer War broke out in South Africa. The great novel of the day, *David Harum,* a novel that became a stage hit and many years later a movie with Will Rogers in the title role, was the story of a down-to-earth countryman of upper New York State. *When Knighthood Was in Flower* was the first best-selling novel to bear the Indianapolis imprint of the Bowen-Merrill Company, later the Bobbs-Merrill Company, a firm which developed a technique of exploiting popular fiction that greatly influenced American publishing. *When Knighthood Was in Flower, Janice Meredith,* and *Richard Carvel* are perhaps the best-remembered of the novels of this great era of historical fiction. *Richard Carvel* introduced Winston Churchill to the best seller lists, an American author who was to attain leading places on many later annual lists and whose name was much better known then in America than that of Winston Spencer Churchill of England. Also on the 1899 list appeared *Mr. Dooley,* Finley Peter Dunne's humorous character who was quoted for many years.

1900

Fiction

1. To Have and to Hold, by *Mary Johnston*. Houghton Mifflin
2. Red Pottage, by *Mary Cholmondeley*. Harper
3. Unleavened Bread, by *Robert Grant*. Scribner
4. The Reign of Law, by *James Lane Allen*. Macmillan
5. Eben Holden, by *Irving Bacheller*. Lothrop
6. Janice Meredtih, by *Paul Leicester Ford*. Dodd, Mead
7. The Redemption of David Corson, by *Charles Frederic Goss*. Bowen-Merrill
8. Richard Carvel, by *Winston Churchill*. Macmillan
9. When Knighthood Was in Flower, by *Charles Major*. Bowen-Merrill
10. Alice of Old Vincennes, by *Maurice Thompson*. Bowen-Merrill

1900 WAS THE YEAR of the Boxer Rebellion in China, the great hurricane and flood in Galveston, Texas, and the first excavation for the New York subway. In Kansas, Carry Nation began her hatchet raids on saloons. Four thousand "horseless carriages," most of them powered by electric batteries or steam, were manufactured during the first year of the new century. Historical novels dominated the nation's reading: *To Have and to Hold, Janice Meredith, Alice of Old Vincennes,* and others. *David Harum* had a follower in the field of rural wisdom in *Eben Holden,* which for a short time brought D. Lothrop & Co. (of *Five Little Peppers* fame) into the field of adult publishing. Bowen-Merrill was prominent on the list with three titles, two of them by Hoosier novelists Charles Major and Maurice Thompson.

1901

Fiction

1. The Crisis, by *Winston Churchill*. Macmillan
2. Alice of Old Vincennes, by *Maurice Thompson*. Bowen-Merrill
3. The Helmet of Navarre, by *Bertha Runkle*. Century
4. The Right of Way, by *Gilbert Parker*. Harper
5. Eben Holden, by *Irving Bacheller*. Lothrop
6. The Visits of Elizabeth, by *Elinor Glyn*. John Lane
7. The Puppet Crown, by *Harold MacGrath*. Bowen-Merrill
8. Richard Yea-and-Nay, by *Maurice Hewlett*. Macmillan
9. Graustark, by *George Barr McCutcheon*. Stone & Kimball
10. D'ri and I, by *Irving Bacheller*. Lothrop

PRESIDENT MCKINLEY was shot while attending the Pan-American Exposition, and Theodore Roosevelt took office on September 14. Though this was a year of financial panic, famous novels sold in the hundreds of thousands. The first book of a previously unknown author, *The Helmet of Navarre*, made such a success as a serial in *The Century* that it was published in an unprecedented first printing of 100,000 copies. Turning from the Revolutionary setting of *Richard Carvel* to the Civil War scene for his new book, Winston Churchill established *The Crisis* as the best seller of the year. *Alice of Old Vincennes* climbed from tenth place on the best seller list of the previous year to second place, via national advertising and promotion such as books had seldom before been given. *Graustark*, with the Chicago imprint of Stone & Kimball, established a lasting reputation for George Barr McCutcheon, another of the Hoosier school of writers. Together with Harold MacGrath's *The Puppet Crown*, it marked a new trend in fiction—toward the light romance of intrigue and adventure in high society.

1902

Fiction

1. The Virginian, by *Owen Wister*. Macmillan
2. Mrs. Wiggs of the Cabbage Patch, by *Alice Caldwell Hegan*. Century
3. Dorothy Vernon of Haddon Hall, by *Charles Major*. Macmillan
4. The Mississippi Bubble, by *Emerson Hough*. Bowen-Merrill
5. Audrey, by *Mary Johnston*. Houghton Mifflin
6. The Right of Way, by *Gilbert Parker*. Harper
7. The Hound of the Baskervilles, by *A. Conan Doyle*. McClure, Phillips
8. The Two Vanrevels, by *Booth Tarkington*. McClure, Phillips
9. The Blue Flower, by *Henry van Dyke*. Scribner
10. Sir Richard Calmady, by *Lucas Malet*. Dodd, Mead

WHILE "RAGTIME" swept America, Debussy's *Pélleas et Mélisande* was a popular success in Paris. The first "skyscrapers" were being built. Historical fiction, still riding high, comprised more than half the best seller list. Advance orders for Mary Johnston's *Audrey* exceeded 100,000 copies. Several new writing reputations were established by 1902 sales— those of Owen Wister, Emerson Hough, and Alice Caldwell Hegan (later Mrs. Rice). The book, the play, in which Dustin Farnum acted for ten years, and the movie in which Gary Cooper portrayed "The Virginian" have made the hero's famous words "When you call me that, *smile,*" familiar in many an American household. In the sixties *The Virginian* became the basis for a TV serial. Eventually it sold in the millions. Owen Wister dedicated the book to his lifelong friend, Theodore Roosevelt. The Hoosier school added Booth Tarkington to its best-selling membership with his third book, *The Two Vanrevels*. His first novel, *The Gentleman from Indiana,* had been published in 1899. On this list, too, a detective story appeared for the first time. It was *The Hound of the Baskervilles,* by that most famous writer of detective fiction, the creator of Sherlock Holmes.

1903

Fiction

1. Lady Rose's Daughter, by *Mrs. Humphry Ward.* Harper
2. Gordon Keith, by *Thomas Nelson Page.* Scribner
3. The Pit, by *Frank Norris.* Doubleday, Page
4. Lovey Mary, by *Alice Hegan Rice.* Century
5. The Virginian, by *Owen Wister.* Macmillan
6. Mrs. Wiggs of the Cabbage Patch, by *Alice Hegan Rice.* Century
7. The Mettle of the Pasture, by *James Lane Allen.* Macmillan
8. Letters of a Self-Made Merchant to His Son, by *George Horace Lorimer.* Small, Maynard
9. The One Woman, by *Thomas Dixon, Jr.* Doubleday, Page
10. The Little Shepherd of Kingdom Come, by *John Fox, Jr.* Scribner

1903 was the year of the first successful airplane flight, made by the Wright brothers on December 17. The past few years had been a period of financial crisis; now the era of great industrial expansion was beginning. With *Lovey Mary,* Alice Hegan Rice repeated the success of her *Mrs. Wiggs of the Cabbage Patch.* Both were in the Century Company's famous series of short dollar novels, a series which reached its sales climax with *The Lady of the Decoration* in 1907. A new author, John Fox, Jr., appeared with the first of two novels that were to become almost synonymous with the words "best seller." There was only one English author on the list, Mrs. Humphry Ward; but her *Lady Rose's Daughter* was in number one position. Big business as a subject for fiction has cropped up over the years ever since *The Pit* and the famous *Saturday Evening Post* editor's *Letters of a Self-Made Merchant to His Son* became best sellers.

1904

Fiction

1. The Crossing, by *Winston Churchill*. Macmillan
2. The Deliverance, by *Ellen Glasgow*. Doubleday, Page
3. The Masquerader, Anonymous (*Katherine Cecil Thurston*). Harper
4. In the Bishop's Carriage, by *Miriam Michelson*. Bobbs-Merrill
5. Sir Mortimer, by *Mary Johnston*. Harper
6. Beverly of Graustark, by *George Barr McCutcheon*. Dodd, Mead
7. The Little Shepherd of Kingdom Come, by *John Fox, Jr.* Scribner
8. Rebecca of Sunnybrook Farm, by *Kate Douglas Wiggin*. Houghton Mifflin
9. My Friend Prospero, by *Henry Harland*. McClure, Phillips
10. The Silent Places, by *Stewart Edward White*. McClure, Phillips

THE RUSSO-JAPANESE WAR was raging, and Americans were, on the whole, sympathetic to Japan. Advertisements of the year offered new rolls for phonographs, automobile road maps, one-piece collar buttons, and Sapolio. The World's Fair was on in St. Louis, the New York subway was opened, the Panama Canal was begun, and the first successful tunnel under the Hudson River was completed. In the magazines and newspapers the "literature of exposure" was appearing. Lincoln Steffens was writing; Thomas W. Lawson produced *Friday the Thirteenth*; and Ida Tarbell's *History of the Standard Oil Company* was running in *McClure's Magazine*. Among books, historical and romantic fiction dominated the best seller lists and the "sex problem" reared its head. Again Winston Churchill topped all other novelists of the year. An edition of 110,000 copies of Ellen Glasgow's *The Deliverance* was published; like most of these early 20th-century novels, it was priced at $1.50. The famous house of best sellers, Bowen-Merrill, became Bobbs-Merrill.

1905

Fiction

1. The Marriage of William Ashe, by *Mrs. Humphry Ward*. Harper
2. Sandy, by *Alice Hegan Rice*. Century
3. The Garden of Allah, by *Robert Hichens*. Stokes
4. The Clansman, by *Thomas Dixon, Jr*. Doubleday, Page
5. Nedra, by *George Barr McCutcheon*. Dodd, Mead
6. The Gambler, by *Katherine Cecil Thurston*. Harper
7. The Masquerader, Anonymous (*Katherine Cecil Thurston*). Harper
8. The House of Mirth, by *Edith Wharton*. Scribner
9. The Princess Passes, by *C. N.* and *A. M. Williamson*. Holt
10. Rose o' the River, by *Kate Douglas Wiggin*. Houghton Mifflin

NOVELS WERE beginning to utilize motor cars and wireless telegraphy, the new inventions of the period, in their plots. "Realism" was a literary trend. Novels and plays on business themes were popular. One of the year's stage hits was Charles Klein's *The Lion and the Mouse,* a play about a department store. Maxine Elliott and Mrs. Fiske were stars of the period. The first issue of *Variety* was published on December 16. *The Clansman,* Thomas Dixon's novel of the Ku Klux Klan, which was to become, as *The Birth of a Nation,* one of the most famous feature pictures of the silent movies, was well up on this year's best seller list. The Williamsons made the list with one of their first automobile romances. They specialized in the type of story in which the heroine falls in love with her chauffeur, who is actually the scion of a titled British family. "Motormania" hit the nation in a big way and practically all the publicity pictures of authors showed them at the wheels of their 1905 automobiles.

1906

Fiction

1. Coniston, by *Winston Churchill*. Macmillan
2. Lady Baltimore, by *Owen Wister*. Macmillan
3. The Fighting Chance, by *Robert W. Chambers*. Appleton
4. The House of a Thousand Candles, by *Meredith Nicholson*. Bobbs-Merrill
5. Jane Cable, by *George Barr McCutcheon*. Dodd, Mead
6. The Jungle, by *Upton Sinclair*. Doubleday, Page
7. The Awakening of Helena Ritchie, by *Margaret Deland*. Harper
8. The Spoilers, by *Rex Beach*. Harper
9. The House of Mirth, by *Edith Wharton*. Scribner
10. The Wheel of Life, by *Ellen Glasgow*. Doubleday, Page

ONE of the most influential novels ever published in this country, Upton Sinclair's *The Jungle,* awoke the American public to the menace of the "meat trust" and was influential in the passage of the Pure Food and Drugs Act. Theodore Roosevelt, who took the "big stick" to some of the big corporations, championed simplified spelling as well as trust busting. John Philip Sousa was the March King of the nation. William Vaughn Moody's *The Great Divide* was a Broadway success. William Randolph Hearst was defeated for the governorship of New York State. Here for the first time was an all-American best seller list, which Winston Churchill headed for the third time, with another novel which, like *The Crisis* and *The Crossing* made good use of the letter C. Robert W. Chambers' *The Fighting Chance* was published in a first printing of 50,000 copies, in six weeks went to 100,000 and soon to 200,000. One of the first hits in the mystery-adventure field which was not a costume romance was Meredith Nicholson's *House of a Thousand Candles.*

1907

1907 WAS a year of financial panic. Harrison Fisher was the popular artist of the time, along with Howard Chandler Christy, who illustrated *Beverly of Graustark,* and James Montgomery Flagg. The Harrison Fisher "gift book" annual was called *A Dream of Fair Women,* each colored illustration inspired by a popular poem. Ian Maclaren died in 1907. He was the great popular novelist of the previous decade and author of the first best seller of these yearly lists, *Beside the Bonnie Brier Bush.* Novelist Stewart Edward White was photographed in his two-cylinder Maxwell runabout; Mrs. Pat Campbell arrived to tour the country; Farrar and Chaliapin were singing at the Metropolitan, and Mary Garden at the Manhattan Opera House; the *Lusitania* made its first voyage to New York; and *The Man from Home,* by Booth Tarkington and Harry Leon Wilson, was the theatrical hit of the year. The Century Company's short dollar fiction series, which had started with the publication of *Mrs. Wiggs of the Cabbage Patch,* reached another high with *The Lady of the Decoration.* Robert W. Chambers' new novel, *The Younger Set,* marking the interest in sophisticated society romance, had sales of 200,000 copies, equaling the sale of his *The Fighting Chance* in 1906. Bobbs-Merrill, Indianapolis publishers, had four titles on this list, to the envy of many an eastern publisher.

1908

Fiction

1. Mr. Crewe's Career, by *Winston Churchill*. Macmillan
2. The Barrier, by *Rex Beach*. Harper
3. The Trail of the Lonesome Pine, by *John Fox, Jr.* Scribner
4. The Lure of the Mask, by *Harold MacGrath*. Bobbs-Merrill
5. The Shuttle, by *Frances Hodgson Burnett*. Stokes
6. Peter, by *F. Hopkinson Smith*. Scribner
7. Lewis Rand, by *Mary Johnston*. Houghton Mifflin
8. The Black Bag, by *Louis J. Vance*. Bobbs-Merrill
9. The Man from Brodney's, by *George Barr McCutcheon*. Dodd, Mead
10. The Weavers, by *Gilbert Parker*. Harper

BELGIUM ANNEXED the Congo. Maude Adams was playing in Barrie's *What Every Woman Knows,* and Augustus Thomas' *The Witching Hour* was another theatrical success. Maxine Elliott became the first American actress to own and operate her own theatre. The Harrison Fisher annual was *Bachelor Belles*. Winston Churchill was again first on the best seller list, having deserted his southern historical scenes for a New Hampshire setting. The first printing of *The Trail of the Lonesome Pine,* third on the list, was sold out in a few months. One of the best-known popular songs used the book's title—a songwriting habit that has persisted. Frances Hodgson Burnett was still a best seller twenty-two years after her greatest hit, *Little Lord Fauntleroy.* Nine of the authors were Americans, but all were "repeaters" from previous years, a characteristic of the fiction lists, which report favorite writers year after year.

1909

Fiction

1. The Inner Shrine, Anonymous (*Basil King*). Harper
2. Katrine, by *Elinor Macartney Lane*. Harper
3. The Silver Horde, by *Rex Beach*. Harper
4. The Man in Lower Ten, by *Mary Roberts Rinehart*. Bobbs-Merrill
5. The Trail of the Lonesome Pine, by *John Fox, Jr.* Scribner
6. Truxton King, by *George Barr McCutcheon*. Dodd, Mead
7. 54-40 or Fight, by *Emerson Hough*. Bobbs-Merrill
8. The Goose Girl, by *Harold MacGrath*. Bobbs-Merrill
9. Peter, by *F. Hopkinson Smith*. Scribner
10. Septimus, by *William J. Locke*. John Lane

WILLIAM HOWARD TAFT was inaugurated as President of the United States; the first "Model T" Ford rolled off the assembly line; Peary reached the North Pole; and suffragettes were chaining themselves to London railings in this year 1909. Rube Goldberg's *Foolish Questions* was a regular feature of the New York *Evening Mail*. Frances Starr was appearing in *The Easiest Way,* and Mary Garden triumphed as Salome. "The art of the moving picture is still in its infancy," wrote Frederic Taber Cooper. Dr. Eliot's *Five-Foot Shelf,* its advertising a milestone in merchandising, made its first appearance. In the publication of Basil King's *The Inner Shrine,* best-selling book of 1909, Harper used anonymity to build up curiosity. The same publisher had also employed that method in selling Katherine Cecil Thurston's hit book of 1904 and 1905, *The Masquerader,* and was to use it again in 1910 with Basil King's *The Wild Olive.* This promotion stunt can be used only infrequently or its effect is blunted. Another example of its success, twenty years later, was the publication of Ursula Parrott's *Ex-Wife* in 1929 by Cape & Smith. *The Man in Lower Ten,* by Mary Roberts Rinehart, was the first American detective story to make the annual best seller list. It was illustrated in color by Howard Chandler Christy. William J. Locke, who had long been popular and is best remembered for his *Beloved Vagabond,* was introduced to the list, in tenth place, with one of his typically whimsical tales.

1910

Fiction

1. The Rosary, by *Florence Barclay,* Putnam
2. A Modern Chronicle, by *Winston Churchill.* Macmillan
3. The Wild Olive, Anonymous (*Basil King.*) Harper
4. Max, by *Katherine Cecil Thurston.* Harper
5. The Kingdom of Slender Swords, by *Hallie Erminie Rives.* Bobbs-Merrill
6. Simon the Jester, by *William J. Locke.* John Lane
7. Lord Loveland Discovers America, by *C. N.* and *A. M. Williamson.* Doubleday, Page
8. The Window at the White Cat, by *Mary Roberts Rinehart.* Bobbs-Merrill
9. Molly Make-Believe, by *Eleanor Abbott.* Century
10. When a Man Marries, by *Mary Roberts Rinehart.* Bobbs-Merrill

THE END of an era had come with the death of Edward VII of England. 1910 was also the year of the death, in her ninety-second year, of Julia Ward Howe, author of *The Battle Hymn of the Republic.* Japan annexed Korea. The *Mauretania* was queen of the Atlantic. Edmond Rostand's *Chantecler* was produced in Paris; and Maeterlinck's *Blue Bird,* in London. Montague Glass' *Potash and Perlmutter* stories were running in the *Saturday Evening Post,* and the newspaper "funnies" of the day were *The Hall Room Boys* and Bud Fisher's *Mutt and Jeff.* Everyone was humming Ethelbert Nevin's song, "The Rosary," which was used in the plot of the year's best-selling novel—the first to take precedence over a new Churchill novel at the top of the list in a number of years. So popular and profitable was the book that its publisher's new building on West 45th Street, in New York, was dubbed "The Rosary." But its author, Florence Barclay, along with such other authors as the Williamsons and Eleanor Abbott, was soon forgotten. On the other hand, Mary Roberts Rinehart, represented by two books on the 1910 list, was a best-selling author for over half a century.

1911

Fiction

1. The Broad Highway, by *Jeffrey Farnol*. Little, Brown
2. The Prodigal Judge, by *Vaughan Kester*. Bobbs-Merrill
3. The Winning of Barbara Worth, by *Harold Bell Wright*. Book Supply Co.
4. Queed, by *Henry Sydnor Harrison*. Houghton Mifflin
5. The Harvester, by *Gene Stratton Porter*. Doubleday, Page
6. The Iron Woman, by *Margaret Deland*. Harper
7. The Long Roll, by *Mary Johnston*. Houghton Mifflin
8. Molly Make-Believe, by *Eleanor Abbott*. Century
9. The Rosary, by *Florence Barclay*. Putnam
10. The Common Law, by *Robert W. Chambers*. Appleton

"ALEXANDER'S RAGTIME BAND" was the song of the year. It swept the country in 1911, and staged a return some twenty-seven years later. As a result of the 1938 movie of that title, an additional 1,000,000 copies of the song were sold. Along with ragtime came the first big wave of mechanized music—the player piano and the phonograph, forerunners of radio, talking screen and TV. The New York Public Library at 42nd Street and Fifth Avenue, which, with other libraries, is a final repository for many of the forgotten best sellers of yesterday, was opened on May 23. Top seller of the year, *The Broad Highway,* by the new English writer, Jeffrey Farnol, marked the last high spot of this long era of the historical novel. A total of 305,000 copies were sold in both original and reprint editions. Here was the first appearance of Harold Bell Wright, who built an extraordinary following, perhaps largely among a public not generally buyers of books. Gene Stratton Porter, many of whose books are among the big American best sellers of all time, made her first appearance on these lists with *The Harvester. Freckles* had been published in 1904 but had missed making an annual list largely because its great sale came after it had gone into a 50-cent reprint edition. *The Winning of Barbara Worth* was priced at $1.30 and *Queed,* a first novel that caught the public fancy, at $1.35—both prices typical of their time.

1912

Fiction

1. The Harvester, by *Gene Stratton Porter*. Doubleday, Page
2. The Street Called Straight, by *Basil King*. Harper
3. Their Yesterdays, by *Harold Bell Wright*. Book Supply Co.
4. The Melting of Molly, by *Maria Thompson Daviess*. Bobbs-Merrill
5. A Hoosier Chronicle, by *Meredith Nicholson*. Houghton Mifflin
6. The Winning of Barbara Worth, by *Harold Bell Wright*. Book Supply Co.
7. The Just and the Unjust, by *Vaughan Kester*. Bobbs-Merrill
8. The Net, by *Rex Beach*. Harper
9. Tante, by *Anne Douglas Sedgwick*. Century
10. Fran, by *J. Breckenridge Ellis*. Bobbs-Merrill

Nonfiction

1. The Promised Land, by *Mary Antin*. Houghton Mifflin
2. The Montessori Method, by *Maria Montessori*. Stokes
3. South America, by *James Bryce,* Macmillan
4. A New Conscience and an Ancient Evil, by *Jane Addams*. Macmillan
5. Three Plays, by *Eugène Brieux*. Brentano
6. Your United States, by *Arnold Bennett*. Harper
7. Creative Evolution, by *Henri Bergson*. Holt
8. How to Live on Twenty-Four Hours a Day, by *Arnold Bennett*. Doran
9. Woman and Labor, by *Olive Schreiner*. Stokes
10. Mark Twain, by *Albert Bigelow Paine*. Harper

WOODROW WILSON was elected President of the United States, defeating both William Howard Taft and Theodore Roosevelt: the latter's Bull Moose candidacy split the Republican party. Arizona and New Mexico were admitted to the Union. The dramatic sinking of the great new luxury liner *Titanic,* with many notables on board and with enormous loss of life, stunned two continents. In this year began the heyday of the

Harold Bell Wright-Gene Stratton Porter novels. Both their 1911 best sellers reappeared on the 1912 list, Mrs. Porter's reaching top place. Anne Douglas Sedgwick's *Tante* gave a note of literary distinction to a none too distinguished group of novels. *The Publishers' Weekly* added nonfiction best-selling records this year and again in 1913, then dropped them for three years until the sales of books about World War I made nonfiction titles big sellers again. Previously fiction and nonfiction had been lumped together, with the result that the list consisted almost entirely of fiction and a book of general literature seldom if ever reached a yearly best seller list. Not until the 1920's did nonfiction sales equal those of fiction, when such books as H. G. Wells' *Outline of History* began to come along. Nonfiction best sellers tell more about the subjects in which the public was interested than which authors were their favorites. The first nonfiction best-seller list was no lightweight assembly. It featured "self-help" books, biography, travel, social and economic problems, philosophy—recurring topics through all the later years. Notable was the appearance of two books by Arnold Bennett on the list, and one by Jane Addams. There began a revival of interest in the teaching methods of Maria Montessori 50 years after *The Montessori Method* reached second place among nonfiction best sellers.

1913

Fiction

1. The Inside of the Cup, by *Winston Churchill*. Macmillan
2. V.V.'s Eyes, by *Henry Sydnor Harrison*, Houghton Mifflin
3. Laddie, by *Gene Stratton Porter*. Doubleday, Page
4. The Judgment House, by *Sir Gilbert Parker*. Harper
5. Heart of the Hills, by *John Fox, Jr*. Scribner
6. The Amateur Gentleman, by *Jeffrey Farnol*. Little, Brown
7. The Woman Thou Gavest Me, by *Hall Caine*. Lippincott
8. Pollyanna, by *Eleanor H. Porter*. Page
9. The Valiants of Virginia, by *Hallie Erminíe Rives*. Bobbs-Merrill
10. T. Tembarom, by *Frances Hodgson Burnett*. Century

Nonfiction

1. Crowds, by *Gerald Stanley Lee*. Doubleday, Page
2. Germany and the Germans, by *Price Collier*. Scribner
3. Zone Policeman 88, by *Harry A. Franck*. Century
4. The New Freedom, by *Woodrow Wilson*. Doubleday, Page
5. South America, by *James Bryce*. Macmillan
6. Your United States, by *Arnold Bennett*. Harper
7. The Promised Land, by *Mary Antin*. Houghton Mifflin
8. Auction Bridge To-Day, by *Milton C. Work*. Houghton Mifflin
9. Three Plays, by *Eugène Brieux*. Brentano
10. Psychology and Industrial Efficiency, by *Hugo Munsterberg*. Houghton Mifflin

IN 1901, 1904, 1906, 1908, and again in 1913 a novel by Winston Churchill headed fiction sales. Hall Caine's *The Woman Thou Gavest Me* sold 346,000 in the year. *Pollyanna* made her first appearance, beginning a series that continued to sell over many years, although latterly as juvenile reading. Nonfiction included (a year before the outbreak of World War I) a book on Germany, by Price Collier, and President Wilson's statement of his program, *The New Freedom*. Brieux's plays appeared for the second year—one of the few books of drama in all these lists. The discussion of one of the plays, *Damaged Goods,* when performed in New York probably accounted for the book's large sale. It was based on a theme startling for those times, the problem of venereal disease. Milton Work, first bridge authority to achieve a national sale for his instruction books, was succeeded as a best seller many years later by Ely Culbertson and then by Charles Goren. 1913 was the year in which the Secretary of State declared the first federal income tax law in effect, after the 16th Amendment to the Constitution had been ratified by 42 of the 48 states.

1914

Fiction

1. The Eyes of the World, by *Harold Bell Wright*. Book Supply Co.
2. Pollyanna, by *Eleanor H. Porter.* Page
3. The Inside of the Cup, by *Winston Churchill.* Macmillan
4. The Salamander, by *Owen Johnson*. Bobbs-Merrill
5. The Fortunate Youth, by *William J. Locke.* John Lane
6. T. Tembarom, by *Frances Hodgson Burnett.* Century
7. Penrod, by *Booth Tarkington.* Doubleday, Page
8. Diane of the Green Van, by *Leona Dalrymple.* Reilly & Britton
9. The Devil's Garden, by *W. B. Maxwell.* Bobbs-Merrill
10. The Prince of Graustark, by *George Barr McCutcheon.* Dodd, Mead

IN MIDSUMMER an Austrian archduke was murdered in the obscure Balkan town of Sarajevo, and by fall all Europe was at war. The United States had just opened the Panama Canal to the world's seaborne traffic. At home, everyone was singing one of Jerome Kern's first great song hits, "They Didn't Believe Me," from *The Girl from Utah*. Harold Bell Wright attained first place as most popular novelist of the year, closely followed by Eleanor Porter with *Pollyanna* and Winston Churchill with his story of a liberal minister, which had been the 1913 leader. Among the new names were those of Owen Johnson, already known for his appealing stories of Lawrenceville School, Leona Dalrymple, with *Diane of the Green Van* under the new Chicago imprint of Reilly & Britton (later Reilly & Lee), and W. B. Maxwell. It is interesting to note that in this year of 1914 two best sellers were adult novels about boys. Once in a long while such a story hits the hearts of its readers—as did J. D. Salinger's *Catcher in the Rye* many years later. Perhaps the most famous book on this list is that novel of youth, whose hero, Penrod, belongs in the permanent roll of American literature.

1915

Fiction

1. The Turmoil, by *Booth Tarkington.* Harper
2. A Far Country, by *Winston Churchill.* Macmillan
3. Michael O'Halloran, by *Gene Stratton Porter.* Doubleday, Page
4. Pollyanna Grows Up, by *Eleanor H. Porter.* Page
5. K, by *Mary Roberts Rinehart.* Houghton Mifflin
6. Jaffery, by *William J. Locke.* John Lane
7. Felix O'Day, by *F. Hopkinson Smith.* Scribner
8. The Harbor, by *Ernest Poole.* Macmillan
9. The Lone Star Ranger, by *Zane Grey.* Harper
10. Angela's Business, by *Henry Sydnor Harrison.* Houghton Mifflin

U.S. WAR INDUSTRIES were booming. The *Lusitania* was sunk by a German submarine on May 7. "Hello Frisco" was the song of the day, celebrating the opening of the New York-San Francisco telephone line; the first trans-atlantic speech was given by radio, and the first telephone message sent across the Atlantic. Poison gas made its appearance on Europe's battle-fields. Billy Sunday was exhorting a good many Americans into repentance. *The Birth of a Nation,* first great feature film, based upon *The Clansman,* a best seller of 1905, opened in New York. F. Hopkinson Smith, author of *Felix O'Day,* a best seller of 1915, whose novels had been best sellers ever since the 1890's died in his seventy-seventh year. *The Turmoil,* Booth Tarkington's first long serious novel, headed the list of fiction. *K,* by Mary Roberts Rinehart, in fifth place, became her best-known non-mystery novel. Here came the first of the many Zane Grey books to appear on the lists, and another new name was that of Ernest Poole, whose novel of New York harbor has a well-established place in American fiction.

1916

Fiction

1. Seventeen, by *Booth Tarkington.* Harper
2. When a Man's a Man, by *Harold Bell Wright.* Book Supply Co.
3. Just David, by *Eleanor H. Porter.* Houghton Mifflin
4. Mr. Britling Sees It Through, by *H. G. Wells.* Macmillan
5. Life and Gabriella, by *Ellen Glasgow.* Doubleday, Page
6. The Real Adventure, by *Henry Kitchell Webster.* Bobbs-Merrill
7. Bars of Iron, by *Ethel M. Dell.* Putnam
8. Nan of Music Mountain, by *Frank H. Spearman.* Scribner
9. Dear Enemy, by *Jean Webster.* Century
10. The Heart of Rachael, by *Kathleen Norris.* Doubleday, Page

THE FIRST WORLD WAR was in its third year. The New York-New Jersey area was rocked by the Black Tom explosion, supposedly engineered by German secret agents. Woodrow Wilson was re-elected on the campaign slogan, "He kept us out of war." "Preparedness' became the watchword of the day. For the second year in succession Booth Tarkington headed the list of best sellers, this time with *Seventeen,* novel of adolescence, almost as well known as his famous *Penrod. Seventeen* has sold over one and a half million. In fourth place was *Mr. Britling Sees It Through,* by H. G. Wells, which gave thousands of Americans a better understanding of the war. Here is the first appearance of Kathleen Norris with *The Heart of Rachael. Dear Enemy* was written by the author of the better-remembered *Daddy-Long-Legs,* which, because of its slow but steady sale, did not appear on any annual list. Along with such books as *Penrod, Seventeen,* and the Pollyanna stories, it marks a noticeable trend through this period toward novels about very young people written to entertain adults.

1917

Fiction

1. Mr. Britling Sees It Through, by *H. G. Wells*. Macmillan
2. The Light in the Clearing, by *Irving Bacheller*. Bobbs-Merrill
3. The Red Planet, by *William J. Locke*. John Lane
4. The Road to Understanding, by *Eleanor H. Porter*. Houghton Mifflin
5. Wildfire, by *Zane Grey*. Harper
6. Christine, by *Alice Cholmondeley*. Macmillan
7. In the Wilderness, by *Robert S. Hichens*. Stokes
8. His Family, by *Ernest Poole*. Macmillan
9. The Definite Object, by *Jeffery Farnol*. Little, Brown
10. The Hundredth Chance, by *Ethel M. Dell*. Putnam

General Nonfiction

1. Rhymes of a Red Cross Man, by *Robert W. Service*. Barse & Hopkins
2. The Plattsburg Manual, by *O. O. Ellis* and *E. B. Garey*. Century
3. Raymond, by *Sir Oliver Lodge*. Doran
4. Poems of Alan Seeger. Scribner
5. God the Invisible King, by *H. G. Wells*. Macmillan
6. Laugh and Live, by *Douglas Fairbanks*. Britton Publishing Co.
7. Better Meals for Less Money, by *Mary Green*. Holt

War Books

1. The First Hundred Thousand, by *Ian Hay*. Houghton Mifflin
2. My Home in the Field of Honor, by *Frances W. Huard*. Doran
3. A Student in Arms, by *Donald Hankey*. Dutton
4. Over the Top, by *Arthur Guy Empey*. Putnam
5. Carry On, by *Coningsby Dawson*. John Lane
6. Getting Together, by *Ian Hay*. Houghton Mifflin
7. My Second Year of the War, by *Frederick Palmer*. Dodd, Mead

8. The Land of Deepening Shadow, by *D. Thomas Curtin*. Doran
9. Italy, France and Britain at War, by *H. G. Wells*. Macmillan
10. The Worn Doorstep, by *Margaret Sherwood*. Little, Brown

THE UNITED STATES declared war on Germany on April 6. The first of the A.E.F. landed in France in June. Liberty Loans were launched and Mary Pickford, Douglas Fairbanks, and Charlie Chaplin drew enormous crowds to buy bonds, as they made appearances in such places as the steps of the New York Public Library. Revolution swept Imperial Russia. Jazz was the rage in America. Large hotels and restaurants introduced *thés dansants* featuring fox trots. As Americans donned khaki and rolled puttees, Britain's *Mr. Britling* rose to top place in fiction, selling 350,000 copies in fifteen months. Irving Bacheller reappeared, after sixteen years, with his *Light in the Clearing* in second place, followed by many other familiar names—Locke, Porter, Grey, Hichens, etc.—though none of these books has been remembered as its author's best. Although most of the fiction was on the mediocre side, nonfiction and war books (both added classifications in this year) showed what the war-minded American public wanted, for most books on this "general nonfiction" list reflected the emotions and emergencies of wartime America. First was the poetry of Robert W. Service, then *The Plattsburg Manual* for future officers. Sir Oliver Lodge aroused great interest when he, a noted scientist, proclaimed his belief in communion with the dead, in this case with his son, who had been killed in the war. Alan Seeger's poem, *I Have a Rendezvous with Death,* was responsible for the continued sale of his book through the war years. *Over the Top,* best-remembered of World War I accounts, glorified the doughboy and sold 350,000 copies in 1917.

1918

Fiction

1. The U. P. Trail, by *Zane Grey*. Harper
2. The Tree of Heaven, by *May Sinclair*. Macmillan
3. The Amazing Interlude, by *Mary Roberts Rinehart*. Doran
4. Dere Mable, by *Edward Streeter*. Stokes
5. Oh, Money! Money! by *Eleanor H. Porter*. Houghton Mifflin
6. Greatheart, by *Ethel M. Dell*. Putnam
7. The Major, by *Ralph Connor*. Revell
8. The Pawns Count, by *E. Phillips Oppenheim*. Little, Brown
9. A Daughter of the Land, by *Gene Stratton Porter*. Doubleday, Page
10. Sonia, by *Stephen McKenna*. Doran

General Nonfiction

1. Rhymes of a Red Cross Man, *by Robert W. Service*. Barse & Hopkins
2. Treasury of War Poetry, by *G. H. Clark*. Houghton Mifflin
3. With the Colors, by *Everard J. Appleton*. Stewart, Kidd
4. Recollections, by *Viscount Morley*. Macmillan
5. Laugh and Live, by *Douglas Fairbanks*. Britton Publishing Co.
6. Mark Twain's Letters, ed. by *Albert Bigelow Paine*. Harper
7. Adventures and Letters of Richard Harding Davis, by *Richard Harding Davis*. Scribner
8. Over Here, by *Edgar Guest*. Reilly & Lee
9. Diplomatic Days, by *Edith O'Shaughnessy*. Harper
10. Poems of Alan Seeger. Scribner

War Books

1. My Four Years in Germany, by *James W. Gerard*. Doran
2. The Glory of the Trenches, by *Coningsby Dawson*. John Lane
3. Over the Top, by *Arthur Guy Empey*. Putnam
4. A Minstrel in France, by *Harry Lauder*. Hearst's International Library Co.

5. Private Peat, by *Harold R. Peat.* Bobbs-Merrill
6. Outwitting the Hun, by *Lieut. Pat O'Brien.* Harper
7. Face to Face With Kaiserism, by *James W. Gerard.* Doran
8. Carry On, by *Coningsby Dawson.* John Lane
9. Out to Win, by *Coningsby Dawson.* John Lane
10. Under Fire, by *Henri Barbusse.* Dutton

"THE LONG LONG TRAIL" wound on into the last year of war, which began with a great German offensive and ended with dancing in the streets as the first premature Armistice Day was celebrated. Zane Grey's *U. P. Trail* was the most popular novel of the year, firmly establishing his reputation as a writer of western adventure that was to last for more than four decades. *The Tree of Heaven* introduced an English writer of consequence to the American best seller list. *Dere Mable,* considered the prototype of soldier humor, flashed into popularity as did *See Here, Private Hargrove* a quarter of a century later. Edward Streeter's book, which might well have been classed as a war book instead of fiction, quickly sold half a million copies. Not for thirty-one years did Edward Streeter's name reappear on the annual lists. His *Father of the Bride* in 1949 made almost as big a hit. E. Phillips Oppenheim, whose stories of intrigue, mystery, and adventure have been read by more than two generations in England and America, made his first appearance on the list. There are four books of poetry among non-fiction, all with wartime appeal—a type of writing that was noticeably missing among World War II best sellers with one exception. Edgar Guest, through his thirty-five years of writing, had probably the largest popular audience for poetry since James Whitcomb Riley in the 1890's. Two important volumes of memoirs received attention in that war year of 1918 —*Mark Twain's Letters* edited by Albert Bigelow Paine and the *Recollections* of Viscount Morley. Ambassador Gerard's books on Germany had a noticeable influence on American public opinion just as William L. Shirer's *Berlin Diary,* Ambassador Davies' *Mission to Moscow,* and Ambassador Grew's *Ten Years in Japan* were to have in World War II. One of the most widely discussed books from a literary point of view was the French *Under Fire.* Three books by Coningsby Dawson, star reporter of World War I and extremely popular lecturer in the United States, appeared on this list of war books.

118

1919

Fiction

1. The Four Horsemen of the Apocalypse, by *V. Blasco Ibañez*. Dutton
2. The Arrow of Gold, by *Joseph Conrad*. Doubleday, Page
3. The Desert of Wheat, by *Zane Grey*. Harper
4. Dangerous Days, by *Mary Roberts Rinehart*. Doran
5. The Sky Pilot in No Man's Land, by *Ralph Connor*. Doran
6. The Re-Creation of Brian Kent, by *Harold Bell Wright*. Book Supply Co.
7. Dawn, by *Gene Stratton Porter*. Houghton Mifflin
8. The Tin Soldier, by *Temple Bailey*. Penn Publishing Co.
9. Christopher and Columbus, by *"Elizabeth."* Doubleday, Page
10. In Secret, by *Robert W. Chambers*. Doran

Nonfiction

1. The Education of Henry Adams, by *Henry Adams*. Houghton Mifflin
2. The Years Between, by *Rudyard Kipling*. Doubleday, Page
3. Belgium, by *Brand Whitlock*. Appleton
4. The Seven Purposes, by *Margaret Cameron*. Harper
5. In Flanders Fields, by *John McCrae*. Putnam
6. Bolshevism, by *John Spargo*. Harper

GENERAL JOHN J. PERSHING and his men of the AEF marched up Fifth Avenue in a great Victory Parade. Then the fight for the League of Nations was on, with Henry Cabot Lodge its most vigorous opponent in the Senate. President Wilson, who was awarded the Nobel Peace Prize in 1919, took his dream of world organization to the people in a nation-wide tour. Calvin Coolidge was settling the Boston police strike, an act that was to win him national fame and help to bring him eventually to the White House. There came a resurgence of the Ku Klux Klan not only in the South but in many northern states. The "high cost of living" made the daily headlines even as the flapper era, of rolled stockings (silk now, instead of cotton), of bobbed hair and of knee-length skirts, dawned. Helen Hayes appeared in a flapper role in Booth Tarkington's play

119

Clarence, which starred Alfred Lunt. The first airplane crossed the Atlantic, a Navy plane that flew from Nova Scotia to Portugal. *The Four Horsemen of the Apocalypse,* an oustanding war novel of more romantic appeal that *Mr. Britling* of 1916-1917, headed 1919 fiction. Dutton used spectacular display advertising to push it. Its price, $1.90, was a new high for a book destined for wide sales. Later, *The Four Horsemen* became one of the first movies to build the great popularity of Rudolph Valentino. With *The Arrow of Gold,* Doubleday, Page succeeded in giving Joseph Conrad the wide audience he deserved. Here is the first appearance of Temple Bailey, whom Charles Shoemaker, of the Penn Publishing Company of Philadelphia, brought to the front and made a competitor of such writers as Kathleen Norris for the great audience of romantic women readers. Nonfiction best seller and war book records were merged in 1919. What has become a classic of our literature, *The Education of Henry Adams,* took top place among nonfiction. Like Alan Seeger's *Poems,* John McCrae's *In Flanders Fields* became a best seller on the strength of a single poem, the title poem in this case. Kipling's *The Years Between* contained some poems about World War I.

1920

Fiction

1. The Man of the Forest, by *Zane Grey*. Harper
2. Kindred of the Dust, by *Peter B. Kyne*. Cosmopolitan Book Co.
3. The Re-Creation of Brian Kent, by *Harold Bell Wright*. Book Supply Co.
4. The River's End, by *James Oliver Curwood*. Cosmopolitan Book Co.
5. A Man for the Ages, by *Irving Bacheller*. Bobbs-Merrill
6. Mary-Marie, by *Eleanor H. Porter*. Houghton Mifflin
7. The Portygee, by *Joseph C. Lincoln*. Appleton
8. The Great Impersonation, by *E. Phillips Oppenheim*. Little, Brown
9. The Lamp in the Desert, by *Ethel M. Dell*. Putnam
10. Harriet and the Piper, by *Kathleen Norris*. Doubleday, Page

Nonfiction

1. Now It Can Be Told, by *Philip Gibbs*. Harper
2. The Economic Consequences of the Peace, by *John M. Keynes*. Harcourt, Brace
3. Roosevelt's Letters to His Children, ed. by *Joseph B. Bishop*. Scribner
4. Theodore Roosevelt, by *William Roscoe Thayer*. Scribner
5. White Shadows in the South Seas, by *Frederick O'Brien*. Century
6. An American Idyll, by *Cornelia Stratton Parker*. Atlantic Monthly Press

THE FIRST ELECTION returns ever broadcast in the United States (by Station KDKA, Pittsburgh) announced the success of Warren G. Harding's campaign for the Presidency. Women voted for the first time in the 1920 election and helped to put across the amendment to the Constitution that ushered in the prohibition era, the era in which such books as *This Side of Paradise, Flaming Youth,* and *The Plastic Age* brought into the limelight the uninhibited "younger generation." Ponzi, bridge expert Joseph Elwell murdered in New York, Big Jim Colosimo awarded an extravagant gangland funeral in Chicago, Fannie Brice singing "My Man," and the many greats of the sports world—Babe Ruth, Red Grange, Jack Dempsey, Gene Tunney, Walter Hagen, Gertrude Ederle, The Four Horsemen, Big Bill Tilden, Helen Wills, Bobby Jones—are names that echo from the decade ushered in by 1920. Zane Grey again topped best-selling fiction with *The Man of the Forest*. William Randolph Hearst was in the book publishing field for a time; his Cosmopolitan Book Company put two favorites—Peter B. Kyne and James Oliver Curwood, both writers of outdoor adventure stories—on the best seller list. Joseph C. Lincoln, teller of homely New England tales, joined the best sellers with *The Portygee*. Heading nonfiction was Philip Gibbs, a favorite reporter of World War I, who found a waiting market for a volume of war episodes, *Now It Can Be Told*. A new publisher, Harcourt, Brace & Company, appeared on the list with a book of historical importance, *The Economic Consequences of the Peace,* by John M. Keynes. Public interest in President Theodore Roosevelt's letters, written with charm and spontaneity, and in the biography of him by William Roscoe Thayer, was highlighted by his recent death. Frederick O'Brien's *White Shadows in the South Seas* started a new vogue in travel literature and aroused the public's interest in exotic lands.

1921

Fiction

1. Main Street, by *Sinclair Lewis*. Harcourt, Brace
2. The Brimming Cup, by *Dorothy Canfield*. Harcourt, Brace
3. The Mysterious Rider, by *Zane Grey*. Harper
4. The Age of Innocence, by *Edith Wharton*. Appleton
5. The Valley of Silent Men, by *James Oliver Curwood*. Cosmopolitan Book Co.
6. The Sheik, by *Edith M. Hull*. Small, Maynard
7. A Poor Wise Man, by *Mary Roberts Rinehart*. Doran
8. Her Father's Daughter, by *Gene Stratton Porter*. Doubleday, Page
9. The Sisters-in-Law, by *Gertrude Atherton*. Stokes
10. The Kingdom Round the Corner, by *Coningsby Dawson*. Cosmopolitan Book Co.

Nonfiction

1. The Outline of History, by *H. G. Wells*. Macmillan
2. White Shadows in the South Seas, by *Frederick O'Brien*. Century
3. The Mirrors of Downing Street, by a Gentleman with a Duster (*Harold Begbie*). Putnam
4. Mystic Isles of the South Seas, by *Frederick O'Brien*. Century
5. The Autobiography of Margot Asquith. Doran
6. Peace Negotiations, by *Robert Lansing*. Houghton Mifflin

WORLD WAR I's Unknown Soldier was enshrined at Arlington Cemetery. Boston banned the movie, "The Birth of a Nation." Caruso died in Naples. Frank Bacon completed a record run on Broadway in "Lightnin'." Albert Einstein was awarded the Nobel Prize in Physics. Emperor Hirohito of Japan went on a world peace tour. "Normalcy" was President Harding's word for the administration he hoped to provide—but the best-selling novel of the year was a "debunker" of normal small-town life, the book that skyrocketed Sinclair Lewis into fame. *Main Street* sold 295,000 copies in 1921 and brought a new realistic vein into American popular literature which had, for many years, been dominated by royal romance and western

123

adventure. Lewis's book was published by the young firm of Harcourt, Brace & Company, which also provided the second novel on the list, *The Brimming Cup*, by Dorothy Canfield, one of the most beloved writers of a quarter century. Edith Wharton, already a literary notable, appeared on the list for the first time since 1906 with her most famous book, *The Age of Innocence*. Here, too, was the first appearance of Gertrude Atherton, and of Coningsby Dawson as a writer of fiction. Next to *Main Street*, the novel that became most famous was *The Sheik*, by Edith M. Hull. The romantic novel sold like wildfire and eventually became the movie vehicle which made Rudolph Valentino the screen idol of his day. A landmark among best sellers headed nonfiction—H. G. Wells' *Outline of History*, which was issued first as a two-volume set at $10.50, was later marketed in one volume at $5.00, and a few years later had an edition of half a million at $1.00. *White Shadows of the South Seas* was even more popular in its second year; a second and similar book by Frederick O'Brien also appeared on this list. One of the first "debunking" biographies was *The Mirrors of Downing Street*, published under a pseudonym. The visit to the U.S.A. of Margot Asquith, wife of a former English Prime Minister, stirred interest in her autobiography, and Wilson's Secretary of State scored a success with his history of World War peace negotiations. This was almost the last of nonfiction best sellers to deal directly with World War I during the three years after its close. In the 1960's, however, World War I again became a subject of importance in nonfiction for the general reader, when such books as Barbara Tuchman's *The Guns of August* achieved high sales.

1922

Fiction

1. If Winter Comes, by *A. S. M. Hutchinson*. Little, Brown
2. The Sheik, by *Edith M. Hull*. Small, Maynard
3. Gentle Julia, by *Booth Tarkington*. Doubleday, Page
4. The Head of the House of Coombe, by *Frances Hodgson Burnett*. Stokes
5. Simon Called Peter, by *Robert Keable*. Dutton
6. The Breaking Point, by *Mary Roberts Rinehart*. Doran
7. This Freedom, by *A. S. M. Hutchinson*. Little, Brown
8. Maria Chapdelaine, by *Louis Hémon*. Macmillan
9. To the Last Man, by *Zane Grey*. Harper
10. {Babbitt, by *Sinclair Lewis*. Harcourt, Brace
    {Helen of the Old House, by *Harold Bell Wright*. Appleton

Nonfiction

1. The Outline of History, by *H. G. Wells*. Macmillan
2. The Story of Mankind, by *Hendrik Willem Van Loon*. Boni & Liveright
3. The Americanization of Edward Bok, by *Edward Bok*. Scribner
4. Diet and Health, by *Lulu Hunt Peters*. Reilly & Lee
5. The Mind in the Making, by *James Harvey Robinson*. Harper
6. The Outline of Science, by *J. Arthur Thomson*. Putnam
7. Outwitting Our Nerves, by *Josephine A. Jackson and Helen M. Salisbury*. Century
8. Queen Victoria, by *Lytton Strachey*. Harcourt, Brace
9. Mirrors of Washington, Anonymous (*Clinton W. Gilbert*). Putnam
10. Painted Windows, by a Gentleman with a Duster (*Harold Begbie*). Putnam

WAISTLINES at the hips—mah-jongg—Paul Whiteman at the Palais Royale —Rudy Vallee, first of the crooners—the Castles and the Astaires—and *Babbitt,* which introduced a new descriptive word into our language, are all reminders of the twenties. 1922 was the year in which the *Reader's*

Digest was launched. It was to have a definite effect upon the sale of books it "digested" and to start a tremendous wave of magazine book digests. The English writer, A. S. M. Hutchinson, had two novels on the best seller list, with *If Winter Comes,* which sold 350,000 copies in its first ten months, in first place. *The Sheik* carried over into its second year, this time next to the leader. *The Head of the House of Coombe* brought Frances Hodgson Burnett into her fourth decade of best sellerdom. *Simon Called Peter,* a war novel dealing with a religious problem, was a sensation on both sides of the Atlantic and sold 152,000 copies. *Maria Chapdelaine,* with its background the northern Quebec woods, was a critical as well as a popular success. *The Outline of History* in its lower-priced edition made top place in nonfiction for the second year. With Hendrik Willem Van Loon's *Story of Mankind,* James Harvey Robinson's *Mind in the Making,* and J. Arthur Thomson's *Outline of Science,* it ushered in a period of "outline" books on various cultural and scientific subjects that was to reach a climax with the sales of *The Story of Philosophy* four years later. Edward Bok, who had made a reputation as editor of the *Ladies' Home Journal,* provided a new version of the American success story. Two health books achieved big sales. Lytton Strachey's first outstanding biography was his life of Queen Victoria. *Mirrors of Washington* and *Painted Windows* followed in the anonymous steps of *The Mirrors of Downing Street.*

126

1923

Fiction

1. Black Oxen, by *Gertrude Atherton*. Boni & Liveright
2. His Children's Children, by *Arthur Train*. Scribner
3. The Enchanted April, by *"Elizabeth."* Doubleday, Page
4. Babbitt, by *Sinclair Lewis*. Harcourt, Brace
5. The Dim Lantern, by *Temple Bailey*. Penn Publishing Co.
6. This Freedom, by *A. S. M. Hutchinson*. Little, Brown
7. The Mine with the Iron Door, by *Harold Bell Wright*. Appleton
8. The Wanderer of the Wasteland, by *Zane Grey*. Harper
9. The Sea-Hawk, by *Rafael Sabatini*. Houghton Mifflin
10. The Breaking Point, by *Mary Roberts Rinehart*. Doran

Nonfiction

1. Etiquette, by *Emily Post*. Funk & Wagnalls
2. The Life of Christ, by *Giovanni Papini*. Harcourt, Brace
3. The Life and Letters of Walter H. Page, ed. by *Burton J. Hendrick*. Doubleday, Page
4. The Mind in the Making, by *James Harvey Robinson*. Harper
5. The Outline of History, by *H. G. Wells*. Macmillan
6. Diet and Health, by *Lulu Hunt Peters*. Reilly & Lee
7. Self-Mastery Through Conscious Auto-Suggestion, by *Emile Coué*. American Library Service
8. The Americanization of Edward Bok, by *Edward Bok*. Scribner
9. The Story of Mankind, by *Hendrik Willem Van Loon*. Boni & Liveright
10. A Man from Maine, by *Edward Bok*. Scribner

ALL America was chanting "Yes, We Have No Bananas." Dance marathons were the latest craze. Sarah Bernhardt died in Paris and Eleanora Duse in Pittsburgh during a farewell American tour. Laurette Taylor was starring in "Peg o' My Heart" in New York. Over in Germany Hitler's beer hall *Putsch* missed fire. President Harding died, and Calvin Coolidge was quietly sworn in as President of the United States by his father in a simple ceremony in his small native Vermont village of Plymouth. All

127

over the country the revived Ku Klux Klan flourished; white-sheeted men marched openly and fiery crosses burned at night. The magazine *Time* was founded in 1923. With *Black Oxen,* based on what was at the time considered the rather sensational theme of physical rejuvenation, Gertrude Atherton achieved the great popular success of her long writing career. *Babbitt* and *This Freedom* held over into a second year on a fiction list of typical wide-audience appeal, marked with first appearances of Arthur Train and Rafael Sabatini. *Etiquette,* by Emily Post, who had previously been known as a novelist, topped nonfiction sales and developed into a staple bookstore item for the years to come. Papini's *Life of Christ,* a presentation of the life of Jesus in terms of the new psychology, sold well over 100,000 copies in 1923. The Page *Letters* made a new record for a two-volume biography, with 75,000 sold in a year. Mrs. Peters' *Diet and Health,* in its second year on the list, had just about reached 200,000. Robinson and Van Loon in their second years, Wells in his third, and Bok in his second, the latter with another book besides his *Americanization* on the list, gave evidence of the long life of nonfiction. It was in these post-World War I years that nonfiction titles of worth and importance won a separate listing of their own, perhaps spurred on by public interest in "war books." Previously "best sellers" meant novels, and often very frothy novels. Coué became a conversational byword through the ideas expressed in his little self-help book—particularly "Day by day in every way I am getting better and better."

128

Fiction

1. So Big, by *Edna Ferber*. Doubleday, Page
2. The Plastic Age, by *Percy Marks*. Century
3. The Little French Girl, by *Anne Douglas Sedgwick*. Houghton Mifflin
4. The Heirs Apparent, by *Philip Gibbs*. Doran
5. A Gentleman of Courage, by *James Oliver Curwood*. Cosmopolitan Book Co.
6. The Call of the Canyon, by *Zane Grey*. Harper
7. The Midlander, by *Booth Tarkington*. Doubleday, Page
8. The Coast of Folly, by *Coningsby Dawson*. Cosmopolitan Book Co.
9. Mistress Wilding, by *Rafael Sabatini*. Houghton Mifflin
10. The Homemaker, by *Dorothy Canfield Fisher*. Harcourt, Brace

Nonfiction

1. Diet and Health, by *Lulu Hunt Peters*. Reilly & Lee
2. The Life of Christ, by *Giovanni Papini*. Harcourt, Brace
3. The Boston Cooking School Cook Book; new ed. by *Fannie Farmer*. Little, Brown
4. Etiquette, by *Emily Post*. Funk & Wagnalls
5. Ariel, by *André Maurois*. Appleton
6. The Cross Word Puzzle Books, by *Prosper Buranelli* and others. Simon & Schuster
7. Mark Twain's Autobiography. Harper
8. Saint Joan, by *Bernard Shaw*. Brentano
9. The New Decalogue of Science, by *Albert E. Wiggam*. Bobbs-Merrill
10. The Americanization of Edward Bok, by *Edward Bok*. Scribner

"TWENTY-FOUR votes for Underwood" rang through the nation as the 1924 Democratic Convention in the old Madison Square Garden on New York's Madison Square went on through the hot summer days and nights. At Aeolian Hall, Paul Whiteman brought jazz into the realm of classical music with his introduction of George Gershwin's *Rhapsody in Blue* to the concert stage. *What Price Glory,* realistic war drama, was the theatrical hit of the year. The Teapot Dome scandal thoroughly discredited the Harding regime, and Calvin Coolidge, who had become President upon Harding's death, was re-elected. Edna Ferber was a new name on best seller lists. Her *So Big* skyrocketed. *The Plastic Age,* a revelation of campus life and the "lost generation," achieved the best sellerdom that F. Scott Fitzgerald's *This Side of Paradise* (1920) had not reached. Attempts to suppress Percy Marks' novel only added to the demand for it. Anne Douglas Sedgwick returned to the list for the first time since 1912. In its third year, *Diet and Health* outsold every other nonfiction title. Papini's *Life of Christ,* approaching 200,000, was in second place for the second year. The *Boston Cooking School Cook Book,* which has sold over 3,000,000 copies through its long career from its first publication in 1896, appeared in a new and best-selling edition. *Etiquette* continued to sell. A French writer, André Maurois, found a big American audience for his biography of Shelley. Shaw's *Saint Joan* was one of the few dramas in all these years to make an annual list. The first and highly successful venture of the new publishing house of Simon and Schuster was that of putting cross word puzzles, long a newspaper feature, into book form. The demand was so great that this firm has continued ever since to publish several volumes of cross word puzzles and the later *Double-Crostics* each year. Since 1924 many novelty books of various kinds from *Ask Me Another, Believe It Or Not* and *Boners* to the photographic books of Clare Barnes, Jr., have been issued successfully by other publishers in the wake of this first experiment in game books.

1925

Fiction

1. Soundings, by *A. Hamilton Gibbs.* Little, Brown
2. The Constant Nymph, by *Margaret Kennedy.* Doubleday, Page
3. The Keeper of the Bees, by *Gene Stratton Porter.* Doubleday, Page
4. Glorious Apollo, by *E. Barrington.* Dodd, Mead
5. The Green Hat, by *Michael Arlen.* Doran
6. The Little French Girl, by *Anne Douglas Sedgwick.* Houghton Mifflin
7. Arrowsmith, by *Sinclair Lewis.* Harcourt, Brace
8. The Perennial Bachelor, by *Anne Parrish.* Harper
9. The Carolinian, by *Rafael Sabatini.* Houghton Mifflin
10. One Increasing Purpose, by *A. S. M. Hutchinson.* Little, Brown

Nonfiction

1. Diet and Health, by *Lulu Hunt Peters.* Reilly & Lee
2. The Boston Cooking School Cook Book; new ed. by *Fannie Farmer.* Little, Brown
3. When We Were Very Young, by *A. A. Milne.* Dutton
4. The Man Nobody Knows, by *Bruce Barton.* Bobbs-Merrill
5. The Life of Christ, by *Giovanni Papini.* Harcourt, Brace
6. Ariel, by *André Maurois.* Appleton
7. Twice Thirty, by *Edward Bok.* Scribner
8. Twenty-Five Years, by *Lord Grey.* Stokes
9. Anatole France Himself, by *J. J. Brousson.* Lippincott
10. The Cross Word Puzzle Books. by *Prosper Buranelli* and others. 1st—4th series. Simon & Schuster

COOLIDGE prosperity—the Scopes case in Tennessee, in which Clarence Darrow and William Jennings Bryan argued the theory of evolution, basis of the play *Inherit the Wind* in 1955—Red Grange—the Florida boom—the crash of the Shenandoah—are all memories of 1925. *Soundings,* first in fiction, sold nearly 100,000 copies. Better remembered is *The Constant Nymph,* made into a stage hit and the basis of both British and American

131

movies. *Glorious Apollo,* woven around the character of Byron, was the start of E. Barrington's (Mrs. L. Adams Beck) extremely successful series of novels about real people of the past. Michael Arlen made a much talked-about hit with what was considered a daring novel, *The Green Hat,* later a highly successful stage play starring Katharine Cornell. Sinclair Lewis' third novel, *Arrowsmith,* confirmed his place in American literature and probably was an important factor in his being awarded the Nobel Prize. *Arrowsmith* dealt with the medical profession as *Babbitt* had with the businessman and as *Elmer Gantry* was to deal, in 1927, with the ministry. Here was the first appearance of Anne Parrish, long a favorite writer. The records of both *Diet and Health* and *The Boston Cooking School Cook Book* gave evidence of the exceptionally energetic distribution of books which gave practical advice on the always popular subject of food. *When We Were Very Young,* permanent contribution to the literature of childhood by A. A. Milne, previously known chiefly as a playwright, was the first book in the field of semi-juvenile, semi-adult writing to hit the lists in many years. Bruce Barton topped Papini's *Life of Christ,* then in its third year on the best seller lists, with an American businessman's version of Jesus' life. Lord Grey's reminiscences gave a foretaste of the advent of more basic books on World War I than the reporters' narratives published during and immediately after the war years.

132

1926

Fiction

1. The Private Life of Helen of Troy, by *John Erskine*. Bobbs-Merrill
2. Gentlemen Prefer Blondes, by *Anita Loos*. Boni & Liveright
3. Sorrell and Son, by *Warwick Deeping*. Knopf
4. The Hounds of Spring, by *Sylvia Thompson*. Little, Brown
5. Beau Sabreur, by *P. C. Wren*. Stokes
6. The Silver Spoon, by *John Galsworthy*. Scribner
7. Beau Geste, by *P. C. Wren*. Stokes
8. Show Boat, by *Edna Ferber*. Doubleday, Page
9. After Noon, by *Susan Ertz*. Appleton
10. The Blue Window, by *Temple Bailey*. Penn Publishing Co.

Nonfiction

1. The Man Nobody Knows, by *Bruce Barton*. Bobbs-Merrill
2. Why We Behave Like Human Beings, by *George A. Dorsey*. Harper
3. Diet and Health, by *Lulu Hunt Peters*. Reilly & Lee
4. Our Times, Vol. I, by *Mark Sullivan*. Scribner
5. The Boston Cooking School Cook Book; new ed. by *Fannie Farmer*. Little, Brown
6. Auction Bridge Complete, by *Milton C. Work*. Winston
7. The Book Nobody Knows, by *Bruce Barton*. Bobbs-Merrill
8. The Story of Philosophy, by *Will Durant*. Simon & Schuster
9. The Light of Faith, by *Edgar A. Guest*. Reilly & Lee
10. Jefferson and Hamilton, by *Claude G. Bowers*. Houghton, Mifflin

THE MIDDLE 1920's were the years of pioneering along the air lanes of the world. Admiral Byrd made the first flight over the North Pole in 1926. Babe Ruth became Sultan of Swat. Philadelphia opened the Sesquicentennial Exhibition. In Germany, Hitler's *Mein Kampf* had been published. The Book-of-the-Month Club, which was to introduce an extremely successful method of marketing books, was founded in 1926.

New fiction writers were coming to the fore in America—John Erskine, with his first great hit, *The Private Life of Helen of Troy,* historical fiction written in a new manner; Warwick Deeping, English author, whose *Sorrell and Son* found a responsive note in thousands of American hearts (his book marking the first appearance of the firm of Alfred A. Knopf, Inc., on the annual best seller lists); and P. C. Wren, whose more popular *Beau Geste* was published late in the previous year and did not make the 1925 list, and whose second book, *Beau Sabreur,* also appeared among 1926 best sellers. Galsworthy was at the height of his American sales, with one of the novels in *A Modern Comedy,* companion volume to *The Forsyte Saga.* Edna Ferber followed *So Big* with the perennially famous *Show Boat,* familiar to the world as book, play, movie, and song. With his *Man Nobody Knows* heading nonfiction, Bruce Barton added an interpretation of the Bible in his series of books on practical religion. George Dorsey rode the wave of the new interest in psychology with *Why We Behave Like Human Beings,* and *Diet and Health* continued on its fifth year, the new edition of *The Boston Cooking School Cook Book* in its third. Mark Sullivan's first volume of *Our Times* marked a new interest in our recent past that was continued some years later by such books as Frederick Lewis Allen's *Only Yesterday* and *Since Yesterday.* Evidence of the bridge craze was the pre-publication print order for 65,000 copies of Milton Work's new manual and the sale of over 100,000 copies of Foster's *Simplified Auction Bridge* within ten months after publication. ("Contract" had not yet come along.) Will Durant's *Story of Philosophy,* which had previously appeared in part in the five-cent booklets published as Little Blue Books by the Haldeman-Julius Co. of Wichita, Kansas, marked the peak of the "outline" era, selling 95,000 copies in 1926 alone.

1927

Fiction

1. Elmer Gantry, by *Sinclair Lewis.* Harcourt, Brace
2. The Plutocrat, by *Booth Tarkington.* Doubleday, Page
3. Doomsday, by *Warwick Deeping.* Knopf
4. Sorrell and Son, by *Warwick Deeping.* Knopf
5. Jalna, by *Mazo de la Roche.* Little, Brown
6. Lost Ecstasy, by *Mary Roberts Rinehart.* Doran
7. Twilight Sleep, by *Edith Wharton.* Appleton
8. Tomorrow Morning, by *Anne Parrish.* Harper
9. The Old Countess, by *Anne Douglas Sedgwick.* Houghton Mifflin
10. A Good Woman, by *Louis Bromfield.* Stokes

Nonfiction

1. The Story of Philosophy, by *Will Durant.* Simon & Schuster
2. Napoleon, by *Emil Ludwig.* Boni & Liveright
3. Revolt in the Desert, by *T. E. Lawrence.* Doran
4. Trader Horn, Vol. I, by *Alfred Aloysius Horn* and *Ethelreda Lewis.* Simon & Schuster
5. We, by *Charles A. Lindbergh.* Putnam
6. Ask Me Another, by *Julian Spafford and Lucien Esty.* Viking Press
7. The Royal Road to Romance, by *Richard Halliburton.* Bobbs-Merrill
8. The Glorious Adventure, by *Richard Halliburton.* Bobbs-Merrill
9. Why We Behave Like Human Beings, by *George A. Dorsey.* Harper
10. Mother India, by *Katherine Mayo.* Harcourt, Brace

MECHANICAL and scientific progress continued in 1927, height of the whole period of invention and exploration that followed World War I. Lindbergh made the flight to Paris that thrilled the world, and later in the year wrote about it in a book that became a best seller. Ford produced his new Model A, the first Ford with a gear shift. The Holland Tunnel

135

under the Hudson River was officially opened. The stock market was booming. The disastrous Mississippi floods occurred the same year that the musical play based upon Edna Ferber's novel of Ol' Man River was produced in New York. The Literary Guild, following book marketing methods similar to those of the Book-of-the-Month Club, started to function in 1927, and one of its first selections, *Trader Horn*, made the yearly list. The publication of *Elmer Gantry* with an initial printing of 100,000 copies and sales of over 200,000 in the first ten weeks found Sinclair Lewis at the peak of popularity. Booth Tarkington was high on the list. So was Warwick Deeping, with two books; *Sorrell and Son*, holding over from 1926, sold 133,830 copies in the two years. Mazo de la Roche, a Canadian contributor to American best seller lists, like Gilbert Parker, Ralph Connor, and Louis Hémon of past years, made a great hit with *Jalna*, first book in a notable series about the Whiteoak family of Canada. The ninth volume in the series, but the earliest chronologically, was published seventeen years afterward, in 1944, and there were more Jalna stories up to the '60's. Louis Bromfield made his first appearance on the list with *A Good Woman*. *The Story of Philosophy* was the outstanding nonfiction title of the year. Emil Ludwig, who was to write so many popular biographies, revived the always latent interest in Napoleon. *Revolt in the Desert* was a book of permanent historical importance by the great English hero of World War I, the mysterious and daring Lawrence of Arabia. Trader Horn came from South Africa to tell tall tales which caught the public's fancy. As Simon & Schuster had done, a new firm, the Viking Press, scored its first best-selling success with a series of novelty books. Its *Ask Me Another* quiz book was an immediate hit, selling 100,000 copies in its first four weeks and becoming the first of a series which made quizzes a popular pastime for years—perhaps germinating radio's "Information Please!" and television's "$64,000 Question." With two best sellers in 1927, Richard Halliburton captured a public which wanted adventure with glamour, a trend in travel and escape reading that had begun with O'Brien's *White Shadows in the South Seas* a number of years before. Dorsey carried on the interest in popular science, and in *Mother India* Katherine Mayo wrote the first book to make a large audience aware of modern India's problems.

136

1928

Fiction

1. The Bridge of San Luis Rey, by *Thornton Wilder*. A. & C. Boni
2. Wintersmoon, by *Hugh Walpole*. Doubleday, Doran
3. Swan Song, by *John Galsworthy*. Scribner
4. The Greene Murder Case, by *S. S. Van Dine*. Scribner
5. Bad Girl, by *Viña Delmar*. Harcourt, Brace
6. Claire Ambler, by *Booth Tarkington*. Doubleday, Doran
7. Old Pybus, by *Warwick Deeping*. Knopf
8. All Kneeling, by *Anne Parrish*. Harper
9. Jalna, by *Mazo de la Roche*. Little, Brown
10. The Strange Case of Miss Annie Spragg, by *Louis Bromfield*. Stokes

Nonfiction

1. Disraeli, by *André Maurois*. Appleton
2. Mother India, by *Katherine Mayo*. Harcourt, Brace
3. Trader Horn, Vol. I, by *Alfred Aloysius Horn* and *Ethelreda Lewis*. Simon & Schuster
4. Napoleon, by *Emil Ludwig*. Liveright
5. Strange Interlude, by *Eugene O'Neill*. Liveright
6. We, by *Charles A. Lindbergh*. Putnam
7. Count Luckner, the Sea Devil, by *Lowell Thomas*. Doubleday, Doran
8. Goethe, by *Emil Ludwig*. Putnam
9. Skyward, by *Richard E. Byrd*. Putnam
10. The Intelligent Woman's Guide to Socialism and Capitalism, by *George Bernard Shaw*. Brentano

WITH the outward scars of World War I healed, war itself outlawed by the Kellogg-Briand Pact, and the big bull market well under way, Americans were flocking to Europe by every conceivable means of the time, from freighter to mammoth liner. Amelia Earhart was the first woman to fly the Atlantic. At home, gangsters, bootleggers, and racketeers were riding high. The first all-talking movie, *The Lights of New York,* was presented, and

Walt Disney was working on his first Mickey Mouse picture. *The Bridge of San Luis Rey,* a novel that attained such fame that the Pulitzer Prize committee departed from its usual custom of giving its award to a story laid in the United States, was leader of 1928 fiction. This novel with a South American background, Thornton Wilder's first great success, sold 240,000 copies in its first year. English writers with devoted American audiences were next on the list. A new writer of detective stories, S. S. Van Dine (pseudonym of Willard Huntington Wright), flashed into the book world with big sales. *The Greene Murder Case* was one of the first of many novels that made Philo Vance almost as familiar a fictional character as Sherlock Holmes, and the first detective story to appear on an annual list since Mary Roberts Rinehart's *The Window at the White Cat* in 1910. Booth Tarkington's *Claire Ambler* had an added interest because it was the first book to be issued under the new imprint of Doubleday, Doran & Co., a merger of the old firms of Doubleday, Page and George H. Doran. Biography was the subject of about half the nonfiction list. André Maurois followed his successful *Ariel* with the life of Disraeli. Emil Ludwig's *Napoleon* held over into its second year and he added a biography of Goethe to the list. American antipathy to all things German having subsided, readers devoured Lowell Thomas' account of a German war hero's exploits. *Mother India* and *We* were both best sellers for the second year. Eugene O'Neill's play, widely publicized for its feat of holding audiences through five hours, with intermission for dinner, sold well in book form. Admiral Byrd followed Lindbergh's account of sky adventure with his story of his 1926 flight to the North Pole. Bernard Shaw addressed the intelligent woman on political theory.

1929

Fiction

1. All Quiet on the Western Front, by *Erich Maria Remarque.* Little, Brown
2. Dodsworth, by *Sinclair Lewis.* Harcourt, Brace
3. Dark Hester, by *Anne Douglas Sedgwick.* Houghton Mifflin
4. The Bishop Murder Case, by *S. S. Van Dine.* Scribner
5. Roper's Row, by *Warwick Deeping.* Knopf
6. Peder Victorious, by *O. E. Rölvaag.* Harper
7. Mamba's Daughters, by *DuBose Heyward.* Doubleday, Doran
8. The Galaxy, by *Susan Ertz.* Appleton
9. Scarlet Sister Mary, by *Julia Peterkin.* Bobbs-Merrill
10. Joseph and his Brethren, by *H. W. Freeman.* Holt

Nonfiction

1. The Art of Thinking, by *Ernest Dimnet.* Simon & Schuster
2. Henry the Eighth, by *Francis Hackett.* Liveright
3. The Cradle of the Deep, by *Joan Lowell.* Simon & Schuster
4. Elizabeth and Essex, by *Lytton Strachey.* Harcourt, Brace
5. The Specialist, by *Chic Sale.* Specialist Publishing Co.
6. A Preface to Morals, by *Walter Lippmann.* Macmillan
7. Believe It or Not, by *Robert L. Ripley.* Simon & Schuster
8. John Brown's Body, by *Stephen Vincent Benét.* Doubleday, Doran
9. The Tragic Era, by *Claude G. Bowers.* Houghton Mifflin
10. The Mansions of Philosophy, by *Will Durant.* Simon & Schuster

THE Coolidge boom turned into Hoover prosperity, only to totter in September with the first warning crash of this country's greatest financial depression. Black Tuesday, October 29, brought this country to the brink of financial disaster, but book sales were still booming. The great anti-war novel of World War I, *All Quiet on the Western Front,* written by the German-born Erich Maria Remarque, appeared eleven years after the war's close, to sell 300,000 in its first year. It was issued here in a first printing of 100,000; 700,000 copies were printed in Germany, many of them later to be burned by the Nazis. Famous all over the world, it was made into a Hollywood super-feature. Sinclair Lewis did another portrait of the American businessman in *Dodsworth,* a book that became a highly successful play, later a movie. S. S. Van Dine's *Bishop Murder Case* was as high on the list as his *Greene Murder Case* had been. Ole Rölvaag's *Peder Victorious* was a sequel to his first novel of the Dakota prairies, *Giants in the Earth* (1927). American regional literature was awakening more and more interest. The South provided two new novelists of distinction, DuBose Heyward of *Porgy* fame, and Julia Peterkin, who won the Pulitzer Prize with her first book. Perfecting its technique for selecting and developing best sellers, the young firm of Simon & Schuster, which had started only five years previously with *The Cross Word Puzzle Book,* was responsible for four books on the nonfiction list. *The Art of Thinking,* by a French writer, caught on with a public interested in self-improvement and sold 125,000 in 1929. The sensational spit-in-the-wind *Cradle of the Deep* followed in Trader Horn's footsteps. *Believe It or Not,* first of Robert Ripley's collections of his popular newspaper features, went over 50,000. *The Mansions of Philosophy* did not become quite the great success that Will Durant's *Story of Philosophy* had been. *Henry the Eighth* and *Elizabeth and Essex* were added to the many notable biographies of the period. Word-of-mouth publicity made Chic Sale's tiny little book of decidedly homely humor a runaway best seller. Since 1929 its sales have exceeded 1,500,000 copies. Walter Lippmann, outstanding political commentator, made his first appearance among best sellers in 1929. *John Brown's Body,* one of the early selections of the Book-of-the-Month Club, attained unusual sales for a book of poetry, in this case one long narrative sequence. Its first printing was 70,000 copies. At that time Book-of-the-Month Club's membership was about 50,000.

1930

Fiction

1. Cimarron, by *Edna Ferber*. Doubleday, Doran
2. Exile, by *Warwick Deeping*. Knopf
3. The Woman of Andros, by *Thornton Wilder*. A. & C. Boni
4. Years of Grace, by *Margaret Ayer Barnes*. Houghton Mifflin
5. Angel Pavement, by *J. B. Priestley*. Harper
6. The Door, by *Mary Roberts Rinehart*. Farrar & Rinehart
7. Rogue Herries, by *Hugh Walpole*. Doubleday, Doran
8. Chances, by *A. Hamilton Gibbs*. Little, Brown
9. Young Man of Manhattan, by *Katharine Brush*. Farrar & Rinehart
10. Twenty-Four Hours, by *Louis Bromfield*. Stokes

Nonfiction

1. The Story of San Michele, by *Axel Munthe*. Dutton
2. The Strange Death of President Harding, by *Gaston B. Means* and *May Dixon Thacker*. Guild Publishing Corp.
3. Byron, by *André Maurois*. Appleton
4. The Adams Family, by *James Truslow Adams*. Little, Brown
5. Lone Cowboy, by *Will James*. Scribner
6. Lincoln, by *Emil Ludwig*. Little, Brown
7. The Story of Philosophy, by *Will Durant*. Garden City Publishing Co.
8. The Outline of History, by *H. G. Wells*. Garden City Publishing Co.
9. The Art of Thinking, by *Ernest Dimnet*. Simon & Schuster
10. The Rise of American Civilization, by *Charles* and *Mary Beard*. Macmillan

1930 was a year of financial depression, bank crashes, and brokers' suicides, with the unemployed selling apples on the streets of New York, and with people turning to the inexpensive diversion of miniature golf to take their minds off money troubles. France started to build the Maginot Line that was designed to protect her forever from military aggression. Edna

Ferber led fiction sales for the second time in six years. Her *Cimarron* was a story of pioneer Oklahoma. The fame of his first novel carried Thornton Wilder's story of ancient Greece high on the list, though interest in it quickly flagged. *Years of Grace* was the first novel by a new writer from Chicago; it won the Pulitzer Prize and made its author one of the established favorites in the fiction scene. *The Good Companions,* published in 1929, had made a great audience for the English novelist, playwright, and essayist, J. B. Priestley, an audience that eagerly bought his new book, *Angel Pavement.* Mrs. Rinehart scored with another mystery novel twenty-one years after her *Man in Lower Ten* had become one of the first best sellers in American detective fiction. Hers was the first best seller on these lists to be published by the new firm of Farrar & Rinehart—established by John Farrar, formerly editor of *The Bookman,* and by two of Mrs. Rinehart's sons. The first book of the *Herries Chronicle* by Hugh Walpole was an immediate favorite and founded a fictional dynasty that rivaled Galsworthy's Forsytes in popularity. A young American writer scored a big success with *Young Man of Manhattan* (also a Farrar & Rinehart publication), combining realism and romance in a story of the uproarious 1920's. In nonfiction, leader of the year was Dr. Axel Munthe's *Story of San Michele,* one of those rare best sellers that start out in a modest way, catch on through recommendation by one reader to another until sales begin to pile up and advertising takes over. This, the first of many best-selling "doctor" books of the period, sold 181,000 copies. The vogue for autobiographies by notables or unusual figures in the professions began, but neither lawyers nor preachers proved as magnetic in the literary field at that time as doctors. The sensational *Strange Death of President Harding* (300,000 sold) had been preceded in 1927 by another book of the same caliber, *The President's Daughter,* revealing unsavory Washington scandal in an era of corruption. *Byron* was Maurois' third consecutive success, and Ludwig again offered a biography to an assured public. James Truslow Adams and the Beards made their first appearances as best-selling historians. Will James rose to popularity with his cowboy reminiscences and drawings. The Durant and Wells books both returned to the lists in new dollar hardbound editions. (The era of paperback reprints of such lengthy and meaty books was far in the future.)

Fiction

1. The Good Earth, by *Pearl S. Buck*. John Day
2. Shadows on the Rock, by *Willa Cather*. Knopf
3. A White Bird Flying, by *Bess Streeter Aldrich*. Appleton
4. Grand Hotel, by *Vicki Baum*. Doubleday, Doran
5. Years of Grace, by *Margaret Ayer Barnes*. Houghton Mifflin
6. The Road Back, by *Erich Maria Remarque*. Little, Brown
7. The Bridge of Desire, by *Warwick Deeping*. McBride
8. Back Street, by *Fannie Hurst*. Cosmopolitan Book Co.
9. Finch's Fortune, by *Mazo de la Roche*. Little, Brown
10. Maid in Waiting, by *John Galsworthy*. Scribner

Nonfiction

1. Education of a Princess, by *Grand Duchess Marie*. Viking Press
2. The Story of San Michele, by *Axel Munthe*. Dutton
3. Washington Merry-Go-Round, Anonymous (*Drew Pearson* and *Robert S. Allen*). Liveright
4. Boners. Viking Press
5. Culbertson's Summary, by *Ely Culbertson*. Bridge World
6. Contract Bridge Blue Book, by *Ely Culbertson*. Bridge World
7. Fatal Interview, by *Edna St. Vincent Millay*. Harper
8. The Epic of America, by *James Truslow Adams*. Little, Brown
9. Mexico, by *Stuart Chase*. Macmillan
10. New Russia's Primer, by *M. Ilin*. Houghton Mifflin

CONTRACT BRIDGE hit the nation with full force in this year of continued depression. Katharine Cornell was appearing on Broadway in *The Barretts of Wimpole Street* (one of the most popular plays presented for American soldiers overseas in World War II) and "De Lawd" made his appearance in *The Green Pastures. Of Thee I Sing,* with George Gershwin's music, was the first musical play ever to win the Pulitzer Prize. *The Good Earth,* by Pearl S. Buck, topped all novels of the year, making a permanent place in our literature for itself and her other novels of China. Mrs. Buck was awarded the Nobel Prize for Literature in 1938. Her book marked the first appearance on these lists of a publication of the John Day Company. There were five novelists new among best sellers in 1931, all of them women, all American but one. Willa Cather's books had been highly esteemed and widely read for years, but not until publication of *Shadows on the Rock* did one of them become a leading best seller. Bess Streeter Aldrich's preceding book, *A Lantern in Her Hand,* had won many readers by word-of-mouth publicity, gaining an audience for her next, *A White Bird Flying. Grand Hotel,* by the only one of the five not an American, is the most famous of them all. Fannie Hurst, fifth new name on the list, already had a great following among magazine and book readers, but it was *Back Street* that put her among the top-ranking best sellers. A new woman writer topped nonfiction as well. She was a member of the Russian royal family; the sale of her autobiography reflected the widespread interest in Russia. Through all these years many memoirs of imperial and revolutionary times in that country were published. The first best seller to illustrate public interest in the Soviet régime was M. Ilin's *New Russia's Primer. Washington Merry-Go-Round* was a natural successor to *Mirrors of Washington* of nearly a decade before, but it packed more dynamite. Published anonymously, it proved to have been written by columnists Drew Pearson and Robert Allen. *Boners* was another fad book in the *Cross Word Puzzle, Ask Me Another* and *Believe It or Not* line. With several succeeding volumes it sold into the hundreds of thousands. As the new contract bridge replaced auction, there was demand for new guides to the game; Ely Culbertson was the one who cashed in on the opportunity in a big way, taking the place held by Milton Work five years before, later to be succeeded himself by Charles Goren with his "point count" system. Edna St. Vincent Millay reached the list for the first time with *Fatal Interview,* and thus became the first new best-selling writer of serious poetry besides Stephen Vincent Benét since World War I days.

1932

Fiction

1. The Good Earth, by *Pearl S. Buck*. John Day
2. The Fountain, by *Charles Morgan*. Knopf
3. Sons, by *Pearl S. Buck*. John Day
4. Magnolia Street, by *Louis Golding*. Farrar & Rinehart
5. The Sheltered Life, by *Ellen Glasgow*. Doubleday, Doran
6. Old Wine and New, by *Warwick Deeping*. Knopf
7. Mary's Neck, by *Booth Tarkington*. Doubleday, Doran
8. Magnificent Obsession, by *Lloyd C. Douglas*. Willett, Clark
9. Inheritance, by *Phyllis Bentley*. Macmillan
10. Three Loves, by *A. J. Cronin*. Little, Brown

Nonfiction

1. The Epic of America, by *James Truslow Adams*. Little, Brown
2. Only Yesterday, by *Frederick Lewis Allen*. Harper
3. A Fortune to Share, by *Vash Young*. Bobbs-Merrill
4. Culbertson's Summary, by *Ely Culbertson*. Bridge World
5. Van Loon's Geography, by *Hendrik Willem Van Loon*. Simon & Schuster
6. What We Live By, by *Ernest Dimnet*. Simon & Schuster
7. The March of Democracy, by *James Truslow Adams*. Scribner
8. Washington Merry-Go-Round, Anonymous (*Drew Pearson* and *Robert S. Allen*). Liveright; Blue Ribbon Books
9. The Story of My Life, by *Clarence Darrow*. Scribner
10. More Merry-Go-Round, Anonymous (*Drew Pearson* and *Robert S. Allen*). Liveright

IN THE WORST YEAR of the depression came the bonus march on Washington and the ensuing battle of Anacostia Flats. James J. Walker resigned under a cloud as Mayor of New York City. Radio was in full swing, with Rudy Vallee its topnotch artist. Father Coughlin's radio talks were gaining listeners. Technocracy was the newest theory on how to cure the depression. Colonel and Mrs. Lindbergh's small son was kidnaped from his crib in Hopewell, N. J. Over in China, Japan seized Shanghai in her undeclared war on that country. *The Good Earth* headed fiction for a second year. Pearl Buck's second novel, continuing the story of the same Chinese family, took third place. *The Fountain,* in second place, received unusual critical attention. Also from England came *Magnolia Street, Inheritance,* with which Macmillan vigorously reentered the field of best-selling fiction, and *Three Loves,* A. J. Cronin's first best seller. Ellen Glasgow and Booth Tarkington both continued their many years' popularity. Lloyd Douglas came rather quietly into the list in eighth place. He was a retired minister, over fifty, when his first novel was published. It was a book that caught on throughout the country, chiefly in the Midwest, by word-of-mouth personal recommendation, the first of many novels on religious themes that were to put him in the highest ranks of best-selling novelists. James Truslow Adams, who had been developing a reputation as an American historian, found a popular audience with two books, one of which, first in nonfiction in 1932, had also appeared on the previous year's list. Frederick Lewis Allen of *Harper's Magazine,* as Mark Sullivan had done with his *Our Times* books, found a waiting audience of people who enjoyed reading about things they remembered, events of the not-too-far-distant past. Vash Young, businessman like Bruce Barton before him, combined inspirational writing with practical advice in a little volume timed for that period of financial depression when salesmen, particularly, needed a lift. Hendrik Van Loon, going under Simon & Schuster's sponsorship, added another volume to his illustrated surveys of human knowledge. Ernest Dimnet followed his *Art of Thinking* with a new book, as did Pearson and Allen with *More Merry-Go-Round.* Their first book was still selling merrily, switching during the course of the year into a reprint edition. The trade policy regarding reprints was changing and nonfiction titles were now released much more quickly in popular-priced editions. Clarence Darrow, who, seven years before, had shared the spotlight in the Scopes trial, wrote a best-selling autobiography.

1933

Fiction

1. Anthony Adverse, by *Hervey Allen*. Farrar & Rinehart
2. As the Earth Turns, by *Gladys Hasty Carroll*. Macmillan
3. Ann Vickers, by *Sinclair Lewis*. Doubleday, Doran
4. Magnificent Obsession, by *Lloyd C. Douglas*. Willett, Clark
5. One More River, by *John Galsworthy*. Scribner
6. Forgive Us Our Trespasses, by *Lloyd C. Douglas*. Houghton Mifflin
7. The Master of Jalna, by *Mazo de la Roche*. Little, Brown
8. Miss Bishop, by *Bess Streeter Aldrich*. Appleton-Century
9. The Farm, by *Louis Bromfield*. Harper
10. Little Man, What Now? by *Hans Fallada*. Simon & Schuster

Nonfiction

1. Life Begins at Forty, by *Walter B. Pitkin*. Whittlesey House
2. Marie Antoinette, by *Stefan Zweig*. Viking Press
3. British Agent, by *R. H. Bruce Lockhart*. Putnam
4. 100,000,000 Guinea Pigs, by *Arthur Kallet and F. J. Schlink*. Vanguard Press
5. The House of Exile, by *Nora Waln*. Little, Brown
6. Van Loon's Geography, by *Hendrik Willem Van Loon*. Simon & Schuster
7. Looking Forward, by *Franklin D. Roosevelt*. John Day
8. Contract Bridge Blue Book of 1933, by *Ely Culbertson*. Bridge World
9. The Arches of the Years, by *Halliday Sutherland*. Morrow
10. The March of Democracy, Vol. II, by *James Truslow Adams*. Scribner

"WHO's Afraid of the Big Bad Wolf?" was the theme song of 1933 as Franklin D. Roosevelt, taking office as chief executive of the nation, quickly declared a bank holiday. The NRA and the AAA were created. The World's Fair opened in Chicago. *Tobacco Road,* which by 1939 was to break the record for successive Broadway performances, was produced.

147

The United States abandoned the gold standard, liquor made a legitimate reappearance with the repeal of the 18th Amendment, the speakeasy era passed out of existence. Jigsaw puzzles became a big popular fad. In Berlin the Reichstag was burned. *Anthony Adverse,* selling 300,000 copies in its first six months, captured readers of many levels of taste and turned public interest definitely toward the historical novel for the first time since the early decades of the century. *Anthony Adverse,* too, began a trend toward the novel of unusual length, a feature which appealed to the public again in *Gone with the Wind.* Continuing its big-time fiction drive begun with Phyllis Bentley's *Inheritance* in 1932, Macmillan found in Gladys Hasty Carroll a new writer from Maine. Lewis, Aldrich, and Bromfield repeated best-seller performances, as did Galsworthy with his third book in the new saga and Mrs. Aldrich with a schoolteacher predecessor of *Mr. Chips* and *Miss Dove.* Lloyd Douglas' *Magnificent Obsession* climbed steadily. In tenth place appeared a new writer from Germany, Hans Fallada, author of the first fiction success for the firm of Simon & Schuster that had up till now been outstanding in nonfiction. A new self-help book hit the nonfiction top for a long run, selling 88,897 copies in 1933. *Life Begins at Forty* added a new axiom to our language. Biography, with characters from France, Russia, China, and a doctor's story, *The Arches of the Years,* took four of the places on the list. Kallet and Schlink issued their interpretation of the claims of modern advertising in *100,000,000 Guinea Pigs,* a volume that led the way for many other books of the "exposure" type and drew increased attention to consumer movements. Culbertson continued to sell year after year. As Woodrow Wilson had done twenty years before, Franklin Roosevelt began his administration with a best-selling book on his policies. For the first time the firms of Whittlesey House, Morrow, and the Vanguard Press made their appearance on these lists. 1933 also saw a best seller from Appleton-Century, a combination of two publishing houses which had been individually responsible for many best-selling titles since the beginning of these records.

1934

Fiction

1. Anthony Adverse, by *Hervey Allen*. Farrar & Rinehart
2. Lamb in His Bosom, by *Caroline Miller*. Harper
3. So Red the Rose, by *Stark Young*. Scribner
4. Good-Bye, Mr. Chips, by *James Hilton*. Little, Brown
5. Within This Present, by *Margaret Ayer Barnes*. Houghton Mifflin
6. Work of Art, by *Sinclair Lewis*. Doubleday, Doran
7. Private Worlds, by *Phyllis Bottome*. Houghton Mifflin
8. Mary Peters, by *Mary Ellen Chase*. Macmillan
9. Oil for the Lamps of China, by *Alice Tisdale Hobart*. Bobbs-Merrill
10. Seven Gothic Tales, by *Isak Dinesen*. Smith & Haas

Nonfiction

1. While Rome Burns, by *Alexander Woollcott*. Viking Press
2. Life Begins at Forty, by *Walter B. Pitkin*. Whittlesey House
3. Nijinsky, by *Romola Nijinsky*. Simon & Schuster
4. 100,000,000 Guinea Pigs, by *Arthur Kallet and F. J. Schlink*. Vanguard Press
5. The Native's Return, by *Louis Adamic*. Harper
6. Stars Fell on Alabama, by *Carl Carmer*. Farrar & Rinehart
7. Brazilian Adventure, by *Peter Fleming*. Scribner
8. Forty-two Years in the White House, by *Ike Hoover*. Houghton Mifflin
9. You Must Relax, by *Edmund Jacobson*. Whittlesey House
10. The Life of Our Lord, by *Charles Dickens*. Simon & Schuster

THE Townsend plan and Upton Sinclair's EPIC party followed on the heels of Technocracy as economic cure-alls. Dillinger, greatest American bandit of the era, was killed, and the Dionne quintuplets were born. Parisians rioted over evidence of government corruption, and F.D.R. signed the Philippine Independence Act. Dust storms devastated Kansas and Oklahoma. *Anthony Adverse* sold 176,100 more copies in 1934, bringing it to the top of the fiction list again, but this was only the beginning! The South contributed two new novelists, Caroline Miller with the Pulitzer Prize novel, *Lamb in His Bosom,* and Stark Young with *So Red the Rose,* both books laid in the old South. Another two-year period of best-sellerdom began with James Hilton's first success, *Good-bye, Mr. Chips,* the first book, too, to achieve country-wide fame through radio commendation—the book about which Alexander Woollcott went "quietly mad." There were seven new names on the list in all. The English writer, Phyllis Bottome, scored a hit with her story of insanity, marking a trend toward novels studying abnormal psychological situations. Mary Ellen Chase, who had taught English to two decades of Smith College girls, proved that she herself could write vigorously. *Mary Peters* was another Maine story and subject of another big Macmillan promotion campaign. Alice Tisdale Hobart wrote a striking story of China; and *Seven Gothic Tales* introduced an author from Denmark whose unique tales created a devoted audience for her work in this country. Alexander Woollcott had become radio's favorite voice and expert story-teller as well as book promoter. People bought his own book, *While Rome Burns,* as well as those he recommended. In 1934 *While Rome Burns* sold 83,545 copies. Eventually it reached a sale of over 500,000. *Life Begins at Forty* was second in 1934, and another self-help book, *You Must Relax,* was in ninth place. Louis Adamic's extremely interesting account of his native Yugoslavia found many readers, as did Carl Carmer's picturesque interpretation of the State of Alabama, a book that inspired a popular song and laid the foundations for the author's reputation in the field of American folklore. A century-old book by the prince of best sellers, Charles Dickens, was rescued for a time from obscurity.

1935

Fiction

1. Green Light, by *Lloyd C. Douglas*. Houghton Mifflin
2. Vein of Iron, by *Ellen Glasgow*. Harcourt, Brace
3. Of Time and the River, by *Thomas Wolfe*. Scribner
4. Time Out of Mind, by *Rachel Field*. Macmillan
5. Good-Bye, Mr. Chips, by *James Hilton*. Little, Brown
6. The Forty Days of Musa Dagh, by *Franz Werfel*. Viking Press
7. Heaven's My Destination, by *Thornton Wilder*. Harper
8. Lost Horizon, by *James Hilton*. Morrow
9. Come and Get It, by *Edna Ferber*. Doubleday, Doran
10. Europa, by *Robert Briffault*. Scribner

Nonfiction

1. North to the Orient, by *Anne Morrow Lindbergh*. Harcourt, Brace
2. While Rome Burns, by *Alexander Woollcott*. Viking Press
3. Life with Father, by *Clarence Day*. Knopf
4. Personal History, by *Vincent Sheean*. Doubleday, Doran
5. Seven Pillars of Wisdom, by *T. E. Lawrence*. Doubleday, Doran
6. Francis the First, by *Francis Hackett*. Doubleday, Doran
7. Mary Queen of Scotland and the Isles, by *Stefan Zweig*. Viking Press
8. Rats, Lice and History, by *Hans Zinsser*. Little, Brown
9. R. E. Lee, by *Douglas Southall Freeman*. Scribner
10. Skin Deep, by *M. C. Phillips*. Vanguard Press

THE NAZIS, in full power in Germany, intensified their anti-Jewish campaign. Mussolini invaded Ethiopia. In the U.S.A. the social security laws were passed and the WPA was inaugurated. Will Rogers was killed in an airplane crash. Boondoggling, Huey Long, and café society were conversational topics. Swing music hit the country, with Benny Goodman its leading exponent. George Gershwin's *Porgy and Bess,* originating in DuBose Heyward's novel, *Porgy,* was the first musical produced by the

151

Theatre Guild. With his third book, which sold 103,286 copies in 1935, Lloyd Douglas became the most popular novelist in the country. Ellen Glasgow, a best-selling author since 1904, achieved a high place with *Vein of Iron*. Six years previously, Thomas Wolfe's *Look Homeward, Angel* had brought him into literary prominence. His second novel, *Of Time and the River,* found a popular audience. Rachel Field, widely known as a writer and illustrator of books for children, made a national reputation with an adult novel. James Hilton's *Mr. Chips* went into its second year. One of his earlier novels, now reissued and also praised by Mr. Woollcott, was close behind it on the list. Eventually *Lost Horizon* became perhaps more famous than *Mr. Chips* and added a new word to our language, Shanghri-La. Both books also became famous movies. Although no yearly records were kept of juvenile best sellers, it is interesting to note that a famous juvenile, *The Little Colonel,* brought out in reprint edition, sold 100,000 copies in 1935. The name of Lindbergh reappeared on the nonfiction list after eight years. This time it was Anne Morrow Lindbergh who wrote of air adventure. It was her literary skill as well as her name, with all its associations from the first Paris flight through the tragic events of kidnapping and trial, that made her book nonfiction top seller of the year, reaching 185,000 copies. *While Rome Burns,* first in 1934, was second in 1935. *Life with Father,* as a book, laid the groundwork for the famous play's record run on Broadway. Vincent Sheean's *Personal History* forecast the important part that newspapermen were to play in the book field during the coming war years. The foundations for the success of *Seven Pillars of Wisdom* had been laid eight years previously by Lawrence's *Revolt in the Desert.* The legend of the man had grown and this, with a notable publicity campaign, accounted for the fact that an expensive book, one that was not "written down" for the sake of appeal to a wide public, was a best seller of the year. *Revolt in the Desert* had been in fact a popularization of part of the original *Seven Pillars of Wisdom.* It was to be the source for many years of books, movies and plays based on the Lawrence legend. Notable biographies by Hackett, Zweig, and Freeman had many readers. Hans Zinsser popularized some interesting aspects of medical lore; and *Skin Deep* became still another best-selling "consumer" book, following *100,000,000 Guinea Pigs.*

1936

Fiction

1. Gone with the Wind, by *Margaret Mitchell.* Macmillan
2. The Last Puritan, by *George Santayana.* Scribner
3. Sparkenbroke, by *Charles Morgan.* Macmillan
4. Drums Along the Mohawk, by *Walter D. Edmonds.* Little, Brown
5. It Can't Happen Here, by *Sinclair Lewis.* Doubleday, Doran
6. White Banners, by *Lloyd C. Douglas.* Houghton Mifflin
7. The Hurricane, by *Charles Nordhoff* and *James Norman Hall.* Little, Brown
8. The Thinking Reed, by *Rebecca West.* Viking Press
9. The Doctor, by *Mary Roberts Rinehart.* Farrar & Rinehart
10. Eyeless in Gaza, by *Aldous Huxley.* Harper

Nonfiction

1. Man the Unknown, by *Alexis Carrel.* Harper
2. Wake Up and Live! by *Dorothea Brande.* Simon & Schuster
3. The Way of a Transgressor, by *Negley Farson.* Harcourt, Brace
4. Around the World in Eleven Years, by *Patience, Richard,* and *Johnny Abbe.* Stokes
5. North to the Orient, by *Anne Morrow Lindbergh.* Harcourt, Brace
6. An American Doctor's Odyssey, by *Victor Heiser.* Norton
7. Inside Europe, by *John Gunther.* Harper
8. Live Alone and Like It, by *Marjorie Hillis.* Bobbs-Merrill
9. Life with Father, by *Clarence Day.* Knopf
10. I Write As I Please, by *Walter Duranty.* Simon & Schuster

THE Rome-Berlin Axis was announced and Germany entered the Rhineland. Edward VIII of England renounced his throne to marry the woman he loved. Revolution against the Republican government in Spain broke out in bloody civil war. American inventiveness turned to air conditioning and streamlining. Destructive floods rolled through the East and Mid-

153

west. Published in June, *Gone with the Wind* was to dominate all fiction sales for two years, creating publishing history with sales never before reached by fiction in so short a time. One million copies were sold in its first six months, and the book and its author, whose first novel it was and who never wrote another, established themselves firmly in American literary legend. George Santayana, Spanish by birth and long a professor of philosophy at Harvard, wrote a best-selling novel, *The Last Puritan,* first of a number of novels by various authors on patrician and intellectual Boston. Walter Edmonds was a new name in historical fiction, adding to the period's growing trend toward long historical novels which was started by *Anthony Adverse* and pointed up again by *Gone with the Wind.* Nordhoff and Hall were a writing team from the South Seas who had first written after World War I of their experiences in France and who had previously made a big hit with *Mutiny on the Bounty,* a sea chronicle based on old records. Rebecca West and Aldous Huxley, notable English writers, appeared for the first time on an American annual best seller list. The nonfiction list was typical of the variety of authorship and subject matter which often comes to the fore in public approval. A surgeon writing for the layman headed the list, followed by a self-improvement book and a newspaperman's story. Fourth came the travel experiences of three smart youngsters, delightedly read by adults. Travel of all kinds predominated the list in this year when the rumblings of coming war were growing louder. Mrs. Lindbergh's book was still a best seller, followed by the narrative of the experiences in out-of-the-way countries of a doctor with a notable career throughout the world in medical research, which also marked the first appearance of the W. W. Norton imprint on these lists. *Inside Europe* was the first book in his long and excellent series on political interpretation the world over by reporter John Gunther. *Live Alone and Like It,* which sold 100,000 copies in 1936, was another self-help book written in humorous and entertaining fashion. Tenth was one of the first and one of the most notable books on the new Russia that foreign correspondents were to write.

1937

Fiction

1. Gone with the Wind, by *Margaret Mitchell*. Macmillan
2. Northwest Passage, by *Kenneth Roberts*. Doubleday, Doran
3. The Citadel, by *A. J. Cronin*. Little, Brown
4. And So—Victoria, by *Vaughan Wilkins*. Macmillan
5. Drums Along the Mohawk, by *Walter D. Edmonds*. Little, Brown
6. The Years, by *Virginia Woolf*. Harcourt, Brace
7. Theatre, by *W. Somerset Maugham*. Doubleday, Doran
8. Of Mice and Men, by *John Steinbeck*. Covici, Friede
9. The Rains Came, by *Louis Bromfield*. Harper
10. We Are Not Alone, by *James Hilton*. Little, Brown

Nonfiction

1. How to Win Friends and Influence People, by *Dale Carnegie*. Simon & Schuster
2. An American Doctor's Odyssey, by *Victor Heiser*. Norton
3. The Return to Religion, by *Henry C. Link*. Macmillan
4. The Arts, by *Hendrik Willem Van Loon*. Simon & Schuster
5. Orchids on Your Budget, by *Marjorie Hillis*. Bobbs-Merrill
6. Present Indicative, by *Noel Coward*. Doubleday, Doran
7. Mathematics for the Million, by *Lancelot Hogben*. Norton
8. Life with Mother, by *Clarence Day*. Knopf
9. The Nile, by *Emil Ludwig*. Viking Press
10. The Flowering of New England, by *Van Wyck Brooks*. Dutton

U.S. TRAVELERS flocked to Paris for the Exposition and to London for the coronation of King George VI. Japan began her long war against China. The dirigible *Hindenburg* burst into fire as it made its first landing at Lakehurst, N.J. Charlie McCarthy, candid cameras, and skiing were current crazes in America, which was also swept by a wave of the new "sit-down" strikes. *Pins and Needles,* produced by the Labor Stage, was to break musical show records by 1939. *Gone with the Wind* swung into an even more triumphant leadership of fiction sales, eventually selling high in the millions. Translation rights were being sought in a score of languages and GWTW became as well-known initials as NBC or WPA. Kenneth Roberts of Maine had published four other historical novels before he achieved national recognition with *Northwest Passage*. A. J. Cronin was more popular than ever, with one of his best-liked novels, *The Citadel,* which sold 161,108 copies in 1937. A new writer of historical fiction from England, Vaughan Wilkins, made his debut on the list, as did Virginia Woolf and W. Somerset Maugham, although their books had had large American audiences for many years. John Steinbeck's first selling success came with *Of Mice and Men.* His *Tortilla Flat,* in 1935, had made its mark with the critics. Louis Bromfield departed from his usual American scene with a novel of India. Half the fiction was contributed in 1937 by English writers, half by American. The best-known self-help book of them all, *How to Win Friends and Influence People,* topped all nonfiction with sales of 729,000 copies in 1937, in addition to its 12,000 from the previous year. With its reappearance in a 25-cent edition (the paperback price of its time), it was to sell well into the millions. *The Return to Religion,* one of the few titles in the nonfiction religious field to reach the annual lists in some time, in contrast to the predominance of religion in both earlier and later years, sold 83,000 copies. Continuing his series of books on various fields of human knowledge, Hendrik Van Loon produced a best seller whose illustrations and format added to its sales appeal. Marjorie Hillis followed her *Live Alone and Like It* with another entertaining book along self-help lines, and Noel Coward first appeared among best sellers with his autobiography. *Mathematics for the Million* was not written down for mass interest; on the contrary, the public had to rise to the scholarly but effective presentation of a difficult subject. Clarence Day continued his delightful family chronicle with *Life with Mother.* Emil Ludwig deserted, temporarily, the lives of great men for the biography of a river. With *The Flowering of New England,* a distinguished literary critic began a series of books on American cultural history, though this was not the first volume chronologically.

1938

Fiction

1. The Yearling, by *Marjorie Kinnan Rawlings*. Scribner
2. The Citadel, by *A. J. Cronin*. Little, Brown
3. My Son, My Son! by *Howard Spring*. Viking Press
4. Rebecca, by *Daphne du Maurier*. Doubleday, Doran
5. Northwest Passage, by *Kenneth Roberts*. Doubleday, Doran
6. All This, and Heaven Too, by *Rachel Field*. Macmillan
7. The Rains Came, by *Louis Bromfield*. Harper
8. And Tell of Time, by *Laura Krey*. Houghton Mifflin
9. The Mortal Storm, by *Phyllis Bottome*. Little, Brown
10. Action at Aquila, by *Hervey Allen*. Farrar & Rinehart

Nonfiction

1. The Importance of Living, by *Lin Yutang*. John Day
2. With Malice Toward Some, by *Margaret Halsey*. Simon & Schuster
3. Madame Curie, by *Eve Curie*. Doubleday, Doran
4. Listen! the Wind, by *Anne Morrow Lindbergh*. Harcourt, Brace
5. The Horse and Buggy Doctor, by *Arthur E. Hertzler*. Harper
6. How to Win Friends and Influence People, by *Dale Carnegie*. Simon & Schuster
7. Benjamin Franklin, by *Carl Van Doren*. Viking Press
8. I'm a Stranger Here Myself, by *Ogden Nash*. Little, Brown
9. Alone, by *Richard E. Byrd*. Putnam
10. Fanny Kemble, by *Margaret Armstrong*. Macmillan

"PEACE in our time" was declared at Munich after the Czech crisis and after Hitler had annexed Austria. American jitters were induced by a Martian radio attack, with Orson Welles as entrepreneur. *God Bless America,* which Irving Berlin had written in 1917, was revived by Kate Smith to become what some chose to call our second national anthem. Bingo and the big apple were fads of the year, and "Wrong-Way" Corrigan amused two continents. "Information Please!" the quiz program that topped all radio quiz programs, presented many authors as well as its "regulars" and, emceed by Clifton Fadiman, then literary critic of *The New Yorker*, added to the interest in and knowledge of books on the part of its vast radio audience. *The Yearling*, novel of a Florida boy and his beloved fawn, outsold other fiction and took its place as an American classic read by both young and old. *The Citadel*, third in 1937, went up to second place in 1938. From England came two writers new to the list and quickly taken up by the public, Howard Spring and Daphne du Maurier. *Rebecca* has gone on selling in reprint editions and was natural material for an extremely popular movie. *Northwest Passage* and *The Rains Came*, perhaps Bromfield's greatest fiction seller, carried on into their second years. Rachel Field's best-known novel, which also became a feature movie, was based upon events in her own family history. *And Tell of Time* was a historical story of Texas by a second new American woman writer on this list. Hervey Allen turned to American Civil War history with his first novel since the great *Anthony*. With the Sino-Japanese war going into its second year, an interpretation of China by a Chinese man of letters outsold all other nonfiction, reaching 124,415 copies in 1938. This included book club sales. Book club first printings were about 75,000 at this time. Margaret Halsey scored the British in her clever and humorous *With Malice Toward Some*. The daughter of Madame Curie told the story of her mother's life, which was taken to the hearts of readers aware of the woman scientist's greatness. *Listen! the Wind*, Mrs. Lindbergh's second account of flying experiences with her famous husband, followed her *North to the Orient* as a best seller. The autobiography of a country doctor was halfway down the list. The response to Carl Van Doren's definitive life of Franklin was enthusiastic. Another new best-selling American biographer was Margaret Armstrong, with *Fanny Kemble*. Ogden Nash was a constantly quoted favorite from the pages of *The New Yorker* and other magazines, even before the publication of *I'm a Stranger Here Myself*, one of the rare books of poetry to reach best-seller lists. Admiral Byrd gave his record of months in the Antarctic, newspaper accounts of which had previously thrilled and mystified millions.

1939

Fiction

1. The Grapes of Wrath, by *John Steinbeck.* Viking Press
2. All This, and Heaven Too, by *Rachel Field.* Macmillan
3. Rebecca, by *Daphne du Maurier.* Doubleday, Doran
4. Wickford Point, by *John P. Marquand.* Little, Brown
5. Escape, by *Ethel Vance.* Little, Brown
6. Disputed Passage, by *Lloyd C. Douglas.* Houghton Mifflin
7. The Yearling, by *Marjorie Kinnan Rawlings.* Scribner
8. The Tree of Liberty, by *Elizabeth Page.* Farrar & Rinehart
9. The Nazarene, by *Sholem Asch.* Putnam
10. Kitty Foyle, by *Christopher Morley.* Lippincott

Nonfiction

1. Days of Our Years, by *Pierre van Paassen.* Hillman-Curl
2. Reaching for the Stars, by *Nora Waln.* Little, Brown
3. Inside Asia, by *John Gunther.* Harper
4. Autobiography with Letters, by *William Lyon Phelps.* Oxford University Press
5. Country Lawyer, by *Bellamy Partridge.* Whittlesey House
6. Wind, Sand and Stars, by *Antoine de St. Exupéry.* Reynal & Hitchcock
7. Mein Kampf, by *Adolf Hitler.* Reynal & Hitchcock
8. A Peculiar Treasure, by *Edna Ferber.* Doubleday, Doran
9. Not Peace But a Sword, by *Vincent Sheean.* Doubleday, Doran
10. Listen! the Wind, by *Anne Morrow Lindbergh.* Harcourt, Brace

THE New York World's Fair opened, with exhibits from nearly all the countries of the world except Germany, and was visited by the King and Queen of England George VI and Elizabeth. The Spanish Civil War ended with the surrender of the Loyalists. Late in the year Germany invaded Poland—the period of peace between two world wars had ended. A novel of the "Okies," those dispossessed by the dust storms of 1934, made John Steinbeck top best seller of the nation. Bookstores sold 300,000 copies during the year. *All This, and Heaven Too* and *Rebecca* both

159

climbed higher on the best-seller ladder in their second year. John P. Marquand had written a penetrating novel of Boston, *The Late George Apley,* in 1937. Known popularly as the writer of the "Mr. Moto" spy stories, he attained critical and commercial success with his first serious novel, though it did not make the list of the year in which it was published. As often happens with a newly prominent writer, the second book after a first success achieved greater national sales in its first year of publication, though not necessarily total sales, than did the earlier book. *Escape,* written by Grace Zaring Stone under the pseudonym of Ethel Vance, was the first best-selling fiction based upon events in Hitler's Germany. Continuing the trend of the long historical novel was *The Tree of Liberty.* Another trend—toward fiction of Biblical times—was marked by the sales of *The Nazarene,* scholarly story by a writer new to this country, whose work was translated from the Yiddish. Christopher Morley, long-beloved poet, essayist, and novelist, found a best-selling audience with his portrayal of a modern working girl, *Kitty Foyle,* later played on the screen by Ginger Rogers. Contemporary history began to loom large in the world of books. Best seller of nonfiction was written by Pierre van Paassen, a Hollander who took a world view of political events in his reminiscences, as had Vincent Sheean in 1935. In *Reaching for the Stars,* Nora Waln described the tragedy of life in Germany under the Nazis as she had witnessed it. Gunther continued his political surveys with *Inside Asia.* Long an influential commentator on books, Professor Phelps of Yale had an assured audience for his autobiography and Oxford University Press (American branch) had its first big popular seller. *Country Lawyer,* amusing narrative of old-time upstate New York life, introduced the legal profession into best sellerdom, where medical lives were already well established. *Wind, Sand and Stars,* by a French writer and aviator, added to the literature of flight. *Mein Kampf,* Bible of Nazi Germany, was published with its full text for the first time over here. A best seller over many years in the fiction field, Edna Ferber wrote best-selling nonfiction as well with her autobiography, *A Peculiar Treasure.*

1940

Fiction

1. How Green Was My Valley, by *Richard Llewellyn*. Macmillan
2. Kitty Foyle, by *Christopher Morley*. Lippincott
3. Mrs. Miniver, by *Jan Struther*. Harcourt, Brace
4. For Whom the Bell Tolls, by *Ernest Hemingway*. Scribner
5. The Nazarene, by *Sholem Asch*. Putnam
6. Stars on the Sea, by *F. van Wyck Mason*. Lippincott
7. Oliver Wiswell, by *Kenneth Roberts*. Doubleday, Doran
8. The Grapes of Wrath, by *John Steinbeck*. Viking Press
9. Night in Bombay, by *Louis Bromfield*. Harper
10. The Family, by *Nina Fedorova*. Little, Brown

Nonfiction

1. I Married Adventure, by *Osa Johnson*. Lippincott
2. How to Read a Book, by *Mortimer Adler*. Simon & Schuster
3. A Smattering of Ignorance, by *Oscar Levant*. Doubleday, Doran
4. Country Squire in the White House, by *John T. Flynn*. Doubleday, Doran
5. Land Below the Wind, by *Agnes Newton Keith*. Little, Brown
6. American White Paper, by *Joseph W. Alsop, Jr.*, and *Robert Kintnor*. Simon & Schuster
7. New England: Indian Summer, by *Van Wyck Brooks*. Dutton
8. As I Remember Him, by *Hans Zinsser*. Little, Brown
9. Days of Our Years, by *Pierre van Paassen*. Dial Press
10. Bet It's a Boy, by *Betty B. Blunt*. Stephen Daye Press

AFTER MONTHS of the so-called "phony" war, the German blitz broke loose, engulfing Holland, Belgium, Luxembourg, France. Millions in America grabbed each new edition of the newspapers as the Nazis stormed nearer Paris. War gloom was at its deepest as Hitler attacked England from the air, and American sympathy went out to the besieged and bombarded Britishers. In the fall Wendell Willkie polled an enormous popular vote, but Franklin D. Roosevelt was elected President of the

161

United States for a third term. A novel of the Welsh coal miners, beautifully written and with emotional appeal, quickly made the best-seller grade, and brought a new name to the head of the fiction list. *How Green Was My Valley* sold 176,280 copies through the bookstores in 1940. Third, by a new English writer, was *Mrs. Miniver,* the central character of which charmed the American public in the book and the movie. Its author, Jan Struther, was possibly the most frequent guest on "Information, Please!" *For Whom the Bell Tolls,* Ernest Hemingway's first great best seller, told of an American in the Spanish Civil War. A new name in historical fiction was F. van Wyck Mason, though, like John P. Marquand, he had long been liked in another field of fiction—as a writer of international adventure stories featuring an Army Intelligence hero. The first in his series of novels on the early maritime history of this country, *Three Harbours,* did not reach an annual list, but the second, *Stars on the Sea,* did. It was a novel of unusual length, as was *Oliver Wiswell,* another Kenneth Roberts historical novel. *I Married Adventure,* Osa Johnson's narrative of years in far, wild countries with her explorer husband, Martin Johnson, topped nonfiction with sales of 288,000, including book club copies. *How to Read a Book* was an interesting success. "Information, Please!" contributed another book success when one of its most popular stars, the whimsical and musical Oscar Levant, entertained with *A Smattering of Ignorance. Country Squire in the White House,* campaign literature of 1940, sold over 100,000 copies. *Land Below the Wind* was an Atlantic-Little, Brown prize-winning book about Borneo. With the exception of *American White Paper* and *Days of Our Years* (the first Dial Press book on these lists), it is amazing to note that by the end of the first year of the war no nonfiction best seller could in any way be considered a "war book." *New England: Indian Summer* was the second volume of Van Wyck Brooks' best-selling literary history. *As I Remember Him* was the biography of his "romantic self" by Hans Zinsser, author of *Rats, Lice and History. Bet It's a Boy,* a little cartoon book of obstetrical humor, sold over 100,000 in the year, a forerunner of the many popular "non-books" of the sixties.

1941

Fiction

1. The Keys of the Kingdom, by *A. J. Cronin*. Little, Brown
2. Random Harvest, by *James Hilton*. Little, Brown
3. This Above All, by *Eric Knight*. Harper
4. The Sun Is My Undoing, by *Marguerite Steen*. Viking Press
5. For Whom the Bell Tolls, by *Ernest Hemingway*. Scribner
6. Oliver Wiswell, by *Kenneth Roberts*. Doubleday, Doran
7. H. M. Pulham, Esquire, by *John P. Marquand*. Little, Brown
8. Mr. and Mrs. Cugat, by *Isabel Scott Rorick*. Houghton Mifflin
9. Saratoga Trunk, by *Edna Ferber*. Doubleday, Doran
10. Windswept, by *Mary Ellen Chase*. Macmillan

Nonfiction

1. Berlin Diary, by *William L. Shirer*. Knopf
2. The White Cliffs, by *Alice Duer Miller*. Coward-McCann
3. Out of the Night, by *Jan Valtin*. Alliance Book Corp.
4. Inside Latin America, by *John Gunther*. Harper
5. Blood, Sweat and Tears, by *Winston S. Churchill*. Putnam
6. You Can't Do Business with Hitler, by *Douglas Miller*. Little, Brown
7. Reading I've Liked, ed. by *Clifton Fadiman*. Simon & Schuster
8. Reveille in Washington, by *Margaret Leech*. Harper
9. Exit Laughing, by *Irvin S. Cobb*. Bobbs-Merrill
10. My Sister and I, by *Dirk van der Heide*. Harcourt, Brace

"NEVER had so many owed so much to so few" as England's gallant airmen defended their island. The worst threat of invasion was over but Germany had attacked Russia and held nearly all the continent as her own *Festung Europa*. One Sunday afternoon toward the end of the year, when most American families had their radios tuned to the Philharmonic, came the stunning announcement that the Japanese had attacked Pearl Harbor. The United States immediately entered the war against Japan, Germany, and Italy. War books predominated the 1941 list of best sellers, although we were actually at war only during the last month of the year.

163

In fiction two best-selling war novels, both by English authors, were in second and third places. James Hilton had already written several best sellers (his *Random Harvest* was about World War I), but Eric Knight, later killed in a plane crash, was best known as the author of an outstanding dog story, *Lassie Come-Home*. First on the list was the latest Cronin novel, rival in popularity to *The Citadel*. *The Keys of the Kingdom* sold 236,496 copies through the trade, plus 234,328 through the Book-of-the-Month Club, whose membership had reached a figure far beyond that of its early years. Marguerite Steen, author of many novels, joined best sellers with a long historical novel. *For Whom the Bell Tolls* and *Oliver Wiswell* appeared in their second year, and John P. Marquand added another portrait of consequence to his gallery of Bostonians. *Mr. and Mrs. Cugat,* introduced another new author. Edna Ferber had a story of Saratoga's heyday, and Mary Ellen Chase a second best seller about Maine. The war led in earnest in nonfiction. Correspondent William Shirer's *Berlin Diary* made history by forming opinion and preparing American understanding of one of the enemies with whom we were to be at war by December. It sold 213,769 copies through the bookstores, 236,496 through the Book-of-the-Month Club in 1941. *The White Cliffs,* first Coward-McCann best seller on these lists, a narrative poem of wartime England, later basis of a movie and a popular song, made a record sale for a book of poetry, reaching 250,000 copies in its first three years. The underground life of Gestapo vs. Communist came into Jan Valtin's *Out of the Night.* John Gunther followed his *Inside Europe* and *Inside Asia* with a third best seller. American interest in England's great crisis was reflected in the sales of Prime Minister Winston Churchill's speeches. *You Can't Do Business with Hitler* struck an important prewar note. The touching story of a Dutch refugee boy, *My Sister and I,* a title which also inspired a popular song of the day, made a total of seven books on the 1941 nonfiction list that were concerned with the war in one way or another. The other three places were filled by Clifton Fadiman's anthology, *Reading I've Liked,* arousing interest in a wide audience because of his great popularity on "Information, Please!" and as book critic of *The New Yorker*; by a historical portrait of Washington, D.C., *Reveille in Washington*; and by the autobiography of a long-time favorite author and humorist, Irvin S. Cobb.

1942

Fiction

1. The Song of Bernadette, by *Franz Werfel.* Viking Press
2. The Moon Is Down, by *John Steinbeck.* Viking Press
3. Dragon Seed, by *Pearl S. Buck.* John Day
4. And Now Tomorrow, by *Rachel Field.* Macmillan
5. Drivin' Woman, by *Elizabeth Pickett.* Macmillan
6. Windswept, by *Mary Ellen Chase.* Macmillan
7. The Robe, by *Lloyd C. Douglas.* Houghton Mifflin
8. The Sun Is My Undoing, by *Marguerite Steen.* Viking Press
9. Kings Row, by *Henry Bellamann.* Simon & Schuster
10. The Keys of the Kingdom, by *A. J. Cronin.* Little, Brown

Nonfiction

1. See Here, Private Hargrove, by *Marion Hargrove.* Holt
2. Mission to Moscow, by *Joseph E. Davies.* Simon & Schuster
3. The Last Time I Saw Paris, by *Elliot Paul.* Random House
4. Cross Creek, by *Marjorie Kinnan Rawlings.* Scribner
5. Victory Through Air Power, by *Major Alexander P. de Seversky.* Simon & Schuster
6. Past Imperfect, by *Ilka Chase.* Doubleday, Doran
7. They Were Expendable, by *W. L. White.* Harcourt, Brace
8. Flight to Arras, by *Antoine de St. Exupéry.* Reynal & Hitchcock
9. Washington Is Like That, by *W. M. Kiplinger.* Harper
10. Inside Latin America, by *John Gunther.* Harper

THE EARLY MONTHS of 1942 marked the low point of the war as far as the United States was concerned. The Philippines were overrun after MacArthur's desperate stand on Corregidor, Australia and our lifelines to that continent were threatened, and Singapore fell. Then in April we struck our first offensive blow with the bombing of Tokyo. In August came the first attack on Guadalcanal. Americans were introduced to rationing, and pleasure-driving in automobiles was prohibited. The death of ex-Kaiser Wilhelm of Germany in exile caused little stir in comparison

165

with tremendous daily developments in World War II. Again the appeal of religious fiction was evidenced by the great sale of *The Song of Bernadette,* which reached almost half a million copies in 1942. With its reprint edition, timed for the release of a notable movie, it sold over 900,000 in two years. John Steinbeck's *The Moon Is Down,* later a stage play, was a story of the German occupation of Norway; it, like *Bernadette,* approached the 500,000 mark in 1942. Pearl Buck's novel of war in China, *Dragon Seed,* sold around 400,000 copies in its original edition and was also made into a notable 1944 movie. *The Robe,* published in October, a novel of the time of Christ, started toward its record-breaking sales figure—it was still high on best seller lists the country over two years later. In that time it was never less than fifth on the monthly National Best Seller List of *Publishers' Weekly,* and it passed the 1,000,000 mark on its second birthday. In 1953 with the release of the movie based upon it, *The Robe* in a cheaper "movie edition" was the best selling novel of the year. The rookie of World War II, Private Hargrove, was the star of the hit book of 1942 nonfiction; sales in all editions went over 2,000,000, far outdistancing the comparable *Dere Mable* of World War I. Seven war books dominated the nonfiction list. Besides *Private Hargrove* there were Ambassador Davies' report on Russia (later a controversial movie); *The Last Time I Saw Paris* (first Random House best seller of these lists), nostalgic portrait of the Paris that had been, by Elliot Paul, whose *Life and Death of a Spanish Town* had previously portrayed the coming of fascism to Spain; *Victory Through Air Power,* a noted flyer, plane designer, and manufacturer's forecast of strategy; *They Were Expendable,* first American record of personal exploits in World War II to become a national best seller, by correspondent W. L. White, the first book to be named an "Imperative" by the newly formed Council on Books in Wartime; *Flight to Arras,* war experiences of the French aviator who had written *Wind, Sand and Stars*; and *Inside Latin America* in its second year. Marjorie Rawlings, of *The Yearling* fame in fiction, contributed charming sketches of her Florida countryside. A highly entertaining autobiography by a star of stage, movie, and radio, and a picture of Washington life completed the unwarlike part of the list.

1943

Fiction

1. The Robe, by *Lloyd C. Douglas.* Houghton Mifflin
2. The Valley of Decision, by *Marcia Davenport.* Scribner
3. So Little Time, by *John P. Marquand.* Little, Brown
4. A Tree Grows in Brooklyn, by *Betty Smith.* Harper
5. The Human Comedy, by *William Saroyan.* Harcourt, Brace
6. Mrs. Parkington, by *Louis Bromfield.* Harper
7. The Apostle, by *Sholem Asch.* Putnam
8. Hungry Hill, by *Daphne du Maurier.* Doubleday, Doran
9. The Forest and the Fort, by *Hervey Allen.* Farrar & Rinehart
10. The Song of Bernadette, by *Franz Werfel.* Viking Press

Nonfiction

1. Under Cover, by *John Roy Carlson.* Dutton
2. One World, by *Wendell L. Willkie.* Simon & Schuster
3. Journey Among Warriors, by *Eve Curie.* Doubleday, Doran
4. On Being a Real Person, by *Harry Emerson Fosdick.* Harper
5. Guadalcanal Diary, by *Richard Tregaskis.* Random House
6. Burma Surgeon, by *Lt. Col. Gordon Seagrave.* Norton
7. Our Hearts Were Young and Gay, by *Cornelia Otis Skinner* and *Emily Kimbrough.* Dodd, Mead
8. U. S. Foreign Policy, by *Walter Lippmann.* Little, Brown
9. Here Is Your War, by *Ernie Pyle.* Holt
10. See Here, Private Hargrove, by *Marion Hargrove.* Holt

WITH the landing of a great Allied armada in North Africa came the turning point of the war. Our troops moved on into Sicily and Italy. From Britain, Germany and the occupied countries of Europe were blasted from the air. In the Pacific our Navy began moving in on Jap-held islands. Again a religious novel topped fiction—*The Robe,* which had been published late the previous year. With paper supply cut to 90 per cent of the 1942 level, Houghton Mifflin was hard put to meet the demand. As new printings of *The Robe* appeared, the book shrank in height and thickness, though the text was not cut. Marcia Davenport was a new best-selling author whose

Valley of Decision, story of a Pennsylvania mine-owning family, met with great success. The daughter of Alma Gluck, she had already written two well-liked books with musical background, a biography of Mozart and a novel, *Of Lena Geyer.* By the end of 1943, *Valley of Decision* had been on 14 consecutive monthly lists and *Bernadette* on 13. Novels reflected the war only slightly; it was the background for only two best sellers of the year, *So Little Time,* in which John Marquand deserted his customary Boston scene, and William Saroyan's tender and moving story of a California family, which became a memorable movie as well. This was Saroyan's first appearance on an annual best seller list. A new author with a first novel whose title was to become as familiar as *Gone with the Wind* was Betty Smith, who put neglected Brooklyn on the fiction map. The four other authors were all familiar names among best sellers—Sholem Asch with his second religious novel, Daphne du Maurier with a successor to *Rebecca,* Hervey Allen with the first book of his projected series of American historical novels, and Franz Werfel with *The Song of Bernadette* in its second year. Three novels on the 1943 list were religious in theme. Only two titles on the nonfiction list were not "war books." These were Dr. Fosdick's *On Being a Real Person,* which sold over 200,000, and the gay reminiscences of a trip to pre-World War I Europe by Cornelia Otis Skinner and Emily Kimbrough. *Under Cover,* an opinion-making report of subversive activities in this country, sold 600,000 copies in its original edition. Wendell Willkie's wartime trip around the world created an eager market for his report, which then absorbed 1,500,000 copies. Since it was published simultaneously in a cloth and a paperbound edition, the latter greatly outselling the former and having a wide newsstand and drugstore sale, Willkie's book might well have stood at the head of this list. But these lists were based upon bookstore sales only, and therefore the reports on *Under Cover* outdistanced those on *One World. One World* was also an "Imperative" of the Council on Books in Wartime, has been translated into sixteen languages, and has sold well over 3,000,000 copies throughout the world. Eve Curie was again a best seller, this time with an account of her trip to the war fronts of the globe. *Guadalcanal Diary* was a correspondent's report of our hard-fought campaign. *Burma Surgeon* related the experiences of a doctor who became an Army medical officer when the Japanese took over the country in which he had labored long as a medical missionary. Walter Lippmann, influential newspaper columnist who had been a best seller in 1929 with *A Preface to Morals,* gave his views on what our foreign policy had been and should be, another Council "Imperative." In *Here Is Your War* newspaperman Ernie Pyle revealed the human qualities of the infantryman as he saw them in North Africa—a book that found country-wide response as had the newspaper articles upon which it was based. *See Here, Private Hargrove* was still going strong in its second year.

1944

Fiction

1. Strange Fruit, by *Lillian Smith*. Reynal & Hitchcock
2. The Robe, by *Lloyd C. Douglas*. Houghton Mifflin
3. A Tree Grows in Brooklyn, by *Betty Smith*. Harper
4. Forever Amber, by *Kathleen Winsor*. Macmillan
5. The Razor's Edge, by *W. Somerset Maugham*. Doubleday, Doran
6. The Green Years, by *A. J. Cronin*. Little, Brown
7. Leave Her to Heaven, by *Ben Ames Williams*. Houghton Mifflin
8. Green Dolphin Street, by *Elizabeth Goudge*. Coward-McCann
9. A Bell for Adano, by *John Hersey*. Knopf
10. The Apostle, by *Sholem Asch*. Putnam

Nonfiction

1. I Never Left Home, by *Bob Hope*. Simon & Schuster; Home Guide
2. Brave Men, by *Ernie Pyle*. Holt
3. Good Night, Sweet Prince, by *Gene Fowler*. Viking Press
4. Under Cover, by *John Roy Carlson*. Dutton
5. Yankee from Olympus, by *Catherine Drinker Bowen*. Little, Brown
6. The Time for Decision, by *Sumner Welles*. Harper
7. Here Is Your War, by *Ernie Pyle*. Holt
8. Anna and the King of Siam, by *Margaret Landon*. John Day
9. The Curtain Rises, by *Quentin Reynolds*. Random House
10. Ten Years in Japan, by *Joseph C. Grew*. Simon & Schuster

THE NEWS of the invasion of northern Europe that the world had been waiting and hoping for so long was broadcast early on the morning of June 6. With the Allies closing in on Germany from all sides, confidence rose that the end of the war was in sight. In the fall, as Dewey and Roosevelt campaigned for the Presidency, two influential and greatly admired men on the national political scene died within a few days of each other. Al Smith and Wendell Willkie, the latter also the author of one of the great best sellers, *One World. Strange Fruit,* poignant first novel of white and black in the South, published by the comparatively new firm of Reynal & Hitchcock, was first on the fiction list of the year. It was later banned in Boston as was another first novel, fourth among best sellers, *Forever Amber.* Kathleen Winsor was the much publicized and photogenic author of *Forever Amber,* a novel of Restoration England which emphasized the bawdiness of the period. There were two religious novels on the list—*The Robe* in its third year of best-sellerdom and *The Apostle* in its second. Another first novel, *A Tree Grows in Brooklyn,* was in third place. It had been fourth the year before. The war was the background in only two novels, in *The Razor's Edge* and in *A Bell for Adano,* which was John Hersey's first novel but third book about the war. It was the story of an American AMG officer in Italy and of the problems he faced in administering the affairs of a region recently swept of the Nazis. Ben Ames Williams, long a favorite fiction and magazine writer, appeared on a yearly list for the first time. *Green Dolphin Street* was a historical novel which won for its author, Elizabeth Goudge, the $125,000 prize offered by the film producers Metro-Goldwyn-Mayer. War books of 1944, seven out of the ten in nonfiction, were notable because of their timeliness, their coverage of the diverse phases of the war, and their excellence of presentation. One was written by a comedian who journeyed to the war fronts to entertain the troops (Bob Hope, over 20 years later, was still making Christmas trips to entertain American soldiers fighting on foreign soil); three by war correspondents; one by an investigator of subversive activities; and two by statesmen. Bob Hope's book, published in a paper as well as a cloth edition, far outstripped the rest in sales, going well over the million mark. Ernie Pyle was the newspaperman responsible for two books on the list. He was awarded a Pulitzer Prize for his reporting from the war fronts where he was later to be killed. Quentin Reynolds had written many excellent books, from the war correspondent's vantage point, since the start of the war, but not until *The Curtain Rises* was published did he make the annual list. The books by former Under Secretary of State Sumner Welles and former Ambassador Grew were outstanding examples of those which, like *Berlin Diary* and *One World,* influenced American thinking. First of the three non-war books of the year was *Good Night, Sweet Prince,* a biography of one of the most famous stars of stage and screen, John Barrymore of the glamorous theatrical family. The other two non-war books were also biographies. *Yankee from Olympus,* in fifth place, was primarily the story of Justice Holmes but included as well other members of a family that held a prominent place in American life and letters over many years.

Anna and the King of Siam was the interesting story of a woman who went to Siam in the 19th century as governess to the King's daughters. It became, many years later, basis of a movie and as "The King and I," the basis of a popular musical, and another movie.

1945

Fiction

1. Forever Amber, by *Kathleen Winsor*. Macmillan
2. The Robe, by *Lloyd C. Douglas*. Houghton Mifflin
3. The Black Rose, by *Thomas B. Costain*. Doubleday
4. The White Tower, by *James Ramsey Ullman*. Lippincott
5. Cass Timberlane, by *Sinclair Lewis*. Random House
6. A Lion Is In the Streets, by *Adria Locke Langley*. Whittlesey House
7. So Well Remembered, by *James Hilton*. Little, Brown
8. Captain from Castile, by *Samuel Shellabarger*. Little, Brown
9. Earth and High Heaven, by *Gwethalyn Graham*. Lippincott
10. Immortal Wife, by *Irving Stone*. Doubleday

Nonfiction

1. Brave Men, by *Ernie Pyle*. Holt
2. Dear Sir, by *Juliet Lowell*. Duell, Sloan & Pearce
3. Up Front, by *Bill Mauldin*. Holt
4. Black Boy, by *Richard Wright*. Harper
5. Try and Stop Me, by *Bennett Cerf*. Simon & Schuster
6. Anything Can Happen, by *George and Helen Papashvily*. Harper
7. General Marshall's Report. Simon & Schuster
8. The Egg and I, by *Betty MacDonald*. Lippincott
9. The Thurber Carnival, by *James Thurber*. Harper
10. Pleasant Valley, by *Louis Bromfield*. Harper

THE WORLD was shocked at Roosevelt's death at Warm Springs in April. The long-awaited VE day came in May and, in August, VJ day, after the atomic bomb had exploded over Hiroshima and Nagasaki. The UN charter was signed in San Francisco. War shortages still prevailed in the book industry; though "thin" books were necessary to conserve paper and other production materials a very "fat" book was 1945's best-selling novel, the already-famous *Forever Amber,* selling 868,630 copies in its second year. Two hundred and seventy thousand copies of the second novel on the 1945 list were sold during that year, also its second year, bringing the total of *The Robe* close to 2,000,000 at that time. These two novels at the top of the 1945 list were the only ones that year that were not book club selections or dividends or issued in the Armed Services Editions of which 90,000,000 books had been distributed to men in the service. The war years were the peak years for the book clubs: their paper quotas were high, under paper rationing, compared to the publishers'. This fact accounted for some of the big sales of fiction, particularly historical fiction. Nearly all the novels on the 1945 list sold over half a million copies, including such extra-bookstore distribution. Three new novelists achieved prominence—James Ramsey Ullman, Adria Locke Langley, and Gwethalyn Graham—most of the others were well-known and popular writers. There were no war novels on the 1945 fiction list; historical fiction predominated. War books, however, took first, second, third and seventh places in nonfiction. *Brave Men,* published late in 1944 and second for that year, sold 687,450 copies through the bookstores, and, with its book club sales, well over a million. *Dear Sir,* the little book of war humor, unexpectedly showed up with the total of 654,391. The leading autobiography of 1945, *Black Boy,* sold 195,000 copies, and, with book club, 546,000. *General Marshall's Report* sold 133,770 copies, of which 15,000 were clothbound, 118,770, paperbound—representing a trend toward two editions, in cloth and paper, of a single title which was further developed in succeeding years. In general nonfiction did not attain the high sales of fiction, though *Brave Men* (its author had been killed early in the year by a Japanese sniper's bullet) outdistanced every book in both classifications.

1946

Fiction

1. The King's General, by *Daphne du Maurier*. Doubleday
2. This Side of Innocence, by *Taylor Caldwell*. Scribner
3. The River Road, by *Frances Parkinson Keyes*. Messner
4. The Miracle of the Bells, by *Russell Janney*. Prentice-Hall
5. The Hucksters, by *Frederic Wakeman*. Rinehart
6. The Foxes of Harrow, by *Frank Yerby*. Dial Press
7. Arch of Triumph, by *Erich Maria Remarque*. Appleton-Century
8. The Black Rose, by *Thomas B. Costain*. Doubleday
9. B. F.'s Daughter, by *John P. Marquand*. Little, Brown
10. The Snake Pit, by *Mary Jane Ward*. Random House

Nonfiction

1. The Egg and I, by *Betty MacDonald*. Lippincott
2. Peace of Mind, by *Joshua L. Liebman*. Simon & Schuster
3. As He Saw It, by *Elliott Roosevelt*. Duell, Sloan & Pearce
4. The Roosevelt I Knew, by *Frances Perkins*. Viking Press
5. Last Chapter, by *Ernie Pyle*. Holt
6. Starling of the White House, by *Thomas Sugrue* and *Col. Edmund Starling*. Simon & Schuster
7. I Chose Freedom, by *Victor Kravchenko*. Scribner
8. The Anatomy of Peace, by *Emery Reves*. Harper
9. Top Secret, by *Ralph Ingersoll*. Harcourt, Brace
10. A Solo in Tom-Toms, by *Gene Fowler*. Viking Press

1946 WAS the year in which the American public first listened to an atomic explosion—at Bikini Atoll, via radio. The end of World War II was officially proclaimed by President Truman. Mother Cabrini was the first American citizen to be raised to sainthood. *Call Me Mister* and *Annie Get Your Gun* were popular stage productions and *The Best Years of Our Lives,* the movie of the year. Daphne du Maurier, whose *The King's General* headed the 1946 best seller list, was a novelist familiar to readers of best sellers. Her *Hungry Hill* was a best seller of 1943 and her famous *Rebecca* appeared on the lists of both 1938 and 1939. Through

174

the bookstores, 228,235 copies of *The King's General* were sold in 1946; including sales through three book clubs, its total in 1946 was 1,095,571. Besides *The King's General,* there were four other historical novels on the 1946 list of best-selling fiction. *This Side of Innocence,* by Taylor Caldwell, took second place with a bookstore sale of about 221,000 copies. This novel had, in addition, the largest sale ever attained at that time by any Literary Guild selection, over 1,055,000. Another longtime popular novelist, Frances Parkinson Keyes, reached the annual list for the first time with her *River Road,* with sales of 225,000, plus a book club sale adding up to 950,000. Fourth of the historical novels was a first novel by Frank Yerby, later to become one of the biggest-selling novelists of the '40's and '50's. *The Foxes of Harrow* sold 172,000 through the bookstores, and, with sales from three book clubs, attained a total of 1,200,000 during the year. Eighth was *The Black Rose,* a Thomas B. Costain historical. A widely publicized first novel, *The Miracle of the Bells,* by Russell Janney, reached fourth place, the only title on the fiction list which was not the selection of any book club. Another writer new to the best seller lists, Frederic Wakeman, had a trade sale of over 180,000 for his sensational novel about the advertising business, *The Hucksters,* with a total of 712,434, including book club sales. *Arch of Triumph,* by Erich Maria Remarque, whose great novel of World War I, *All Quiet on the Western Front,* topped the 1929 best seller list, was in seventh place. *B. F.'s Daughter,* by John P. Marquand, a favorite novelist over many years, sold 129,000 copies through the trade plus 680,000 book club copies. *The Snake Pit,* by Mary Jane Ward, who made her first appearance on the list and started a trend for novels about psychiatric problems, sold about 125,000, which, with the book club sale, made a total of 600,000. All these figures for fiction in the first postwar year seemed staggering in the cold light of less prosperous earlier and later years. With production problems still keeping publishers busy trying to keep up with demand, hardbound books were sold in quantities never before reached, though the actual number of new titles was at its lowest in about 40 years. Said *Publishers' Weekly,* "Never before have so few titles gone to so many readers . . . the major book clubs . . . think nothing of printing a half-million copies of a current selection." Nonfiction figures were not quite so startling. Though Betty MacDonald's first book, *The Egg and I,* sold 496,000 copies through the bookstores and a total of 1,038,500 with its book club sale, Joshua L. Liebman's *Peace of Mind,* which was to be the nonfiction best seller of 1947 and still on the annual list in 1948, reached second place with a mere 242,000 copies. There were two biographies of the late President among 1946 best sellers, and a volume of White House reminiscences, two war books, a book on the peace, and two biographies, one a Russian political autobiography.

175

1947

Fiction

1. The Miracle of the Bells, by *Russell Janney*. Prentice-Hall
2. The Moneyman, by *Thomas B. Costain*. Doubleday
3. Gentleman's Agreement, by *Laura Z. Hobson*. Simon & Schuster
4. Lydia Bailey, by *Kenneth Roberts*, Doubleday
5. The Vixens, by *Frank Yerby*. Dial Press
6. The Wayward Bus, by *John Steinbeck*. Viking Press
7. House Divided, by *Ben Ames Williams*. Houghton Mifflin
8. Kingsblood Royal, by *Sinclair Lewis*. Random House
9. East Side, West Side, by *Marcia Davenport*. Scribner
10. Prince of Foxes, by *Samuel Shellabarger*. Little, Brown

Nonfiction

1. Peace of Mind, by *Joshua L. Liebman*. Simon & Schuster
2. Information Please Almanac, 1947, ed. by *John Kieran*. Garden City Publishing Co.
3. Inside U.S.A., by *John Gunther*. Harper
4. A Study of History, by *Arnold J. Toynbee*. Oxford University Press
5. Speaking Frankly, by *James F. Byrnes*. Harper
6. Human Destiny, by *Pierre Lecomte du Noüy*. Longmans, Green
7. The Egg and I, by *Betty MacDonald*. Lippincott
8. The American Past, by *Roger Butterfield*. Simon & Schuster
9. The Fireside Book of Folk Songs, ed. by *Margaret B. Boni*. Simon & Schuster
10. Together, by *Katharine T. Marshall*. Tupper & Love

THE Taft-Hartley Act was passed by Congress in 1947 and the Marshall Plan announced; the Freedom Train, exhibiting the great historical documents of the U.S.A., and the Friendship Train, bearing food for devastated Europe, were started on their ways. Street-cars disappeared from Manhattan Island and flying saucers were seen in the sky. New Yorkers went to the theatre to see *All My Sons, A Streetcar Named Desire* and the first operas by Gian-Carlo Menotti to be produced here. Henry Ford died at his home in Michigan, leaving an estate of over 500 million dollars. Titles which rang up most sales in the bookstores during 1947 were *The Miracle of the Bells,* a first novel by Russell Janney, in fiction, and *Peace of Mind,* by Rabbi Liebman, in nonfiction. The nonfiction title outsold the fiction title by about 30,000 copies. Both books had also appeared on the 1946 best seller list. *The Miracle of the Bells* had a larger sale, one of over 240,000 copies, in its second year. With book club sales it had reached an overall figure, by the end of 1947, of approximately 400,000. Only two novels and three books of nonfiction on the combined list had no book club or extra-bookstore sales whatever. Half the fiction list in 1947 was made up of historical novels. Thomas B. Costain's *The Moneyman,* in second place in fiction, selling 185,000 through the trade, started out with an advance sale double that of his 1946 best-selling historical romance, *The Black Rose.* The other historical novels on the 1947 list were *Lydia Bailey, The Vixens, House Divided,* and *Prince of Foxes,* all by well-known and popular authors. *The Vixens* sold 152,706 copies through bookstores, plus Fiction Book Club sales of over 125,000. *House Divided,* one of the two "bookstore only" novels on the list, sold just over 125,000. *Prince of Foxes* sold 107,000 copies—with its Literary Guild sales, over 1,125,000. The heightened postwar interest in problems of race relations was reflected in the sale of *Gentleman's Agreement,* by Laura Z. Hobson, dealing with Jewish-Gentile relations, and *Kingsblood Royal,* in which Sinclair Lewis presented what was then the dilemma of a white man who discovered that he had Negro blood. *Gentleman's Agreement* sold 172,615 copies through bookstores, over a million in 1947 through all media. The Lewis book had an overall sale of about 800,000, of which 115,000 were sold in the stores. *The Wayward Bus,* by John Steinbeck, sold 520,000, including trade, book club, and Armed Services Editions. *East Side, West Side,* by Marcia Davenport, the other of the two "bookstore only" novels, had a sale of approximately 111,000. *Peace of Mind,* one of the first of the big sellers in the "inspirational" market that boomed in the '40's and '50's, had a bigger sale in its second year in the bookstores, 270,669. Its overall sale by the end of 1947 was 577,693. Nearly 300,000 copies of the first *Information Please Almanac* were sold—the famous radio program was at the height of its popularity—and the *Almanac* was the second best seller of the year. John Gunther's 1947 "Inside" book, *Inside U.S.A.,* was in third place, with 187,000 copies printed. It was among the four nonfiction best sellers which may be classified as historical and political. The others were Arnold Toynbee's *A Study of History,* with 123,000 trade sale plus 60,000 book club; *Speaking Frankly,* Secretary of State Byrnes' memoirs of the war years, with 125,000 printed; and *The American Past,* picture history by Roger Butterfield, with a sale of about 68,000.

177

Besides *Peace of Mind,* another religious book was a big 1947 seller. *Human Destiny,* by Pierre Lecomte du Noüy, reached sixth place with a sale of 105,000 and a book club printing of 320,000. *The Egg and I,* which had been the 1946 leader in nonfiction, appeared again in 1947 with sales of 101,138 copies in its second year. Its two-year total was in the neighborhood of a million and a quarter. Besides the MacDonald book, the only other 1947 best seller which could be classified as biography, a category that formerly dominated nonfiction lists, was *Together,* the life of General Marshall written by his wife. It sold 59,156 copies through the stores, 300,000 with its book club sales. *The Fireside Book of Folk Songs,* like *The American Past,* a fast seller as a Christmas gift book, reached a sale of about 68,000. Those two and *Speaking Frankly* were the only books among nonfiction best sellers which were not distributed in part through sales agencies other than bookstores.

1948

Fiction

1. The Big Fisherman, by *Lloyd C. Douglas*. Houghton Mifflin
2. The Naked and the Dead, by *Norman Mailer*. Rinehart
3. Dinner at Antoine's, by *Frances Parkinson Keyes*. Messner
4. The Bishop's Mantle, by *Agnes Sligh Turnbull*. Macmillan
5. Tomorrow Will Be Better, by *Betty Smith*. Harper
6. The Golden Hawk, by *Frank Yerby*. Dial Press
7. Raintree County, by *Ross Lockridge, Jr.* Houghton Mifflin
8. Shannon's Way, by *A. J. Cronin*. Little, Brown
9. Pilgrim's Inn, by *Elizabeth Goudge*. Coward-McCann
10. The Young Lions, by *Irwin Shaw*. Random House

Nonfiction

1. Crusade in Europe, by *Dwight D. Eisenhower*. Doubleday
2. How to Stop Worrying and Start Living, by *Dale Carnegie*. Simon & Schuster
3. Peace of Mind, by *Joshua L. Liebman*. Simon & Schuster
4. Sexual Behavior in the Human Male, by *A. C. Kinsey* and others. Saunders
5. Wine, Women and Words, by *Billy Rose*. Simon & Schuster
6. The Life and Times of the Shmoo, by *Al Capp*. Simon & Schuster
7. The Gathering Storm, by *Winston Churchill*. Houghton Mifflin
8. Roosevelt and Hopkins, by *Robert E. Sherwood*. Harper
9. A Guide to Confident Living, by *Norman Vincent Peale*. Prentice-Hall
10. The Plague and I, by *Betty MacDonald*. Lippincott

AMERICANS were talking about the "pumpkin papers" in the Chambers-Hiss case in 1948. They were watching and listening to the first symphony and opera telecasts, and seeing *Mister Roberts* and *Kiss Me Kate* on the stage. *Slow Boat to China, Nature Boy* and Citation became familiar words. Published in mid-November of 1948, Lloyd C. Douglas's second Biblical novel *The Big Fisherman* outdistanced all the other fiction titles

179

of that year. It had an advance of 245,000 copies and, by the end of the year, had sold 366,692. Comparable figures for *The Robe,* issued in 1942, were an advance of 42,000 and a sale of about 100,000 by the end of the year. *The Robe* was a best seller for 32 months, a record at that time. The first outstanding postwar novel about World War II was in second place. This was *The Naked and the Dead,* by Norman Mailer, a new writer who, with his first book, attained his important place in mid-20th century literature. His novel sold 137,185 copies in the stores plus about 60,000 through the Book Find Club. Another World War II novel and also a first novel, though its author, Irwin Shaw, was well known as a playwright and short story writer, reached tenth place on the list. His *The Young Lions* had a sale of 78,050 in 1948. There was another first novelist on 1948's list, also highly regarded by the critics, Ross Lockridge, Jr., who committed suicide not long after his *Raintree County* had achieved great success. All the rest of the best-selling novels of 1948 were by authors of longtime popularity. Frances Parkinson Keyes' *Dinner at Antoine's* was in third place with a sale of 114,249 copies. It was followed by Agnes Sligh Turnbull's novel with a religious theme, *The Bishop's Mantle,* which sold over 100,000 copies through the trade, its Dollar Book Club and other sales bringing it close to the million mark. Betty Smith's successor to *A Tree Grows in Brooklyn, Tomorrow Will Be Better,* was fifth. With its bookstore sale of 102,163 and its Dollar Book Club sales, Frank Yerby's *The Golden Hawk* passed the million mark, making it probably the best-selling novel of the year in sales to the public through all media. Memoirs of the war and war years were prominent among the nonfiction best sellers of the year. General Eisenhower's *Crusade in Europe* topped them with sales in a little over a month, of 239,265 copies plus a large book club sale. Prime Minister Churchill's first volume in his great history of World War II, *The Gathering Storm,* was seventh on the list, and Robert E. Sherwood's *Roosevelt and Hopkins,* eighth. The trend toward big sales for books on man's intimate psychological, spiritual, and physical problems accelerated. Four books on the list could be placed in such categories: *How to Stop Worrying and Start Living, Peace of Mind, Sexual Behavior in the Human Male,* and *A Guide to Confident Living.* Dale Carnegie's book followed his great success, *How to Win Friends and Influence People,* with a sale of 235,636 in its first year. Joshua Liebman's *Peace of Mind,* in its third year as a leading seller was close behind it with 227,705. Book phenomenon of the year, the Kinsey Report, sold about 225,000 copies. Dr. Peale's first best seller, *A Guide to Confident Living,* had sales of 78,000 copies in 1948. Three books in lighter moods completed the list: entrepreneur Billy Rose's *Wine, Women and Words,* with sales of 155,655; cartoonist Al Capp's *The Life and Times of the Shmoo,* selling 141,977; and egg fancier Betty MacDonald's *The Plague and I.*

180

1949

Fiction

1. The Egyptian, by *Mika Waltari*. Putnam
2. The Big Fisherman, by *Lloyd C. Douglas*. Houghton Mifflin
3. Mary, by *Sholem Asch*. Putnam
4. A Rage to Live, by *John O'Hara*. Random House
5. Point of No Return, by *John P. Marquand*. Little, Brown
6. Dinner at Antoine's, by *Frances Parkinson Keyes*. Messner
7. High Towers, by *Thomas B. Costain*. Doubleday
8. Cutlass Empire, by *Van Wyck Mason*. Doubleday
9. Pride's Castle, by *Frank Yerby*. Dial Press
10. Father of the Bride, by *Edward Streeter*. Simon & Schuster

Nonfiction

1. White Collar Zoo, by *Clare Barnes, Jr.* Doubleday
2. How to Win at Canasta, by *Oswald Jacoby*. Doubleday
3. The Seven Storey Mountain, by *Thomas Merton*. Harcourt, Brace
4. Home Sweet Zoo, by *Clare Barnes, Jr.* Doubleday
5. Cheaper by the Dozen, by *Frank B. Gilbreth, Jr.* and *Ernestine Gilbreth Carey*. Crowell
6. The Greatest Story Ever Told, by *Fulton Oursler*. Doubleday
7. Canasta, the Argentine Rummy Game, by *Ottilie H. Reilly*. Ives Washburn
8. Canasta, by *Josephine Artayeta de Viel* and *Ralph Michael*. Pellegrini & Cudahy
9. Peace of Soul, by *Fulton J. Sheen*. Whittlesey House
10. A Guide to Confident Living, by *Norman Vincent Peale*. Prentice-Hall

As President Truman began a second term, people were disturbed by high coffee prices and returned to coffee hoarding. New Yorkers were asked to conserve water because of shortage—until the disastrous floods came to the northeastern states in the latter part of 1949. Tickets for *South Pacific,* the biggest musical hit in years, were only obtainable at impossible prices. Historical novels came back into their own in 1949, comprising more than half the fiction list, two of the six built on Biblical characters. Best-selling novel was *The Egyptian,* by Mika Waltari. It was a story of ancient Egypt and the Near East, a translation from the Finnish of a writer not previously published in this country. Though sales of *The Big Fisherman* were much smaller in 1949 than in 1948, when it topped the annual list, it was, nevertheless, second for the year, selling 162,615 in comparison with 1948's 366,692. Another Biblical novel, *Mary,* by Sholem Asch, was third. Historical romances by the perennially best-selling authors, Costain, Mason, and Yerby were in seventh, eighth and ninth places. *High Towers* had a trade sale of 84,710 plus a Dollar Book Club sale of 824,434. *Cutlass Empire* also had a large book club sale in addition to its 80,668 through bookstores. *Pride's Castle* sold 73,503 plus a Dollar Book Club sale that brought it up over the million mark. On a theme far from Biblical was modern novelist John O'Hara's *A Rage to Live.* Its sales were 135,000 copies. *Point of No Return,* by John P. Marquand, later to be the basis of a very successful stage play, as was his *Late George Apley,* was fifth with 128,164 copies sold through the trade and a total sale, including book club, of 528,164. *Dinner at Antoine's,* which had been third on the 1948 list, sold 95,000 more copies in 1949. With its Dollar Book Club sale it reached over a million. Thirty-one years after publication of his big seller of World War I *Dere Mable,* Edward Streeter reappeared as the author of an entertaining novel, *Father of the Bride* (later a movie), which sold 73,281 copies plus Book-of-the-Month Club distribution. Feature of 1949 nonfiction was the predominance of what could be called non-reading books—picture books and game books. The hilarious "Zoo" books by Clare Barnes, Jr., photographs of animals caricaturing human behavior, were the big hits of the year. *White Collar Zoo* took first place with its sale of 395,000 copies. *Home Sweet Zoo,* published on December 2, wound up in fourth place, selling 262,000 copies in the last month of the year. The Canasta craze that hit the U.S. was reflected in the high sales of three Canasta books. Oswald Jacoby's *How to Win at Canasta* was second on the list with a sale of 385,333. *Canasta, the Argentine Rummy Game,* by Ottilie H. Reilly, sold 206,000 copies. *Canasta,* by Josephine Artayeta de Viel and Ralph Michael, sold over 200,000 in the bookstores and, in a cheaper edition, about 400,000 more through other outlets. Thomas Merton's *The Seven Storey Mountain* led the religious titles which made up most of the remainder of the non-fiction list. It sold 307,400 copies in 1949. Fulton Oursler's *The Greatest Story Ever Told* was sixth with 205,426 sold through the trade, 286,906 through book clubs. *Peace of Soul,* the then Monsignor Fulton J. Sheen's rejoinder to Dr. Liebman's *Peace of Mind,* was ninth with a total of 182,652. *A Guide to Confident Living,* which had been ninth on the

1948 list, was tenth in 1949, selling 158,000 copies, 15,000 of them in the month of December. The remaining "reading" book on the list, in fact the only one not religious, not a picture or game book, was the humorous family biography, *Cheaper by the Dozen,* by Frank B. Gilbreth, Jr. and Ernestine Gilbreth Carey. It sold 241,093 copies in the stores and 257,000 through the Book-of-the-Month Club.

1950

Fiction

1. The Cardinal, by *Henry Morton Robinson*. Simon & Schuster
2. Joy Street, by *Frances Parkinson Keyes*. Messner
3. Across the River and Into the Trees, by *Ernest Hemingway*. Scribner
4. The Wall, by *John Hersey*. Knopf
5. Star Money, by *Kathleen Winsor*. Appleton-Century-Crofts
6. The Parasites, by *Daphne du Maurier*. Doubleday
7. Floodtide, by *Frank Yerby*. Dial Press
8. Jubilee Trail, by *Gwen Bristow*. Crowell
9. The Adventurer, by *Mika Waltari*. Putnam
10. The Disenchanted, by *Budd Schulberg*. Random House

Nonfiction

1. Betty Crocker's Picture Cook Book. McGraw-Hill
2. The Baby. Simon & Schuster
3. Look Younger, Live Longer, by *Gayelord Hauser*. Farrar, Straus & Young
4. How I Raised Myself from Failure to Success in Selling, by *Frank Bettger*. Prentice-Hall
5. Kon-Tiki, by *Thor Heyerdahl*. Rand McNally
6. Mr. Jones, Meet the Master, by *Peter Marshall*. Revell
7. Your Dream Home, by *Hubbard Cobb*. Wise
8. The Mature Mind, by *H. A. Overstreet*. Norton
9. Campus Zoo, by *Clare Barnes, Jr.* Doubleday
10. Belles on Their Toes, by *Frank Gilbreth, Jr.* and *Ernestine Gilbreth Carey*. Crowell

TELEVISION came into its own in 1950 with the tremendous interest shown in the Kefauver committee's crime investigation hearings. The President recalled General MacArthur after the start of the Korean War and authorized continued work on the H bomb. The theatre-in-the-round was arousing interest, and people were humming *Goodnight, Irene*. Heavyweight champion Joe Louis met defeat before the gloves of Ezzard Charles.

184

George Bernard Shaw died at the age of 94. The majority of the 1950 fiction best sellers were modern stories in contrast to the predominance of historical novels in 1949. *The Cardinal,* top seller of the year, was by an author new to the best seller lists, as also were *Jubilee Trail* and *The Disenchanted.* All the others were by authors who had appeared on annual best seller lists at least once. Trade interest in *The Cardinal* was heightened by its publication in both cloth and paperbound editions, the first major trial of this merchandising method for a best-selling novel. It sold 435,516 copies in paper, 152,879 in cloth, a total of 588,395. Frances Parkinson Keyes' *Joy Street,* second in fiction sales, reached its place with only one month in the bookstores. It was published on December 1 with an advance of 110,000. Re-orders made its total, by the end of the year, 140,285. Third and fourth were two novels by well-known writers in which World War II was the background—a much less important background in Ernest Hemingway's *Across the River and Into the Trees* than in John Hersey's fine novel of the Jewish quarter in Nazi-occupied Warsaw. *Across the River and Into the Trees* sold 104,000 copies. *The Wall* sold 97,860 plus a Book-of-the-Month Club distribution of 230,000. Kathleen Winsor followed up the success of *Forever Amber* with the story of a modern girl, *Star Money.* The total sale of *The Parasites* by Daphne du Maurier, including that of the Book League, was 401,891. Its trade sale was 82,347 copies. From seventh to ninth places came the only best-selling historical novels of the year. Frank Yerby's *Floodtide,* 81,000, outsold his *Pride's Castle* of 1949. In addition, it had a large Dollar Book Club sale. *Jubilee Trail,* by Gwen Bristow, was over half a million with its Literary Guild copies. Ninth was *The Adventurer,* by Mika Waltari, whose *The Egyptian* had topped the 1949 list. Budd Schulberg's novel, presumably based on the life of F. Scott Fitzgerald, *The Disenchanted,* wound up the fiction. It sold 70,000 through the trade, 255,000 including book club copies. Again in 1950 "reading" books were scarce among the top ten sellers in nonfiction. Eight out of the ten fell into "how to," picture book, or "self-help" categories, if the Marshall and Overstreet books may be included in the last-named group. The two remaining titles, *Kon-Tiki,* by Thor Heyerdahl and *Belles on Their Toes,* by the Gilbreth writing team, sold respectively 128,848 copies and over 300,000 with book club copies. Leading the bookstore list of 1950 nonfiction best sellers was *Betty Crocker's Picture Cook Book,* with a trade sale of 300,000. General Mills sold about 200,000 more. *The Baby,* humorous picture book, sold about 250,000 copies in the bookstores, with a sale, including newsstands, of 322,236. *Look Younger, Live Longer,* by Gayelord Hauser, sold about 200,000 copies in bookstores, with its health food store sale, 275,135. Frank Bettger's *How I Raised Myself from Failure to Success in Selling,* in fourth position, sold 195,000 copies. Sixth was *Mr. Jones, Meet the*

185

Master, by Peter Marshall, Chaplain of the U.S. Senate, reaching a sale of 125,000. *Your Dream Home,* by Hubbard Cobb, sold over 100,000 copies through bookstores, close to one million by mail, making it actually the top best seller of the year through all channels. *The Mature Mind,* by H. A. Overstreet, was the only title among the first ten that appeared on every monthly list through 1950. It sold 91,341 copies plus a Book-of-the-Month Club sale of 247,500. *Campus Zoo,* another humorous picture book, compiled by Clare Barnes, Jr., two of whose "Zoo" books were on the 1949 list, sold 81,724.

1951

Fiction

1. From Here to Eternity, by *James Jones*. Scribner
2. The Caine Mutiny, by *Herman Wouk*. Doubleday
3. Moses, by *Sholem Asch*. Putnam
4. The Cardinal, by *Henry Morton Robinson*. Simon & Schuster
5. A Woman Called Fancy, by *Frank Yerby*. Dial Press
6. The Cruel Sea, by *Nicholas Monsarrat*. Knopf
7. Melville Goodwin, U.S.A., by *John P. Marquand*. Little, Brown
8. Return to Paradise, by *James A. Michener*. Random House
9. The Foundling, by *Cardinal Spellman*. Scribner
10. The Wanderer, by *Mika Waltari*. Putnam

Nonfiction

1. Look Younger, Live Longer, by *Gayelord Hauser*. Farrar, Straus & Young
2. Betty Crocker's Picture Cook Book. McGraw-Hill
3. Washington Confidential, by *Jack Lait and Lee Mortimer*. Crown
4. Better Homes and Gardens Garden Book. Meredith
5. Better Homes and Gardens Handyman's Book. Meredith
6. The Sea Around Us, by *Rachel L. Carson*. Oxford University Press
7. Thorndike-Barnhart Comprehensive Desk Dictionary, ed. by *Clarence L. Barnhart*. Doubleday
8. Pogo, by *Walt Kelly*. Simon & Schuster
9. Kon-Tiki, by *Thor Heyerdahl*. Rand McNally
10. The New Yorker Twenty-Fifth Anniversary Album. Harper

NEARLY seven years after the end of World War II an Army novel with a Pearl Harbor finale topped the fiction sales of the year, and three other novels with war backgrounds were high on the list. In England Winston Churchill resumed his post as Prime Minister, two British diplomats disappeared behind the Iron Curtain, and King George opened the Festival of Britain. Sinclair Lewis and Henri-Philippe Pétain died, the former

187

aged 65; the latter, 95. In the United States, people were stirred by General MacArthur's address to Congress after his recall from the Far East command. Joe DiMaggio retired from baseball, and Ben Hogan won the Open Golf Championship. "The King and I," staring Gertrude Lawrence and Yul Brunner, based upon the 1944 best seller *Anna and the King of Siam,* was one of the great musicals of the New York season. Television was developing into a threat to the motion picture theatres. War novels were a feature of the 1951 fiction best seller list. *From Here to Eternity,* James Jones' first novel, outsold every other fiction title in the bookstores, reaching a total of 240,000. *The Caine Mutiny,* by Herman Wouk, story of the wartime Navy, was not far behind it with a sale of 236,000 copies. In sixth place was another war novel of the sea, *The Cruel Sea,* by Nicholas Monsarrat, which sold approximately 70,000 copies. Seventh, was John P. Marquand's latest best seller, with a war background, *Melville Goodwin, USA.* Religious novels took third, fourth and ninth places: *Moses,* by Sholem Asch; *The Cardinal,* by Henry Morton Robinson, which was the top 1950 seller and which sold 88,709 copies in 1951; and *The Foundling,* by Cardinal Spellman, with sales of 61,000. There were only two historical novels on the list: *A Woman Called Fancy,* by Frank Yerby (75,666), and *The Wanderer,* by Mika Waltari. James A. Michener's postwar *Return to Paradise* sold 65,000 copies. This was Michener's first novel to make the annual list. His *Tales of the South Pacific,* on which the famous musical "South Pacific" was based, was published in 1947. On the nonfiction list the title which was third in 1950 took top place in 1951, Gayelord Hauser's *Look Younger, Live Longer.* Including the sales of the new edition which came out in 1951, but not including sales through health food stores, its total for the year was 286,735. *Betty Crocker's Picture Cook Book,* which was first in 1950, was second in 1951 with sales of 233,500 copies. Third was one of only three books on the nonfiction list that can be called "reading" books to distinguish them from the "subject" and picture books that comprise seven out of the ten. That was *Washington Confidential,* the first of the "Confidential" books by Jack Lait and Lee Mortimer to make an annual list. It sold 227,131 copies. The two other "reading" titles were Rachel L. Carson's *The Sea Around Us,* with a sale of 167,181, and *Kon-Tiki,* by Thor Heyerdahl (fifth in 1950), which sold 140,461 copies in 1951. Continuing the "subject" books, two *Better Homes and Gardens* titles, the *Garden Book* and the *Handyman's Book,* were fourth and fifth, with sales through bookstores of 221,213 and 206,989 copies. The *Thorndike-Barnhart Comprehensive Desk Dictionary* sold 162,623 copies, not including book club or school distribution. Eighth and tenth were the two "picture" books, Walt Kelly's comic strip book for adults, *Pogo,* selling 145,731 copies, and the cartoon collection, *The New Yorker Twenty-Fifth*

188

Anniversary Album. As a rule standard works like dictionaries and cook books were not included on these *Publishers' Weekly* annual best seller lists except in the years when they were originally published as brand new titles. That is why the Thorndike-Barnhart dictionary was included on the 1951 list but other standard works like the *World Almanac,* Lasser's *Your Income Tax,* other leading cook books, dictionaries, reference works, and Bibles were not.

1952

Fiction

1. The Silver Chalice, by *Thomas B. Costain*. Doubleday
2. The Caine Mutiny, by *Herman Wouk,* Doubleday
3. East of Eden, by *John Steinbeck*. Viking Press
4. My Cousin Rachel, by *Daphne du Maurier*. Doubleday
5. Steamboat Gothic, by *Frances Parkinson Keyes*. Messner
6. Giant, by *Edna Ferber*. Doubleday
7. The Old Man and the Sea, by *Ernest Hemingway*. Scribner
8. The Gown of Glory, by *Agnes Sligh Turnbull*. Houghton Mifflin
9. The Saracen Blade, by *Frank Yerby*. Dial Press
10. The Houses in Between, by *Howard Spring*. Harper

Nonfiction

1. The Holy Bible: Revised Standard Version. Nelson
2. A Man Called Peter, by *Catherine Marshall*. McGraw-Hill
3. U.S.A. Confidential, by *Jack Lait and Lee Mortimer*. Crown
4. The Sea Around Us, by *Rachel L. Carson*. Oxford University Press
5. Tallulah, by *Tallulah Bankhead*. Harper
6. The Power of Positive Thinking, by *Norman Vincent Peale*. Prentice-Hall
7. This I Believe, ed. by *Edward P. Morgan;* foreword by *Edward R. Murrow*. Simon & Schuster
8. This Is Ike, ed. by *Wilson Hicks*. Holt
9. Witness, by *Whittaker Chambers*. Random House
10. Mr. President, by *William Hillman*. Farrar, Straus & Young

IN CONTRAST to the best sellers of a few preceding years, those of 1952 showed few new trends, and, in general, their sales totals were lower. The year was notable, however, for the appearance of Ernest Hemingway's short novel *The Old Man and the Sea* which became a classic in the author's lifetime. All the novels on the list were by well-established authors, most of whom had appeared on annual best seller lists many

190

times. In 1951 there were four war novels among the best sellers; in 1952 the only one was a repeat, *The Caine Mutiny*. There were two historical novels as there were the previous year; two with religious themes as compared with 1951's three. Because of a very large December sale *The Silver Chalice* won top place in fiction to the surprise even of its publisher because the second place title, *The Caine Mutiny,* also a Doubleday book and a best seller for 21 months, had been running ahead throughout the year. When their sales were totaled, however, *The Silver Chalice* turned up with a sale of 221,000 copies, *The Caine Mutiny* with 189,000. *East of Eden* sold 140,000; *My Cousin Rachel* 130,000; *Steamboat Gothic* over 120,000; *Giant* 119,000; *The Gown of Glory* 62,500 and *The Saracen Blade* over 55,000. Outstanding on the 1952 nonfiction list was the Bible, Revised Standard Version, with its close to two-million-copy sale. Three other titles of religious interest among the 1952 best sellers again pointed up the continuing popular appeal of religious books. *A Man Called Peter,* the biography of the late Chaplain of the U.S. Senate, written by his wife, which had been on the list for 15 months, was second with sales of 205,000 copies. *The Power of Positive Thinking* was in sixth place with a total of 102,340 sold and *This I Believe* seventh with 98,500. *U.S.A. Confidential,* third, sold 163,961 copies. *The Sea Around Us,* on the list for 17 months and seventh in 1951 with a sale of 167,181, was fourth for 1952, selling 105,795. Four biographies, two of them of political figures, as befitted the election year, made up the rest of the nonfiction list: *Tallulah; This Is Ike,* which sold about 90,000 copies, including both cloth and paperbound editions; *Witness,* selling 80,000 copies; and *Mr. President* totalling 77,246. Sales of nonfiction titles on the best seller list were larger than those of fiction but still they did not equal by any means the sales of the titles on the similar list in 1951. One reason is that "how-to" books, with their very large sales, made up most of 1951's list. For 1952, the cook books which had been out for several years and the cartoon books, which were current popular novelty items, were omitted in order to give a better picture from the literary point of view of what general topics interested the public most. Outside the book field, TV played its part, for the first time in an election campaign, the campaign in which General Eisenhower defeated Adlai Stevenson. The McCarthy campaign continued as did the FBI raids on Communists. Juvenile delinquency was an urgent problem. Pizzas, scrabble, nylon and dacron, and chlorophyll products were all taken up in a big way by the American consumer.

1953

Fiction

1. The Robe, by *Lloyd C. Douglas.* Houghton Mifflin
2. The Silver Chalice, by *Thomas B. Costain.* Doubleday
3. Désirée, by *Annemarie Selinko.* Morrow
4. Battle Cry, by *Leon M. Uris.* Putnam
5. From Here to Eternity, by *James Jones.* Scribner
6. The High and the Mighty, by *Ernest K. Gann.* Sloane
7. Beyond This Place, by *A. J. Cronin.* Little, Brown
8. Time and Time Again, by *James Hilton.* Little, Brown
9. Lord Vanity, by *Samuel Shellabarger.* Little, Brown
10. The Unconquered, by *Ben Ames Williams.* Houghton Mifflin

Nonfiction

1. The Holy Bible: Revised Standard Version. Nelson
2. The Power of Positive Thinking, by *Norman Vincent Peale.* Prentice-Hall
3. Sexual Behavior in the Human Female, by *Alfred C. Kinsey* and others. Saunders
4. Angel Unaware, by *Dale Evans Rogers.* Revell
5. Life Is Worth Living, by *Fulton J. Sheen.* McGraw-Hill
6. A Man Called Peter, by *Catherine Marshall.* McGraw-Hill
7. This I Believe, ed. by *Edward P. Morgan;* foreword by *Edward R. Murrow.* Simon & Schuster
8. The Greatest Faith Ever Known, by *Fulton Oursler* and *G. A. O. Armstrong.* Doubleday
9. How to Play Your Best Golf, by *Tommy Armour.* Simon & Schuster
10. A House Is Not a Home, by *Polly Adler.* Rinehart

THERE WERE record-breaking floods in the low-lying countries of Europe in 1953. Josef Stalin died in Moscow early in the year. King George VI of England had died in 1952; Elizabeth II was crowned in June 1953. General George C. Marshall was awarded the Nobel Peace Prize and Winston Churchill the Nobel Prize in literature. Eugene O'Neill died in

192

Boston on November 27. An armistice in the Korean War was signed on July 27. Edmund Hillary and Tenzing Norkey conquered the world's highest peak, Mount Everest. The unusual aspect of 1953's fiction best seller list was that the leading novel and two others were popularly-priced editions of older novels, which had been best sellers several years previously in their original editions. Two were re-priced and re-publicized to coincide with new movies based upon them. The biggest fiction sales of 1953 were chalked up by the $1.98 movie edition of *The Robe,* which had been originally published in 1942. It was the top seller of 1943, second in 1944 and in 1945. It is remarkable that, eleven years after its first publication, it topped all fiction with its sale of 180,000. In addition, 8,000 copies of the $3.75 edition were sold. The movie of the same title was the first film to be shown in the then new CinemaScope process. In second place on the fiction list was 1952's best seller, *The Silver Chalice.* After a sale of 221,000 copies in 1952, it sold 135,000 in 1953 including about 89,000 in the $1.98 edition, which was on sale only in the last three months of the year. *Désirée,* leader of sales among novels that were published in 1953, was third with 115,773 copies. It was one of five historical novels, half the list, in comparison with two each in 1952 and in 1951. The author was one of three new to the annual best seller lists. The other two were Leon M. Uris, author of *Battle Cry,* and Ernest K. Gann, author of *The High and the Mighty,* which sold 63,857 copies in the bookstores. *Battle Cry* was the only war novel on the list unless one can so consider the army novel, *From Here to Eternity,* which was fifth with 68,500 copies sold in its $2.69 movie edition. It had been 1951's top-selling novel in its original edition. If outlets other than bookstores had been considered for these annual lists, *From Here to Eternity* would have outdistanced by far any other novel, for 2,000,000 copies of its paperbound 75-cent edition, brought out to coincide with the appearance of the movie, were sold. It was at just about this time that paperback reprints of popular novels became the impressive big sellers. These best seller lists, have, however continued to be confined to hardbound originals. The theme of religion dominated nonfiction best sellers in 1953 as it had in many preceding years, and nonfiction continued, title for title, to outsell fiction in the bookstores. For the second year the *Revised Standard Version* of the Bible outsold all other current titles. It had been averaging 49,700 copies a month in buckram and 41,790 in leather throughout the year. With its big December sale, it went over 1,100,000 for the year. Of the other six books of religious appeal Norman Vincent Peale's *The Power of Positive Thinking* was second with a sale of 340,000 (it had been sixth on the 1952 list); *Angel Unaware* fourth with sales of 257,176; *Life Is Worth Living,* with sales of 142,000, fifth; in sixth place, *A Man Called Peter,* sales in 1953, 130,000; *This I Believe* seventh, as it had been in 1952, its 1953 sales 115,000; and eighth, *The Greatest Faith Ever Known,* selling 96,000. The three remaining non-religious, nonfiction best sellers of the year were *Sexual Behavior in the Human Female,* second of the Kinsey Reports, in third place with sales of 275,000 copies; *How to Play Your Best Golf,* by golf pro Tommy Armour, sales 90,000; and *A House Is Not a Home,* by Polly Adler, a pro of a different kind, in tenth place with 86,000 sold.

1954

Fiction

1. Not As a Stranger, by *Morton Thompson*. Scribner
2. Mary Anne, by *Daphne du Maurier*. Doubleday
3. Love Is Eternal, by *Irving Stone*. Doubleday
4. The Royal Box, by *Frances Parkinson Keyes*. Messner
5. The Egyptian, by *Mika Waltari*. Putnam
6. No Time for Sergeants, by *Mac Hyman*. Random House
7. Sweet Thursday, by *John Steinbeck*. Viking Press
8. The View from Pompey's Head, by *Hamilton Basso*. Doubleday
9. Never Victorious, Never Defeated, by *Taylor Caldwell*. McGraw-Hill
10. Benton's Row, by *Frank Yerby*. Dial Press

Nonfiction

1. The Holy Bible: Revised Standard Version. Nelson
2. The Power of Positive Thinking, by *Norman Vincent Peale*. Prentice-Hall
3. Better Homes and Gardens New Cook Book. Meredith
4. Betty Crocker's Good and Easy Cook Book. Simon & Schuster
5. The Tumult and the Shouting, by *Grantland Rice*. A. S. Barnes
6. I'll Cry Tomorrow, by *Lillian Roth, Gerold Frank* and *Mike Connolly*. Frederick Fell
7. The Prayers of Peter Marshall, ed. by *Catherine Marshall*. McGraw-Hill
8. This I Believe, 2, ed. by *Raymond Swing*. Simon & Schuster
9. But We Were Born Free, by *Elmer Davis*. Bobbs-Merrill
10. The Saturday Evening Post Treasury, ed. by *Roger Butterfield*. Simon & Schuster

As AMERICANS watched the McCarthy hearings on TV, were hopeful about the Salk polio tests, lived through hurricanes Carol to Hazel, and learned to pronounce Dien Bien Phu, they also bought more copies of the Bible in the *Revised Standard Version* than of any other book. In

195

1954 R.S.V.B. held its top position among best sellers for the third consecutive year. Its sales were smaller than they had been in preceding
years, but large enough to outsell any other title, fiction or nonfiction,
by almost 200,000. It sold 710,359 copies in 1954, making a three-year
total of 3,141,670. The majority of novels among the ten best sellers
of the year were by authors whose names have appeared on these lists
many times before, authors of well-established popularity. The exceptions
were: the top title of the year, *Not As a Stranger,* by Morton Thompson,
which pointed up the perennial interest in "medical" stories; *No Time for
Sergeants,* the only first novel on the list, its author, Mac Hyman, bringing
out delightfully some of the more humorous aspects of life in the U.S.
armed forces; and *The View from Pompey's Head.* The author of the
last-named title, Hamilton Basso, although a well-known writer, had not
previously placed among the top ten. *No Time for Sergeants* sold 66,216
copies plus a 100,000 book club sale; *The View from Pompey's Head*
sold 58,000 plus book club copies. Fifth on the fiction list was *The
Egyptian.* It had been the top-selling fiction title of 1949, brought back
in a $1.98 edition to coincide with the release of the movie based upon it.
More than half the fiction list was made up of period novels. Along with
The Egyptian there were *Mary Anne* with a sale of 127,000; *Love Is
Eternal* with an 88,000-copy sale; *The Royal Box,* which sold 83,234;
Never Victorious, Never Defeated, sales 57,442; and *Benton's Row,*
which, in one month, sold 54,724. The one remaining novel, neither historical nor by an author making his first appearance on an annual list,
was *Sweet Thursday,* which sold 65,000 copies and which later became a Broadway play. Sales of the nonfiction titles in the top ten places
of the year were greater by over 1,600,000 than the sales of the top ten
novels, and nonfiction also outsold fiction title by title right down the
list. Besides the number one book, the Bible, there were three other best
sellers of religious interest in comparison with 1953's six. *The Power of
Positive Thinking,* which was second also in 1953 and sixth in 1952, sold
531,336 copies in 1954, making a total of 971,336 for the three years.
In seventh place *The Prayers of Peter Marshall* sold 91,000, followed by
the second series of *This I Believe* selling 89,867—19,887 in the clothbound edition, 69,980 in the paperbound. Two cook books took third and
fourth places among nonfiction, The *Better Homes and Gardens New Cook
Book* with a sale of 359,468 copies and *Betty Crocker's Good and Easy
Cook Book,* which sold 290,000 copies, both these sales only through the
trade, exclusive of sales through magazines and manufacturers. Two autobiographies—that of Grantland Rice, late sports columnist, and of Lillian
Roth of the entertainment world, were in fifth and sixth places, both somewhat surprise sellers. *The Tumult and the Shouting* sold 133,498 copies;

196

I'll Cry Tomorrow, 115,000. *But We Were Born Free,* by Elmer Davis, was the only book on current affairs on the list. *The Saturday Evening Post Treasury,* handsome, illustrated gift book, did especially well at Christmas time, selling 73,159 copies in two months.

Fiction

1. Marjorie Morningstar, by *Herman Wouk*. Doubleday
2. Auntie Mame, by *Patrick Dennis*. Vanguard Press
3. Andersonville, by *MacKinlay Kantor*. World Publishing Co.
4. Bonjour Tristesse, by *Françoise Sagan*. Dutton
5. The Man in the Gray Flannel Suit, by *Sloan Wilson*. Simon & Schuster
6. Something of Value, by *Robert Ruark*. Doubleday
7. Not As a Stranger, by *Morton Thompson*. Scribner
8. No Time for Sergeants, by *Mac Hyman*. Random House
9. The Tontine, by *Thomas B. Costain*. Doubleday
10. Ten North Frederick, by *John O'Hara*. Random House

Nonfiction

1. Gift from the Sea, by *Anne Morrow Lindbergh*. Pantheon Books
2. The Power of Positive Thinking, by *Norman Vincent Peale*. Prentice-Hall
3. The Family of Man, by *Edward Steichen*. Simon & Schuster and Maco Magazine Corp.
4. A Man Called Peter, by *Catherine Marshall*. McGraw-Hill
5. How to Live 365 Days a Year, by *John A. Schindler*. Prentice-Hall
6. Better Homes and Gardens Diet Book. Meredith
7. The Secret of Happiness, by *Billy Graham*. Doubleday
8. Why Johnny Can't Read, by *Rudolf Flesch*. Harper
9. Inside Africa, by *John Gunther*. Harper
10. Year of Decisions, by *Harry S. Truman*. Doubleday

THE PUBLIC's choice of novels during 1955 ranged from some concerned with young love to others about the complex problems of modern life, from one laid in the South during the Civil War, to scenes of strife in South Africa. No trends were particularly discernible, except that there were fewer historical novels than usual on the list, only two. Four of the year's best-selling novels were by new or little-known writers—Patrick Dennis, Françoise Sagan, Sloan Wilson and Mac Hyman. Top novel in sales was *Marjorie Morningstar,* by Herman Wouk, whose *The Caine Mutiny* was second in 1952. *Marjorie Morningstar* sold 191,349 copies during the year. *Auntie Mame* was second with 150,000 copies sold. *Andersonville* was published late in the year but had a total of 121,000 exclusive of book club sales. *Bonjour Tristesse* was by a young French writer, Françoise Sagan, the only author on both fiction and nonfiction lists not an American, and the only woman author on the fiction list. It sold 120,000 copies. *The Man in the Gray Flannel Suit* sold just under 100,000. Total for *Something of Value* was 93,757. *Not As a Stranger* was the top fiction seller of 1954. Sales of the original edition and of the $2.69 edition, timed with the movie based upon it, brought it in its second year to seventh place. *No Time for Sergeants,* also in its second year, and the basis of a Broadway hit, sold 92,000 copies in 1955. Its two-year total plus a book club sale was over a quarter of a million. *The Tontine* was by a writer long familiar to readers of best sellers. It sold 75,298 copies. *Ten North Frederick,* published on Thanksgiving Day, sold 65,900 in just over a month. In reporting the nonfiction best sellers of each year, it had become *Publishers' Weekly's* policy not to include standard works such as dictionaries and cook books, and, in the case of the 1955 list, the Bible, after such volumes had appeared on the lists for one, two, or more years. *The Bible, Revised Standard Version,* had headed the annual list for three years. Its sales of 800,000 copies, more than in 1954, would have made it top for 1955 as well. It seemed to be an established fact up through the mid-twentieth century, that the Bible, in whatever version, was always the best seller. Therefore, in order to mirror more transient contemporary reading taste, it was omitted from this list and *Gift from the Sea* took first place with its sale of 430,000. There were three books of religious interest on the 1955 best-seller list: *The Power of Positive Thinking,* appearing for the fourth consecutive year, sold 378,000; *A Man Called Peter,* with 275,000 sold in its $1.98 movie edition; and *The Secret of Happiness,* by the popular evangelist, which sold 115,697. Third for 1955 was the beautiful book of photographs plus text, by Edward Steichen, *The Family of Man,* which had its big sale, of 364,000 copies, in the paperbound edition. In addition there was a hardbound edition sale of about 15,000. The self-help book, *How to Live 365 Days a Year,* was fifth with a sale of 235,000. The *Better Homes and Gardens Diet Book* sold 130,021 copies in 1955. Winding up the list, in eighth, ninth, and tenth places, were three books of topical importance: *Why Johnny Can't Read, Inside Africa,* and *Year of Decisions* by former President Harry S. Truman. This first volume in President Truman's autobiography sold 74,820 copies. Following the recent

199

trend, the ten top nonfiction titles outsold the ten top fiction by almost two to one. The total sale of the nonfiction through the bookstores amounted to 2,168,701 volumes; that of the fiction, 1,102,761. As 1955 ended the country was still in alarm over President Eisenhower's illness, wondering whether he could again be a candidate for the presidency. The stock market was high, unemployment at a low figure. A new generation had learned all about Davy Crockett. Winston Churchill had retired as British Prime Minister and had been knighted by Queen Elizabeth. Most imminent cloud in the political sky was the threat of a clash in the Near East. On the interplanetary scene came the government's announcement of its project for the launching of manmade satellites.

1956

Fiction

1. Don't Go Near the Water, by *William Brinkley.* Random House
2. The Last Hurrah, by *Edwin O'Connor.* Little, Brown
3. Peyton Place, by *Grace Metalious.* Messner
4. Auntie Mame, by *Patrick Dennis.* Vanguard Press
5. Eloise, by *Kay Thompson.* Simon & Schuster
6. Andersonville, by *MacKinlay Kantor.* World Publishing Co.
7. A Certain Smile, by *Françoise Sagan.* Dutton
8. The Tribe That Lost Its Head, by *Nicholas Monsarrat.* Sloane
9. The Mandarins, by *Simone de Beauvoir.* World Publishing Co.
10. Boon Island, by *Kenneth Roberts.* Doubleday

Nonfiction

1. Arthritis and Common Sense. Revised Edition, by *Dan Dale Alexander.* Witkower Press
2. Webster's New World Dictionary of the American Language. Concise Edition, edited by *David B. Guralnik.* World Publishing Co.
3. Betty Crocker's Picture Cook Book. Revised and Enlarged Second Edition. McGraw-Hill
4. Etiquette, by *Frances Benton.* Random House
5. Better Homes and Gardens Barbecue Book. Meredith
6. The Search for Bridey Murphy, by *Morey Bernstein.* Doubleday
7. Love or Perish, by *Smiley Blanton, M.D.* Simon & Schuster
8. Better Homes and Gardens Decorating Book. Meredith
9. How To Live 365 Days a Year, by *John A. Schindler.* Prentice-Hall
10. The Nun's Story, by *Kathryn Hulme.* Little, Brown

THE SECOND NOVELS by two prominent writers topped fiction: reference, "how-to" and cook books dominated the nonfiction list in this year which saw the re-election of Eisenhower and Nixon. It was the year in which

Grace Kelly married Prince Rainier, in which the Egyptian government seized the Suez Canal, and in which the last veteran of the Civil War Union Army died and the G.A.R. officially went out of existence. There were terrorist activities in Cyprus, disputes between Israel and Jordan, Russia crushed the Hungarian uprising, and the F.B.I. reported more major crimes committed in the U.S. than in any previous year. Elvis Presley was singing "Love Me Tender" and people had given up trying to get seats for "My Fair Lady," Broadway's biggest hit. William Brinkley's *Don't Go Near the Water,* biggest hit novel of the year, a humorous story of Navy life on a Pacific isle during World War II, sold 165,000 copies in the bookstores, plus a book club sale, and was bought for movie production for $350,000. Also making a six-figure movie sale was a first novel, *Peyton Place,* which, in the long run, proved to be one of the top-selling American novels of all time, though it only managed to reach third place in fiction in its first year of publication. *Auntie Mame* was in its second year, racking up some 124,000 copies in 1956. It, too, was destined for bigger triumphs—as a starring vehicle for Rosalind Russell, as a movie, as a great paperback seller, and, over ten years later, as a Broadway musical hit. *Eloise,* terror of the Plaza, took her first bow in the book by Kay Thompson, with illustrations by Hilary Knight. It sold 100,000 copies in 1956 as did MacKinlay Kantor's great Civil War novel and Pulitzer Prize winner, *Andersonville.* There were two best sellers by French women novelists on the 1956 list. Françoise Sagan followed her *Bonjour Tristesse* with *A Certain Smile.* Simone de Beauvoir made her first appearance among best sellers with *The Mandarins.*

Leading all nonfiction with a sale of over 255,000 in the year was a book offering help to arthritis sufferers. Issued by a small Connecticut publisher, *Arthritis and Common Sense* leapt into prominence when it was recommended on the Arthur Godfrey program. A new dictionary was second on this list with a sale of 250,000 copies. *Etiquette* by Frances Benton, co-edited by the General Federation of Women's Clubs, sold over 156,000. Cookbooks, home guides, helps to business and personal problems filled up almost all the rest of the list, each with sales of well over 100,000. There were two exceptions. One was *The Search for Bridey Murphy,* a curious book that captured the imagination of the public. It told about a Colorado housewife, who, in many hypnotic trances, convinced a good number of people that she was the reincarnation of an eighteenth century Irishwoman. The other was *The Nun's Story,* a book of literary merit which reached tenth place. Kathryn Hulme's biography of a Belgian nun was later brought magnificently to the screen by Audrey Hepburn.

1957

Fiction

1. By Love Possessed, by *James Gould Cozzens.* Harcourt, Brace
2. Peyton Place, by *Grace Metalious.* Messner
3. Compulsion, by *Meyer Levin.* Simon & Schuster
4. Rally Round the Flag, Boys! by *Max Shulman.* Doubleday
5. Blue Camellia, by *Frances Parkinson Keyes.* Messner
6. Eloise in Paris, by *Kay Thompson.* Simon & Schuster
7. The Scapegoat, by *Daphne du Maurier.* Doubleday
8. On the Beach, by *Nevil Shute.* Morrow
9. Below the Salt, by *Thomas B. Costain,* Doubleday
10. Atlas Shrugged, by *Ayn Rand.* Random House

Nonfiction

1. Kids Say the Darndest Things! by *Art Linkletter.* Prentice-Hall
2. The FBI Story, by *Don Whitehead.* Random House
3. Stay Alive All Your Life, by *Norman Vincent Peale.* Prentice-Hall
4. To Live Again, by *Catherine Marshall.* McGraw-Hill
5. Better Homes and Gardens Flower Arranging. Meredith
6. Where Did You Go? Out. What Did You Do? Nothing, by *Robert Paul Smith.* Norton
7. Baruch: My Own Story, by *Bernard M. Baruch.* Holt
8. Please Don't Eat the Daisies, by *Jean Kerr.* Doubleday
9. The American Heritage Book of Great Historic Places. American Heritage Publishing Co. and Simon & Schuster
10. The Day Christ Died, by *Jim Bishop.* Harper

THE INTERNATIONAL GEOPHYSICAL YEAR of 1957-58 was inaugurated on July 1 with scientists from many nations cooperating in studies of the earth and its environment. In the first half of the year both the USSR and the USA had been setting off series of greater and greater nuclear tests. In June the American Cancer Society and the Public Health Service had issued warnings on the association between cigarette smoking and lung cancer. Through the summer and fall the Little Rock school integration disturbances continued. French and Algerian warfare went on. Russia launched Sputnik I and Sputnik II, which carried a dog. Albert Camus won the Nobel Prize for Literature. Eugene O'Neill's "Long Day's Journey into Night" won both the Pulitzer Prize and that of the Drama Critics' Circle. "West Side Story," with score by Leonard Bernstein was an outstanding Broadway musical. Rock 'n' roll vied with the hit song "Around the World in 80 Days." In books, a serious novel by James Gould Cozzens sold about 100,000 more copies in the stores than did *Peyton Place,* in second place in its second year. *By Love Possessed,* which sold 217,000 copies, analyzed closely the professional and emotional problems of a New England lawyer. James Gould Cozzens' *Guard of Honor* had won the Pulitzer Prize in 1948 but it was not until publication of *By Love Possessed* that the author made the annual best seller list. In fourth and fifth places were authors new to these lists, with two novels which could scarcely be of greater contrast. *Compulsion,* by Meyer Levin, was generally considered to be based upon the theme of the Leopold-Loeb murder case in Chicago many years before. A play based upon the novel was produced in 1957, later a movie. Max Shulman's *Rally Round the Flag, Boys!* which also became a movie, gave a humorous picture of what happened to a Connecticut exurban town when it became the site of a missile base. *Eloise* popped up again, this time in Paris, with another 100,000-copy sale. Nevil Shute, long-established writer, made his first appearance on an annual best seller list with his widely-publicized story of a world devastated by fallout, man's last stand in Australia. *On the Beach* was later produced as a movie.

Books of information and entertainment filled the nonfiction list, though the usually ubiquitous "how-to" books were strangely absent. *Better Homes and Gardens Flower Arranging* was the only housewife's aid on the list, in fifth place, with a sale of 116,000. *Please Don't Eat the Daisies,* by Jean Kerr, eighth, with nearly 107,000 sold, was not a garden book, but a volume of witty and delightful essays which became the basis of a popular Broadway play. Top of nonfiction for the year was *Kids Say the Darndest Things!,* made of material from Art Linkletter's TV and radio shows, with illustrations by the popular "Peanuts" cartoonist, Charles M. Schulz. *The FBI Story* was second with a sale of 173,000. Dr. Norman Vincent Peale, who had had many books on the best seller lists over the past decade, returned with *Stay Alive All Your Life.* Following on the list was Catherine Marshall's account of personal adjustment after the death of her husband, Peter Marshall, former Chaplain of the Senate, *To Live Again.* In sixth place was a unique book of childhood reminiscences by Robert Paul Smith, the title of which alone could have made it a best seller, *Where Did You Go? Out. What Did You Do? Nothing.*

204

The autobiography of the elder statesman, Bernard M. Baruch, sold over 110,000 copies. Jim Bishop followed his successful *The Day Lincoln Was Shot* with a book on a similar plan, *The Day Christ Died,* a reconstruction of Christ's last twenty-four hours on earth.

1958

Fiction

1. Doctor Zhivago, by *Boris Pasternak.* Pantheon Books
2. Anatomy of a Murder, by *Robert Traver.* St. Martin's Press
3. Lolita, by *Vladimir Nabokov.* Putnam
4. Around the World with Auntie Mame, by *Patrick Dennis.* Harcourt, Brace
5. From the Terrace, by *John O'Hara.* Random House
6. Eloise at Christmastime, by *Kay Thompson.* Random House
7. Ice Palace, by *Edna Ferber.* Doubleday
8. The Winthrop Woman, by *Anya Seton.* Houghton, Mifflin
9. The Enemy Camp, by *Jerome Weidman.* Random House
10. Victorine, by *Frances Parkinson Keyes.* Messner

Nonfiction

1. Kids Say the Darndest Things! by *Art Linkletter.* Prentice-Hall
2. 'Twixt Twelve and Twenty, by *Pat Boone.* Prentice-Hall
3. Only in America, by *Harry Golden.* World Publishing Co.
4. Masters of Deceit, by *Edgar Hoover.* Holt
5. Please Don't Eat the Daisies, by *Jean Kerr.* Doubleday
6. Better Homes and Gardens Salad Book. Meredith Publishing Co.
7. The New Testament in Modern English, translated by *J. P. Phillips.* Macmillan
8. Aku-Aku, by *Thor Heyerdahl.* Rand McNally
9. Dear Abby, by *Abigail Van Buren.* Prentice-Hall
10. Inside Russia Today, by *John Gunther.* Harper

THINGS WERE a bit quieter in the world at large as the USSR halted its nuclear testing and tentative plans for a summit conference were made. But there was trouble nearer home: violent demonstrations against Vice President Nixon marked his visit to Caracas; Castro started his drive against the Batista government; and Governor Faubus closed all the Little Rock high schools as a counter-move to desegregation. In Europe, the Pope died and a new Pope was elected; General deGaulle became

206

President of the New Fifth Republic of France; and Van Cliburn of Texas won first prize in Moscow in the international Tschaikovsky piano competition. Two leading novels of the year in U.S. bookstores were by authors of Russian origin. Leading the best seller list was *Doctor Zhivago,* which came successfully to the screen some seven years later. In its two months on sale in 1958, the book sold nearly half a million copies, exclusive of book club sale. A story of a Russian doctor-poet's experiences in the harrowing years after the Russian Revolution, it was not published in the USSR, and, because of Soviet pressure, the author refused the Nobel Prize awarded him. The title, *Lolita,* became widely known as a descriptive word in this country, mainly because of the movie, which actually had little resemblance to the novel of more serious intent. *Lolita* reached third place in fiction with a sale of 153,000 copies. In second place in fiction, with a bookstore sale of 166,000 copies was that rarity among annual best sellers, a mystery story. *Anatomy of a Murder* was the story of a murder and a trial in northern Michigan, with authentic court atmosphere provided by its author, Court Justice John D. Voelker, writing under the pen-name of Robert Traver. The following year *Anatomy of a Murder* sold close to three million in its Dell paperback edition. *Lolita* sold more than three million as a Crest paperback. Aside from the top three, the best-selling novels of 1958 were by long-established authors. *From the Terrace,* modern novel by the perennial best-selling author, John O'Hara, sold 96,000 copies in one month of 1958; its later Bantam paperback sale placed it close to two million. Patrick Dennis continued Auntie Mame's fame with a sale of 117,000 copies for *Around the World with Auntie Mame.* Edna Ferber's *Ice Palace* was timed with the approaching statehood of Alaska. Though they had previously published popular books, Anya Seton and Jerome Weidman made their first appearances on an annual list. *The Winthrop Woman* was a historical novel of the Massachusetts Bay Colony. *The Enemy Camp* portrayed the tensions of a Gentile-Jewish marriage.

As usual, during these years of the '50's, few "literary" books became nonfiction best sellers. There was, of course, the fine new modern English translation of the *New Testament* by the English clergyman, J. B. Phillips, which sold 154,000. Harry Golden, editor of the *Carolina Israelite* and television personality, made his first appearance on the list with his book of wise and witty comments on a wide range of subjects, both topical and nostalgic. His *Only in America* sold 165,000 copies. A Pocket Book paperback sale brought it over one and one-quarter million in 1960. *Masters of Deceit* by the head of the FBI described communist activities in this country for a 160,000-copy sale. *Please Don't Eat the Daisies* appeared for a second year with almost a 265,000-copy two-year sale. With its Crest paperback sale, it eventually reached more than two million. *Aku-Aku* was an account of another Thor Heyerdahl expedition, this time exploring the archaeological secrets of Easter Island. *Inside Russia Today* was a new report by John Gunther, whose many "Inside" books were all best sellers. Art Linkletter's *Kids Say the Darndest Things!* was nonfiction leader for the second year, with a 1958 total of 241,000 copies. With its later Pocket Book paperback edition, it went well over three million. In the five weeks of 1958 during which the book by the young movie actor, Pat Boone, who had had a phenomenal rise to popularity, was on sale, it reached a total of 187,000. *'Twixt Twelve and Twenty* contained his conservative advice to teen-agers. *Dear Abby* in ninth place, was a collection of lovelorn letters and the answers to them by Abby Van Buren, syndicated column conductor. The cook book of the year was *Better Homes and Gardens Salad Book,* which sold 156,000 copies in bookstores.

1959

Fiction

1. Exodus, by *Leon Uris*. Doubleday
2. Doctor Zhivago, by *Boris Pasternak*. Pantheon Books
3. Hawaii, by *James Michener*. Random House
4. Advise and Consent, by *Allen Drury*. Doubleday
5. Lady Chatterley's Lover, by *D. H. Lawrence*. Grove Press
6. The Ugly American, by *William J. Lederer* and *Eugene L. Burdick*. Norton
7. Dear and Glorious Physician, by *Taylor Caldwell*. Doubleday
8. Lolita, by *Vladimir Nabokov*. Putnam
9. Mrs. 'Arris Goes to Paris, by *Paul Gallico*. Doubleday
10. Poor No More, by *Robert Ruark*. Holt

Nonfiction

1. 'Twixt Twelve and Twenty, by *Pat Boone*. Prentice-Hall
2. Folk Medicine, by *D. C. Jarvis*. Holt
3. For 2¢ Plain, by *Harry Golden*. World Publishing Co.
4. The Status Seekers, by *Vance Packard*. McKay
5. Act One, by *Moss Hart*. Random House
6. Charley Weaver's Letters from Mamma, by *Cliff Arquette*. Winston
7. Elements of Style, by *William Strunk, Jr.* and *E. B. White*. Macmillan
8. The General Foods Kitchens Cookbook. Random House
9. Only in America, by *Harry Golden*. World Publishing Co.
10. Mine Enemy Grows Older, by *Alexander King*. Simon & Schuster

FALLOUT WARNINGS because of atmosphere nuclear testing and advice on building fallout shelters were perhaps of less immediate concern to U.S. citizens than the reports of contamination of their Thanksgiving cranberries. Tension heightened over Berlin. There were anti-white riots in the Congo. Castro consolidated his position in Cuba and took office as premier early in the year. Congress began inquiries about "rigged" TV quiz shows and radio-TV "payola" in the same year that the long-established "Hit Parade" expired. The movie industry, however, showed signs of resuscitation. "The Nun's Story" was one of the year's big movies and "Gigi," with Maurice Chevalier, won the Oscar. On its international tour, Leonard Bernstein's New York Philharmonic gave 18 concerts in the USSR. The USSR Supreme Court announced that foreign writers were not entitled to royalties on their works published in Russia. Pasternak's *Doctor Zhivago* rolled up its sales in the U.S. to well over half a million copies for two years. Another holdover from the 1958 list was Nabokov's *Lolita*. The best-selling novel of 1959 was *Exodus,* story of the making of modern Israel, by Leon Uris, its hardbound total around the 400,000 mark. Later in the year the Bantam paperback edition ran its sales into the millions. *Hawaii,* James Michener's long novel based on the history of the Islands from the time they first emerged from the sea, was published in November. In only two months it made third place on the list with sales close to 200,000 copies. This was the year in which Hawaii became the fiftieth State of the Union. Novels of political implications reached fourth and sixth places. These were Allen Drury's first novel, *Advise and Consent,* laid in Washington, later a Broadway play, and *The Ugly American,* by William J. Lederer and Eugene L. Burdick, which bade fair to add a new catchword to our language. Its controversial matter concerned American diplomatic behavior in a small southeastern Asian country. Between these two, in fifth place, appeared the unexpurgated edition of the 1932 novel, *Lady Chatterley's Lover,* long a best seller in previous editions. There were court battles over the right to send D. H. Lawrence's celebrated book through the mails as well as various suits between hardbound and paperback publishers. Sales of the Grove Press edition in 1959 were about 160,000. Books by popular novelists completed the list of the ten best: *Dear and Glorious Physician,* Taylor Caldwell's Biblical novel about Luke; *Mrs. 'Arris Goes to Paris,* in which Paul Gallico's popular heroine made her first appearance; and *Poor No More,* story of a ruthless businessman by Robert Ruark, whose *Something of Value* had been a big seller four years before.

"How-to" books loomed large in 1959's nonfiction, the list headed by actor-singer Pat Boone's advice to teen-agers, *'Twixt Twelve and Twenty,* which had been second on the list the previous year. Its two-year total was 457,388 copies. *Folk Medicine: A Vermont Doctor's Guide to Good Health* was in second place with a 1958-59 sale of 265,816 copies. A distinguished and unique best seller, a compact little book on correct style in English, was *Elements of Style* by the late Cornell professor William Strunk, Jr., in a revised edition by E. B. White. It was seventh on the list with combined trade clothbound and paperback college edition sales of more than 150,000. It was also distributed as a dividend by the

Book-of-the-Month Club. Direct mail sales by General Foods (which were not included in this compilation) made the fourth "how-to" best seller, *The General Foods Kitchens Cookbook,* probably the year's best seller. Sales by the book trade brought it to eighth place. Television, specifically their authors' appearances on the Jack Paar Tonight Show, aided the sales of four nonfiction titles, Harry Golden's two books, *For 2¢ Plain* and *Only in America, Charley Weaver's Letters from Mamma,* and Alexander King's first essay in autobiography, *Mine Enemy Grows Older.* The more interesting "reading" books among best-selling nonfiction of the year appeared in fourth and fifth positions. These were *The Status Seekers,* commentary, both biting and entertaining, on American class symbols, by Vance Packard, and *Act One* by Moss Hart, chronicle of the famous playwright's early experiences in the theatre.

1960

Fiction

1. Advise and Consent, by *Allen Drury*. Doubleday
2. Hawaii, by *James A. Michener*. Random House
3. The Leopard, by *Giuseppe di Lampedusa*. Pantheon Books
4. The Chapman Report, by *Irving Wallace*. Simon & Schuster
5. Ourselves To Know, by *John O'Hara*. Random House
6. The Constant Image, by *Marcia Davenport*. Scribner
7. The Lovely Ambition, by *Mary Ellen Chase*. Norton
8. The Listener, by *Taylor Caldwell*. Doubleday
9. Trustee from the Toolroom, by *Nevil Shute*. Morrow
10. Sermons and Soda-Water, by *John O'Hara*. Random House

Nonfiction

1. Folk Medicine, by *D. C. Jarvis*. Holt, Rinehart & Winston
2. Better Homes and Gardens First Aid for Your Family. Meredith Publishing Co.
3. The General Foods Kitchens Cookbook. Random House
4. May This House Be Safe from Tigers, by *Alexander King*. Simon & Schuster
5. Better Homes and Gardens Dessert Book. Meredith Publishing Co.
6. Better Homes and Gardens Decorating Ideas. Meredith Publishing Co.
7. The Rise and Fall of the Third Reich, by *William L. Shirer*. Simon & Schuster
8. The Conscience of a Conservative, by *Barry Goldwater*. Victor Publishing Co.
9. I Kid You Not, by *Jack Paar*. Little, Brown
10. Between You, Me and the Gatepost, by *Pat Boone*. Prentice-Hall

THIS WAS a troubled year, politically, with unrest around the world—in Algeria, Laos, Venezuela, Japan, the Congo, Cuba, and the Dominican Republic—much of it anti-American in tone. No Nobel Peace Prize was

212

awarded in 1960. On May 1 the U.S. U-2 reconnaissance plane piloted by Francis Gary Powers was brought down in Russia. Khrushchev broke off the summit conference in Paris because of the incident. Israeli agents captured Nazi Adolf Eichmann. In September, with the opening of the General Assembly of the UN and the arrival of both Khrushchev and Castro, New York City turned into what looked like an armed state. Heavy police guards were on 24-hour duty at all the Iron Curtain consulates and armed cavalcades dashed back and forth between the UN and the delegates' domiciles at all hours. The U.S. continued to be entertained by foreign movies: the French "Hiroshima Mon Amour," the British "Our Man in Havana," the Greek "Never on Sunday," and the Cannes Grand Prix winner, the Italian "La Dolce Vita." The juke boxes ground out "Teenie Weenie Bikini." In November John Fitzgerald Kennedy and Lyndon Baines Johnson were elected President and Vice President of the United States. In the publishing world, which found in these events of 1960 an abundance of material for future books, there were many mergers of old-line firms. There was a tremendous increase in original paperback publishing both for the mass market and in the so-called "quality" lines. There were 20 new paperback firms established and many long-established hardbound publishers entered the paperback field. Prices of paperbacks went up. The original 25-cent price for reprints of novels was long past. Sixty cents and 95 cents became more usual prices as longer and better novels and nonfiction became important paperback merchandise, with paperback publishers offering high prices for reprint rights. The two leading novels in bookstore sales in 1960 were holdovers from the 1959 list, both published late in 1959. In third and fourth places were novels by the only authors among the ten who were new to annual best seller lists, Giuseppe di Lampedusa and Irving Wallace. *The Leopard,* story of a noble Sicilian family, was the first and only book by the late Italian nobleman. *The Chapman Report,* which became a popular movie, drew its plot from a statistical survey similar to that upon which the Kinsey Report was based. John O'Hara was the first novelist in 25 years, not since James Hilton in 1935, to place two books on an annual list. In 1959, Harry Golden was the first author to have two books on the nonfiction list in 10 years.

During the 1950's, reversing the order of many years before, the ten nonfiction best sellers outsold the ten fiction best sellers in overall total. In 1959, nonfiction had an edge of about 110,000 copies over fiction, but in 1960 the ten nonfiction titles sold almost twice as many copies as the corresponding fiction. Again "how-to" books predominated, comprising more than half the list. *Folk Medicine* moved up from second place the previous year to first, with an additional sale of 262,000 copies for a two-year total of 486,018. The publisher's imprint on this title was no longer

213

Henry Holt & Co. Pointing up the many mergers in the book business, was the three-publisher combine of Holt, Rinehart & Winston. Three *Better Homes and Gardens* books for the homemaker were in second, fifth and sixth places, with trade sales respectively of 213,013, 148,183, and 145,- 471 copies. Third place was occupied by a repeater from 1959. *The General Foods Kitchens Cookbook* added another 180,000 copies through the trade. Pat Boone's 1960 best seller, *Between You, Me and the Gate-post,* following his 1959 leader, *'Twixt Twelve and Twenty,* reached tenth place. Most impressive of the 1960 nonfiction was *The Rise and Fall of the Third Reich,* by William L. Shirer, whose *Berlin Diary* had helped to make history in 1941. In only two months of publication this weighty historical volume, priced at $10, sold 111,871 copies. In addition, the Book-of-the-Month Club printed 270,000 copies. Senator Barry Gold-water's statement of his political faith, *The Conscience of a Conservative,* reached eighth place with a sale of 97,000. The paperback sale brought it close to the half-million mark. Jack Paar, at the height of his television popularity, gave added publicity to the remaining two books of the first ten—his own autobiography, in ninth place, and more Alexander King autobiography mingled with witty comment, *May This House Be Safe from Tigers,* which sold 148,714 copies for fourth position on the list.

1961

Fiction

1. The Agony and the Ecstasy, by *Irving Stone*. Doubleday
2. Franny and Zooey, by *J. D. Salinger*. Little, Brown
3. To Kill a Mockingbird, by *Harper Lee*. Lippincott
4. Mila 18, by *Leon Uris*. Doubleday
5. The Carpetbaggers, by *Harold Robbins*. Simon & Schuster
6. Tropic of Cancer, by *Henry Miller*. Grove Press
7. Winnie Ille Pu, translated by *Alexander Lenard*. Dutton
8. Daughter of Silence, by *Morris West*. Morrow
9. The Edge of Sadness, by *Edwin O'Connor*. Little, Brown
10. The Winter of Our Discontent, by *John Steinbeck*. Viking Press

Nonfiction

1. The New English Bible: The New Testament. Cambridge University Press and Oxford University Press
2. The Rise and Fall of the Third Reich, by *William Shirer*. Simon & Schuster
3. Better Homes and Gardens Sewing Book. Meredith Publishing Co.
4. Casserole Cook Book. Meredith Publishing Co.
5. A Nation of Sheep, by *William Lederer*. Norton
6. Better Homes and Gardens Nutrition for Your Family. Meredith Publishing Co.
7. The Making of the President, 1960, by *Theodore H. White*. Atheneum Press
8. Calories Don't Count, by *Dr. Herman Taller*. Simon & Schuster
9. Betty Crocker's New Picture Cook Book: New Edition. McGraw-Hill
10. Ring of Bright Water, by *Gavin Maxwell*. Dutton

THE YEAR of the "twist" craze, the beginning of the Civil War Centennial celebration, and of major advances in space exploration—Major Yuri Gagarin of Russia was the first man to orbit the earth and Alan B. Shepard, Jr. was the first U.S. astronaut to rocket off in a space capsule—was also the year of such disasters as the Bay of Pigs invasion, the closing of the border between East and West Germany, and the death of UN Secretary General Dag Hammarskjöld in a plane crash in Northern Rhodesia. The 1961 Nobel Prize was awarded to him posthumously. The Peace Corps for service in underdeveloped foreign countries was established. There was continued international exchange of orchestras. The Metropolitan Museum bought a Rembrandt painting for the highest auction price ever paid. Cellist Pablo Casals played a return engagement at the White House; the last time he had played there had been for President Theodore Roosevelt in 1904. The state of the American theatre was called distressing. Although Broadway productions bogged down, many local repertory companies were springing up throughout the rest of the country. The best-selling novels of the year were definitely high in interest and excellence. The leaders of the year, Irving Stone's great novel of the life of Michelangelo, *The Agony and the Ecstasy,* and J. D. Salinger's second novel, *Franny and Zooey* (his *Catcher in the Rye,* which originally made him famous, did not make an annual list), at the head of 1961's fiction, were challenged by a newcomer, first novelist Harper Lee. Her *To Kill a Mockingbird,* a sensitive and compelling story of a small southern town in the 1930's, published in 1960, won the Pulitzer Prize. Its two-year total was close to 200,000 plus sales by three book clubs. Following his *Exodus* of two years before, Leon Uris wrote a story of the Warsaw ghetto in World War II, *Mila 18,* which was fourth on the list with 134,397 sold. Popular novelist Harold Robbins made his first appearance on an annual list with a novel of modern American life considered a *roman à clef, The Carpetbaggers,* with over 108,000 sold. In sixth and seventh places appeared two dissimilar titles, both, however, originally published over 25 years before. Henry Miller's *Tropic of Cancer,* long an under-the-counter item, and considered the most-banned book of its time, was openly published in the less-strictured 1960's. It sold 100,000 copies in hardcover plus a later paperback sale of two and one-half million. *Winnie Ille Pu,* forerunner of a vogue for publishing well-loved English language books in other languages, was a Latin translation by Alexander Lenard of A. A. Milne's *Winnie the Pooh,* which was first published as a children's book in 1926, but, as often happens to such classics, taken over for adult reading. *Winnie Ille Pu* was the first book in a language other than English to appear on any of these yearly lists. Books by Morris West with his first best seller on an annual list and by the perennially popular John Steinbeck wound up the fiction, along with *The Edge of Sadness,* novel about a New England political figure, by another writer new to the lists, Edwin O'Connor. It was the winner of the Pulitzer Prize.

A new translation of the Bible always reaffirms the aphorism that the

216

Bible is the best seller of all time. *The New Testament* issued jointly by Cambridge University Press and Oxford University Press as part of *The New English Bible* easily led nonfiction in 1961, selling 756,575 copies. In second place, in its second year was *The Rise and Fall of the Third Reich,* selling an additional 203,346 in 1961. Its book club sale brought it close to one million. The $265,000 which Dell Publishing Co. had paid for paperback reprint rights to *Return to Peyton Place* in 1959 was a record purchase. But only two years later Fawcett paid $400,000 for the paperback rights to William Shirer's big book, a lengthy one for paperback. Among other nonfiction titles for the general reader on the 1961 list were, in fifth place, selling 135,644 copies, *A Nation of Sheep,* by William Lederer, co-author of *The Ugly American* of two years before. This new book was a critical discussion of U.S. foreign policy and of how news about foreign affairs reaches the public. Another book of political content was Theodore H. White's *The Making of the President, 1960,* which won a Pulitzer Prize. A refreshing book wound up the list, Gavin Maxwell's *Ring of Bright Water,* an account of the author's home on the Scottish coast and of his nature adventures shared with two pet otters. The sales of the five other best sellers, books on sewing, cooking, and nutrition, added greatly to the big overall nonfiction count of the year.

1962

Fiction

1. Ship of Fools, by *Katherine Anne Porter*. Little, Brown
2. Dearly Beloved, by *Anne Morrow Lindbergh*. Harcourt, Brace & World
3. A Shade of Difference, by *Allen Drury*. Doubleday
4. Youngblood Hawke, by *Herman Wouk*. Doubleday
5. Franny and Zooey, by *J. D. Salinger*. Little, Brown
6. Fail-Safe, by *Eugene Burdick* and *Harvey Wheeler*. McGraw-Hill
7. Seven Days in May, by *Fletcher Knebel* and *Charles W. Bailey II*. Harper & Row
8. The Prize, by *Irving Wallace*. Simon & Schuster
9. The Agony and the Ecstasy, by *Irving Stone*. Doubleday
10. The Reivers, by *William Faulkner*. Random House

Nonfiction

1. Calories Don't Count, by *Dr. Herman Taller*. Simon & Schuster
2. The New English Bible: The New Testament. Cambridge University Press and Oxford University Press
3. Better Homes and Gardens Cook Book: New Edition. Meredith Publishing Co.
4. O Ye Jigs & Juleps! by *Virginia Cary Hudson*. Macmillan
5. Happiness Is a Warm Puppy, by *Charles M. Schulz*. Determined Productions
6. The Joy of Cooking: New Edition by *Irma S. Rombauer* and *Marion Rombauer Becker*. Bobbs-Merrill
7. My Life in Court, by *Louis Nizer*. Doubleday
8. The Rothschilds, by *Frederic Morton*. Atheneum Publishers
9. Sex and the Single Girl, by *Helen Gurley Brown*. Bernard Geis
10. Travels with Charley, by *John Steinbeck*. Viking Press

THERE WERE world-shaking events in the year 1962: the Cuban missile crisis; increased tension over the Berlin air corridor; the continuation of the Algerian violence by the OAS after official proclamation of the country's independence; resumption of atmospheric nuclear tests by both the USSR and the U.S.; and widening of the ideological breach between Russia and China. At home there was conflict over the admission of James H. Meredith to the University of Mississippi. American advances in space included our first manned earth orbit, by Lieutenant-Colonel John H. Glenn, Jr. and our first operation of a communications satellite, Telstar. Among notable plays were "Who's Afraid of Virginia Woolf?" Aside from teenagers' rock 'n' roll, the most popular song of the year was Anthony Newley's "What Kind of Fool Am I?" from his musical show, "Stop the World—I Want to Get Off." The New York Philharmonic, under Leonard Bernstein, opened Philharmonic Hall in New York's Lincoln Center for the Performing Arts. In Rome, the Vatican Council was opened. In 1962 the number of books published in the United States reached an all-time high, with paperbacks accounting for 31 per cent of the total. The quality of the fiction best sellers of the year was high, with the names of notable writers appearing on the list. Leading was the novel, *Ship of Fools,* upon which Katherine Anne Porter had been working for 20 years. It sold almost 200,000 copies in the bookstores. Old-line publishers with new imprints issued the best sellers in second and seventh places. These were Harcourt, Brace & World and Harper & Row. Second was *Dearly Beloved,* the first novel ever written by Anne Morrow Lindbergh, whose accounts of pioneer air flights with her famous husband had been great best sellers over 20 years before. Just over the 100,000 mark was the record of books in third and fourth positions, *A Shade of Difference,* another political novel by the author of *Advise and Consent,* and *Youngblood Hawke* by Herman Wouk, author of many best sellers. His latest had a book publishing background, its central character resembling Thomas Wolfe. J. D. Salinger's *Franny and Zooey,* second in 1961, was fifth in 1962. Sixth and seventh were two exciting suspense stories, which, because of topical interest, attracted many readers. They were *Fail-Safe* by Eugene Burdick, co-author of *The Ugly American,* and Harvey Wheeler, and *Seven Days in May,* about a presidential crisis. This was a novel by authors new to these lists, Washington newsmen Fletcher Knebel and Charles W. Bailey II. Both these novels sold more than a million copies each in their later paperback editions. Irving Wallace's *The Prize,* quite different in subject from his 1960 best seller, *The Chapman Report,* was a story about a Nobel Prize winner. *The Agony and the Ecstasy,* leader of 1961 fiction, was next with a two-year trade sale of 287,525 copies. The last book on the list, *The Reivers,* was a serio-comic novel by William Faulkner, who had been awarded the Nobel Prize for Literature for 1949. William Faulkner died just a month after publication of *The Reivers.* This, his last novel, won the Pulitzer Prize for the year.

There were a few more books of creative writing as distinguished from instructional guides and books of fleeting entertainment than there had been in the past few years in best-selling nonfiction. These were, in general, biographical and autobiographical. Surprise seller of the year was *O Ye Jigs & Juleps!* a diary recording observations, both naïve and perceptive, of life in a minister's household in the early 1900's. It was written by Virginia Cary Hudson when she was a child. Lawyer Louis Nizer's *My Life in Court,* which just missed making the first ten in 1961, came up in seventh place in 1962 with a sale of 143,695 copies and a two-year total of 218,410. Eighth was the biography of the famous international banking family *The Rothschilds* by Frederic Morton. John Steinbeck, novelist, 1962 winner of the Nobel Prize for Literature, was one of the authors who had appeared most frequently on these best seller lists during the previous 25 years. In 1962 he appeared for the first time as the author of a best-selling nonfiction title. *Travels with Charley* was John Steinbeck's delightful account of his camper journey with his dog from coast to coast. The book sold 110,000, exclusive of book club copies. *The New Testament (N.E.B.),* top seller in 1961, was second in 1962, with a 629,466 sale in cloth, paper, and leather bindings. Its two-year sale was 1,386,041. Topping nonfiction sales for the year was the controversial *Calories Don't Count* by Dr. Herman Taller, with a 1961-62 sale of 1,100,000. The first of the books by the popular cartoonist, Charles M. Schulz, to be published by the new firm, Determined Productions, was *Happiness Is a Warm Puppy,* which made a hit with 175,000 Christmas buyers. Few volumes of poetry had appeared on all these best seller lists. It was noteworthy that Robert Frost's *In the Clearing,* with a sale of 92,619, a total that might easily have placed it on the list in other years, just missed the first ten.

1963

Fiction

1. The Shoes of the Fisherman, by *Morris L. West*. Morrow
2. The Group, by *Mary McCarthy*. Harcourt, Brace & World
3. Raise High the Roof Beam, Carpenters, and Seymour—An Introduction, by *J. D. Salinger*. Little, Brown
4. Caravans, by *James A. Michener*. Random House
5. Elizabeth Appleton, by *John O'Hara*. Random House
6. Grandmother and the Priests, by *Taylor Caldwell*. Doubleday
7. City of Night, by *John Rechy*. Grove Press
8. The Glass-Blowers, by *Daphne du Maurier*. Doubleday
9. The Sand Pebbles, by *Richard McKenna*. Harper & Row
10. The Battle of the Villa Fiorita, by *Rumer Godden*. Viking Press

Nonfiction

1. Happiness Is a Warm Puppy, by *Charles M. Schulz*. Determined Productions
2. Security Is a Thumb and a Blanket, by *Charles M. Schulz*. Determined Productions
3. J.F.K.: The Man and the Myth, by *Victor Lasky*. Macmillan
4. Profiles in Courage: Inaugural Edition, by *John F. Kennedy*. Harper & Row
5. O Ye Jigs & Juleps! by *Virginia Cary Hudson*. Macmillan
6. Better Homes and Gardens Bread Cook Book. Meredith Publishing Co.
7. The Pillsbury Family Cookbook. Harper & Row
8. I Owe Russia $1200, by *Bob Hope*. Doubleday
9. Heloise's Housekeeping Hints. Prentice-Hall
10. Better Homes and Gardens Baby Book. Meredith Publishing Co.

POPE JOHN XXIII DIED—his *Pacem in Terris* was his last papal encyclical —and a new Pope elected. Pope Paul VI re-opened Vatican II in September. Sir Winston Churchill was proclaimed an honorary United States citizen. The Profumo case shocked the English-speaking world. Later there

221

occurred the Great Mail Train Robbery near London. The USSR accepted the U.S. proposal for a direct communications link between Washington and Moscow to lessen the risk of accidental war—a catastrophe suggested by the 1962 best seller, *Fail-Safe.* Later in the year the U.K., USSR and U.S. signed a treaty banning nuclear testing in the atmosphere, in space, and under water. Anti-segregation demonstrations were augmented throughout many southern states during the summer, with a massive rally for civil rights in Washington late in August. November 22 was one of the most tragic days in American history, the day upon which President John F. Kennedy was assassinated in Dallas.

A novel based upon a religious theme, the story of a newly-elected Pope, topped all 1963's fiction with its 170,000-copy sale. *The Shoes of the Fisherman,* by Morris West, was the fastest-selling title Morrow had ever put on the market. Mary McCarthy, though a writer of note, had never had a really big best seller until *The Group* sold some 130,000 copies and reached second place on the list. This story of the lives of some Vassar girls, revealed ten years after their graduation from college, became the basis of a much-publicized feature movie. J. D. Salinger followed his two-year best seller, *Franny and Zooey,* with more episodes in the life of the Glass family. *Raise High the Roof Beam, Carpenters, and Seymour—An Introduction* sold about 100,000 copies. In fourth, fifth, and sixth places were books by novelists who had built great audiences over the years, James Michener, John O'Hara, and Taylor Caldwell. *Caravans,* Michener's novel of Afghanistan adventure, sold over 90,000 plus its book club sale. O'Hara's *Elizabeth Appleton* was set in his favorite fictional Pennsylvania town. Taylor Caldwell's *Grandmother and the Priests* related episodes of Irish family and religious life. There were two first novelists who achieved best sellerdom in 1963. John Rechy's *City of Night* was a picture of the homosexual world in some of the large American cities. With *The Sand Pebbles,* story of a U.S. Navy gunboat in China in the 1920's, Richard McKenna won the 1963 Harper Prize Novel award. Two of the most popular novelists in this country had new books with sales of some 50,000 copies, just missing the first ten. They were Ian Fleming with *On Her Majesty's Secret Service* and Helen Mac-Innes with *The Venetian Affair.* Sales of both these books zoomed in their later paperback editions. These years of the '60's marked the height of the Ian Fleming craze, with movie after movie appearing to increase the popularity of James Bond—007. "Dr. No" was one of the most popular pictures of the year, along with such other movies made from books as *The Birds, Lord of the Flies, The Leopard,* which won the top award at the Cannes Film Festival, and *Tom Jones,* Oscar winner of the year.

Outstanding on the nonfiction list was John F. Kennedy's Pulitzer Prize-winning *Profiles in Courage* in the Inaugural Edition, issued early in 1961.

222

In paperback form (not the Inaugural Edition) *Profiles in Courage,* of which Pocket Books had already sold about two million copies since 1957, rose in sales, selling about two and one-quarter million in 1963 alone. The clothbound Inaugural Edition was in fourth place on the list. Just preceding it was a political biography sharply critical of Kennedy, *J.F.K.: The Man and the Myth* by Victor Lasky. *O Ye Jigs & Juleps!* continued its 1962 success. The only other nonfiction title among the first ten not a book of specific instruction or seasonal entertainment was Bob Hope's hilarious travel saga, *I Owe Russia $1200.* It sold 111,585 copies plus book club distribution. The two Charles M. Schulz books of pictures with captions which topped all nonfiction were *Happiness Is a Warm Puppy* and *Security Is a Thumb and a Blanket.* The first was fifth in the previous year. In 1963 it sold 825,054 copies for a million-copy total. The newer title racked up 356,000 copies. The other four books on 1963's list were books of information for homemakers, each selling more than 100,000.

1964

Fiction

1. The Spy Who Came in From the Cold, by *John Le Carré*. Coward-McCann
2. Candy, by *Terry Southern and Mason Hoffenberg*. Putnam
3. Herzog, by *Saul Bellow*. Viking Press
4. Armageddon, by *Leon Uris*. Doubleday
5. The Man, by *Irving Wallace*. Simon & Schuster
6. The Rector of Justin, by *Louis Auchincloss*. Houghton Mifflin
7. The Martyred, by *Richard E. Kim*. Braziller
8. You Only Live Twice, by *Ian Fleming*. New American Library
9. This Rough Magic, by *Mary Stewart*. Morrow
10. Convention, by *Fletcher Knebel* and *Charles W. Bailey, II*. Harper & Row

Nonfiction

1. Four Days, by *American Heritage* and *United Press International*. Simon & Schuster
2. I Need All the Friends I Can Get, by *Charles M. Schulz*. Determined Productions
3. Profiles in Courage: Memorial Edition, by *John F. Kennedy*. Harper & Row
4. In His Own Write, by *John Lennon*. Simon & Schuster
5. Christmas Is Together-Time, by *Charles M. Schulz*. Determined Productions
6. A Day in the Life of President Kennedy, by *Jim Bishop*. Random House
7. The Kennedy Wit, compiled by *Bill Adler*. Citadel Press
8. A Moveable Feast, by *Ernest Hemingway*. Scribner
9. Reminiscences, by *General Douglas MacArthur*. McGraw-Hill
10. The John F. Kennedys, by *Mark Shaw*. Farrar, Straus & Giroux

THE WORLD'S FAIR opened in New York; the official celebration of the 400th anniversary of Shakespeare's birth began at Stratford-on-Avon. For the first time since their establishment in 1917, no Pulitzer Prizes were awarded in fiction, drama, or music. Jean-Paul Sartre, French exponent of existentialism, refused the Nobel Prize for Literature. The Nobel Peace Prize went to the Reverend Martin Luther King, Jr., Negro civil rights leader. In January Pope Paul made a three-day flying visit to the Holy Land. He was the first Pope to travel by air and the first Pope to leave Italy in 150 years. Deaths of notables in 1964 included those of Herbert Clark Hoover at the age of 90, Prime Minister Nehru of India, and General Douglas MacArthur. Nikita S. Khrushchev was removed from all his governmental and Communist Party offices. The war in Vietnam was escalated, there was mounting trouble in Cyprus, Panama, and the Congo, and race riots in eight northern cities of the U.S. In November Lyndon B. Johnson and Hubert S. Humphrey were elected President and Vice President. The movies had their most successful year since television had become their chief competitor. Sean Connery portrayed Agent 007 in a number of films based on the Fleming books. Mary Poppins, popular character of children's books for many years, was a big hit in a Walt Disney film. For the first time movies were shown to passengers on air flights. Discothèques became the most popular nighttime resorts, where people danced the frug, the swim, and the watusi. The Beatles were the top performers in England and in America. There were smash musicals on Broadway—"Hello Dolly!," "Funny Girl," "Fiddler on the Roof," and "Golden Boy." In publishing there were acquisitions, consolidations, mergers galore by publishers with eyes on the tremendous expansion of the school market. Many old-line houses "went public" on the stock exchange.

Never before had a "thriller" headed all fiction titles of a year. *The Spy Who Came in from the Cold,* aided by unusual word-of-mouth praise, sold a whopping 230,000 copies through bookstores. In 1965 *The Spy* sold more than two million in paperback. Not only the leader, but two other suspense stories were best sellers, illustrating the great appeal of espionage and romantic mystery in the 1960's. In eighth and ninth places, Ian Fleming and Mary Stewart made their first appearances on an annual list, that of Ian Fleming unfortunately just after his death. *This Rough Magic,* like other Mary Stewart novels, represented the best type of romantic mystery, with colorful background. There were four other best-selling novels of 1964 by authors making their first appearances on a yearly list, but only one of them by a first novelist. He was Richard E. Kim, a young Korean, whose *The Martyred* sold 70,000 copies. This novel also marked the first appearance of the publishing firm of George Braziller, Inc. on an annual list. New American Library as a hardcover publisher and Citadel Press also made their débuts on the lists. In second place was *Candy* by Terry Southern and Mason Hoffenberg, who wrote the story as a spoof on the rising tide of "dirty" books. It sold 140,000 copies in

225

1964, almost one and one-half million in paperback in 1965. Third was the novel that had highest critical praise of the year, *Herzog.* Its author, Saul Bellow, was a long-established writer just reaching a very large audience. In similar situation was Louis Auchincloss, author of *The Rector of Justin.* The other three fiction leaders of the year were by authors who had appeared a number of times on these lists. *Armageddon,* by Leon Uris was one of the two war novels—the other, *The Martyred. The Man* by Irving Wallace and *Convention,* by Fletcher Knebel and Charles W. Bailey II, were both concerned with timely political topics.

In contrast to many previous years, the nonfiction list was free of "how-to" books. This was due, in part, to the great number of best sellers related to the late President Kennedy. They comprised half the list of ten, including his own *Profiles in Courage* issued in February in a Memorial Edition. Top of nonfiction, which, overall, outsold the ten fiction titles two to one, was *Four Days,* documentary and pictorial account of the tragic November days of 1963, with a preface by historian Bruce Catton. It was compiled by *American Heritage* magazine and United Press International. Simon & Schuster distributed a half million copies of the deluxe edition through the trade. U.P.I. sold two and one-half million copies. In sixth place, with sales of 139,000 was Jim Bishop's *A Day in the Life of President Kennedy,* a book which the author had completed just a week before the President's death. It was a chronicle of one day in the President's working and home life, from 7 A.M. to midnight. Following was *The Kennedy Wit,* with sales of 103,000, compiled by Bill Adler from comments made by JFK through his entire political life, both in formal speeches and in off-the-cuff repartee. Winding up the list was *The John F. Kennedys,* subtitled "A Family Album," and containing about 150 photographs of the Kennedy family in Georgetown, Cape Cod, Washington, and other places. Of the remaining five nonfiction best sellers, two were Charles M. Schulz picture books. *I Need All the Friends I Can Get* was second, selling 175,000 copies. *Christmas Is To-gether-Time,* fifth, sold 150,000. In fourth place was the book of poems and stories by Beatle John Lennon. Its 150,000-copy sale was pushed along by the Beatles' visit to the U.S. Two books, very different in background and personality, both autobiographical and both posthumously published, were eighth and ninth on the list. They were *A Moveable Feast* by Ernest Hemingway and *Reminiscences* by General Douglas MacArthur.

1965

Fiction

1. The Source, by *James A. Michener.* Random House
2. Up the Down Staircase, by *Bel Kaufman.* Prentice-Hall
3. Herzog, by *Saul Bellow.* Viking Press
4. The Looking Glass War, by *John Le Carré.* Coward-McCann
5. The Green Berets, by *Robin Moore.* Crown
6. Those Who Love, by *Irving Stone.* Doubleday
7. The Man with the Golden Gun, by *Ian Fleming.* New American Library
8. Hotel, by *Arthur Hailey.* Doubleday
9. The Ambassador, by *Morris West.* Morrow
10. Don't Stop the Carnival, by *Herman Wouk.* Doubleday

Nonfiction

1. How To Be a Jewish Mother, by *Dan Greenburg.* Price/Stern/ Sloan
2. A Gift of Prophecy, by *Ruth Montgomery.* Morrow
3. Games People Play, by *Eric Berne, M.D.* Grove Press
4. World Aflame, by *Billy Graham.* Doubleday
5. Happiness Is a Dry Martini, by *Johnny Carson.* Doubleday
6. Markings, by *Dag Hammarskjöld.* Knopf
7. A Thousand Days, by *Arthur Schlesinger, Jr.* Houghton Mifflin
8. My Shadow Ran Fast, by *Bill Sands.* Prentice-Hall
9. Kennedy, by *Theodore C. Sorensen.* Harper & Row
10. The Making of the President, 1964, by *Theodore H. White.* Atheneum

EARLY in 1965, Sir Winston Churchill, dominating world figure for many years, died at the age of 90. President Johnson's first State of the Union message announced his "Great Society" program, continuing the Kennedy "New Frontier" program. Congress passed the Medicare bill and a bill authorizing federal aid to elementary and secondary education. The latter bill was to have a highly stimulating effect upon the book industry. A

227

Soviet astronaut and a U.S. astronaut became the first men to walk in space. Events of the year arousing great public interest were Pope Paul's one-day visit to the UN in New York, with his celebration of mass at the Yankee Stadium just before his departure, and the power failure that blacked out most of the Northeast States and part of Canada. On the entertainment level go-go dancers and the discothèque were the vogue. Such older night spots as the Stork Club in New York, the Trocadero in London, and the Peppermint Lounge, home of the twist, passed out of existence. The average price of books, which had been $5.29 in 1957-59, rose to $7.65 in 1965, still less than the price of a Broadway musical ticket. Best-selling novel on the year's list, mostly comprised of books by well-known authors, was James Michener's *The Source.* This long novel about Israel past and present sold well over a quarter of a million. The other established authors among the first ten were Saul Bellow, repeating the success of *Herzog* for the second year (it sold more than a million in paperback in 1965, 145,000 in hardcover); John Le Carré, with his second espionage best seller, *The Looking Glass War*; Irving Stone, long a best-selling writer of historical and biographical novels, whose *Those Who Love* was based upon the lives of Abigail and John Adams; Ian Fleming, making his second appearance on the yearly hardcover list with his last full-length James Bond adventure, *The Man with the Golden Gun*; Morris West, whose *The Ambassador* was a story of a U.S. diplomat in South Vietnam; and Herman Wouk with *Don't Stop the Carnival,* entertaining story of a man who retired from the public relations business to run a hotel on a Caribbean island. There were three novelists who appeared for the first time among a year's best sellers. Surprise hardcover seller of the year, second in sales only to *The Source,* was *Up the Down Staircase,* clever and touching story of a New York schoolteacher's lot. This was Bel Kaufman's first novel, selling 222,519 copies. *The Green Berets,* another best seller with a Vietnamese setting, sold close to 100,000 copies in hardcover. The paperback edition of Robin Moore's book, which came out in November, became the phenomenon of the year, with 1,200,000 printed in only two months. A second novel about a big hotel was by Arthur Hailey, also new to the list. His *Hotel* was in tenth place, selling 93,000 copies.

Emphasis in the nonfiction best ten was on little books of humor, books of information, and on special subjects, though there was not the preponderance of "non-books" that there had often been. Leader was *How To Be a Jewish Mother,* an entertaining little book on the complex art of momism by Dan Greenburg, issued by the new firm of Price/Stern/Sloan, with pictures by Gerry Gersten. It sold 270,000 copies. Another best-selling "entertainment" was the Tonight Show MC Johnny Carson's *Happiness Is a Dry Martini.* Typical Carson one-liners were illustrated by

Whitney Darrow, Jr., and sold 172,000, reaching fifth place on the list. Books on unusual topics were in second and third places in nonfiction. Ruth Montgomery's *A Gift of Prophecy,* an account of "the phenomenal Jeane Dixon" and her predictions of future events sold 210,000. In *Games People Play: The Psychology of Human Relationships,* Eric Berne, M.D. explained his theories about the roles people assume, usually to conceal the real facts about themselves from others. His book sold 205,000 copies. One of the few religious best sellers of the past few years reached fourth place with a sale of 198,000. This was evangelist Billy Graham's *World Aflame. Markings* by the late Secretary General of the UN, Dag Hammarskjöld, could be called his spiritual autobiography, containing his poems, thoughts, and short essays arranged chronologically. Published late in 1964, this volume had an impressive two-year total of 270,647. Adding to the five best sellers of 1964 about President Kennedy were two more in 1965. *A Thousand Days* by Arthur Schlesinger, Jr. sold 140,000 copies through bookstores and won the Pulitzer Prize for biography. *Kennedy* by Theodore C. Sorensen was a record of the late President's public life by a close associate, his Special Counsel. Tenth was *The Making of the President, 1964,* second best seller in Theodore H. White's narratives of presidential elections. *My Shadow Ran Fast* was an autobiographical account, by Bill Sands, of his prison experiences as a young man in San Quentin and of his later work organizing rehabilitation programs for convicts and ex-convicts.

1966

Fiction

1. Valley of the Dolls, by *Jacqueline Susann*. Bernard Geis
2. The Adventurers, by *Harold Robbins*. Trident Press
3. The Secret of Santa Vittoria, by *Robert Crichton*. Simon & Schuster
4. Capable of Honor, by *Allen Drury*. Doubleday
5. The Double Image, by *Helen MacInnes*. Harcourt, Brace & World
6. The Fixer, by *Bernard Malamud*. Farrar, Straus & Giroux
7. Tell No Man, by *Adela Rogers St. Johns*. Doubleday
8. Tai-Pan, by *James Clavell*. Atheneum Publishers
9. The Embezzler, by *Louis Auchincloss*. Houghton Mifflin
10. All in the Family, by *Edwin O'Connor*. Atlantic-Little, Brown

Nonfiction

1. How to Avoid Probate, by *Norman F. Dacey*. Crown
2. Human Sexual Response, by *William Howard Masters* and *Virginia E. Johnston*. Little, Brown
3. In Cold Blood, by *Truman Capote*. Random House
4. Games People Play, by *Eric Berne, M.D.* Grove Press
5. A Thousand Days, by *Arthur M. Schlesinger, Jr.* Houghton Mifflin
6. Everything But Money, by *Sam Levenson*. Simon & Schuster
7. The Random House Dictionary of the English Language. Random House
8. Rush to Judgment, by *Mark Lane*. Holt, Rinehart & Winston
9. The Last Battle, by *Cornelius Ryan*. Simon & Schuster
10. Phyllis Diller's Housekeeping Hints, by *Phyllis Diller*. Doubleday

BEST-SELLING books of 1966 were chiefly concerned with history, with sex and psychology, and with entertainment. Some of the outstanding world events of the year may be reflected in the lists of later years: France's withdrawal from NATO; the activation of Medicare in the U. S.;

the escalation of the war in Vietnam; the first television pictures from the moon by Surveyor I; U. S. astronauts' first docking operation and walk in space. The former German Chancellor Konrad Adenauer visited Israel. Some U. S. H-bombs were accidentally dropped on and recovered from Spanish soil and sea. The New Metropolitan Opera House offered a new American opera for its gala opening at Lincoln Center. Most popular records of the year were "Winchester Cathedral" and the album of Jeanette MacDonald and Nelson Eddy favorites. "Man of La Mancha," based upon *Don Quixote,* offered strong rivalry to the Broadway musical hits "Mame" and "Hello Dolly." Publication of the Catholic edition of the Bible in the *Revised Standard Version* was considered a milestone in the mid-century ecumenical movement. A new dictionary, *The Random House Dictionary of the English Language,* sold out its first printing of 150,000 copies in the two months before Christmas.

Leading all sales of the year was an unusual volume, offering advice on making wills and avoiding estate litigation, *How To Avoid Probate* by Norman F. Dacey. It sold 575,000 copies. Like the *Kinsey Reports* of nearly twenty years before, a book planned as a scholarly medical work became a leading best seller. This was *Human Sexual Response* by William Howard Masters and Virginia E. Johnston. Third in nonfiction was the "nonfiction novel" by Truman Capote, *In Cold Blood,* report of a particularly brutal and senseless murder of the members of a Kansas farm family. Fourth and fifth were repeaters from 1965, *Games People Play,* with a two-year total of 465,000 copies, and *A Thousand Days,* which won the Pulitzer Prize in 1966. A second book relating to the late President Kennedy was eighth on the list. Mark Lane's *Rush to Judgment* was the best seller among a number of 1966 books questioning the validity of the *Report of the Warren Commission.*

The ten leading nonfiction titles of the year outsold the ten leading novels two to one. All the first ten in nonfiction sold well over 100,000 copies each; only the three top novels sold in that quantity in the bookstores. Two of these were first novels. Heading the list was *Valley of the Dolls* with a sale of 275,808 copies. Jacqueline Susann's novel described the aspirations of three girls in the entertainment world, telling what the use of barbiturates, pep pills, and alcohol did to those aspirations. In third place was Robert Crichton's *The Secret of Santa Vittoria.* This entertaining story of a little Italian village in 1943 sold 116,704 copies in four months. Between the two first novels, in second place, came Harold Robbins' sexiest novel to date, *The Adventurers.* It sold 187,000 copies during the year, was scheduled for movie production and the largest printing before paperback publication that Pocket Books had ever undertaken, 1,625,000 copies. Two novels of the American political scene, *Capable of Honor* and *All in the Family,* a spy story *The Double*

231

Image, a novel with a religious theme *Tell No Man,* and *The Embezzler* a contemporary novel of manners, all by established authors, appeared on the 1966 list. An author new to best sellers was James Clavell. His *Tai-Pan* was a long historical novel about Hong Kong. Best reviewed best seller of the year was *The Fixer* by Bernard Malamud. This story of a "fixer" or handyman in Czarist Russia, who was victim of a wave of anti-Semitism, became the winner of both the National Book Award and the Pulitzer Prize.

Early Best Sellers

EARLY BEST SELLERS

THESE ARE the titles, published before 1895, when the systematic recording of best sellers began, which have without question sold a total of a million copies or more through the years. It is impossible to arrive at definite sales figures for most of these because each has been issued by a variety of publishers. Many of these firms are no longer in existence and few accurate sales records are obtainable now, especially for the earliest books.

Prayer books, hymn books, textbooks, and similar specialized volumes are not included in this list, although many of the titles that are included have appeared in school editions as well as in trade editions. The list is in chronological order according to American publication.

The Holy Bible: King James, Douay Versions

The Pilgrim's Progress, by *John Bunyan*

Mother Goose

Aesop's Fables

The Vicar of Wakefield, by *Oliver Goldsmith*

Robinson Crusoe, by *Daniel Defoe*

Poems, by *Robert Burns*

Gulliver's Travels, by *Jonathan Swift*

Arabian Nights' Entertainment

Autobiography, by *Benjamin Franklin*

Plays, by *William Shakespeare*

The Sketch Book of Geoffrey Crayon, Gent., by *Washington Irving*

Ivanhoe, by *Sir Walter Scott*

Kenilworth, by *Sir Walter Scott*

The Spy, by *James Fenimore Cooper*

The Last of the Mohicans, by *James Fenimore Cooper*

The Swiss Family Robinson, by *Johann R. Wyss*

American Dictionary of the English Language (in various editions), by *Noah Webster*

The Last Days of Pompeii, by *Edward Bulwer-Lytton*

Oliver Twist, by *Charles Dickens*

235

Tales, by *Edgar Allan Poe*

Two Years Before the Mast, by *Richard Henry Dana, Jr.*

The Deerslayer, by *James Fenimore Cooper*

The Old Curiosity Shop, by *Charles Dickens*

Essays, by *Ralph Waldo Emerson*

Poems, by *Alfred Tennyson*

A Christmas Carol, by *Charles Dickens*

The Three Musketeers, by *Alexandre Dumas*

The Count of Monte Cristo, by *Alexandre Dumas*

Poems, by *Henry Wadsworth Longfellow*

Fairy Tales, by *Hans Christian Andersen*

Jane Eyre, by *Charlotte Brontë*

Vanity Fair, by *William Makepeace Thackeray*

Wuthering Heights, by *Emily Brontë*

The Oregon Trail, by *Francis Parkman*

Poems, by *John Greenleaf Whittier*

David Copperfield, by *Charles Dickens*

Reveries of a Bachelor, by *Ik Marvell*

The Scarlet Letter, by *Nathaniel Hawthorne*

The Wide Wide World, by *Susan Warner*

The House of the Seven Gables, by *Nathaniel Hawthorne*

Moby-Dick, by *Herman Melville*

Bleak House, by *Charles Dickens*

Uncle Tom's Cabin, by *Harriet Beecher Stowe*

Hard Times, by *Charles Dickens*

Tempest and Sunshine, by *Mary Jane Holmes*

Walden, by *Henry David Thoreau*

The Age of Fable, by *Thomas Bulfinch*

Familiar Quotations, by *John Bartlett*

Leaves of Grass, by *Walt Whitman*

The Prince of the House of David, by *J. H. Ingraham*

Lena Rivers, by *Mary Janes Holmes*

John Halifax, Gentleman, by *Dinah Maria Mulock*

The Autocrat of the Breakfast Table, by *Oliver Wendell Holmes*

A Tale of Two Cities, by *Charles Dickens*

East Lynne, by *Mrs. Henry Wood*

Fairy Tales, by *Jakob and Wilhelm Grimm*

Silas Marner, by *George Eliot*

Les Misérables, by *Victor Hugo*

Lady Audley's Secret, by *Mary Elizabeth Braddon*

Ishmael, by *Mrs. E. D. E. N. Southworth*

Self-Raised, or, Out of the Depths, by *Mrs. E. D. E. N. Southworth*

Hans Brinker and His Silver Skates, by *Mary Mapes Dodge*

St. Elmo, by *Augusta J. Evans*

The Man Without a Country, by *Edward Everett Hale*

Alice's Adventures in Wonderland, by *Lewis Carroll*

Little Women, by *Louisa May Alcott*

The Rubaiyat of Omar Khayyam, Translated by *Edward Fitzgerald*

The Story of a Bad Boy, by *Thomas Bailey Aldrich*

Little Men, by *Louisa May Alcott*

Barriers Burned Away, by *E. P. Roe*

Science and Health with Key to the Scriptures, by *Mary Baker Eddy*

The Return of the Native, by *Thomas Hardy*

The Adventures of Tom Sawyer, by *Mark Twain*

The Faith of Our Fathers, by *Cardinal Gibbons*

Ben-Hur, by *Lew Wallace*

Nana, by *Emile Zola*

Madame Bovary, by *Gustave Flaubert*

Five Little Peppers and How They Grew, by *Margaret Sidney*

Poems, by *James Whitcomb Riley*

Heidi, by *Johanna Spyri*

Treasure Island, by *Robert Louis Stevenson*

A Child's Garden of Verses, by *Robert Louis Stevenson*

The Adventures of Huckleberry Finn, by *Mark Twain*

War and Peace, by *Leo Tolstoi*

The Birds' Christmas Carol, by *Kate Douglas Wiggin*

She, by *H. Rider Haggard*

Thelma, by *Marie Corelli*

Robert Elsmere, by *Mrs. Humphry Ward*

Stories, by *Guy de Maupassant*

Barrack-Room Ballads, by *Rudyard Kipling*

Black Beauty, by *Anna Sewell*

Plain Tales from the Hills, by *Rudyard Kipling*

Three Men in a Boat, by *Jerome K. Jerome*

237

The Adventures of Sherlock Holmes, by *A. Conan Doyle*
Steps to Christ, by *Ellen G. White*
Beautiful Joe, by *Marshall Saunders*
Coin's Financial School, by *William H. Harvey*
The Christian's Secret of a Happy Life, by *Hannah Whitall Smith*
Trilby, by *George du Maurier*
Memoirs of a Woman of Pleasure (Fanny Hill), by *John Cleland*

Books and Articles

About Best Sellers

BOOKS AND ARTICLES
ABOUT BEST SELLERS

America's Most Censored Author. *Publishers' Weekly*, May 14, 1949
An interview with Erskine Caldwell.

Anthony Hits a Million! by Sanford Cobb. *Publishers' Weekly*, Aug. 24, 1935
An account of the publication and sales of *Anthony Adverse* in the United States and in other countries.

April 1954—30th Birthday of Crossword Puzzle Books, by John J. Winterich. *Publishers' Weekly*, Apr. 17, 1954

Augusta Evans Wilson, 1833-1900, by William Perry Fidler. University of Alabama Press, 1954
A biography of the author of *St. Elmo*.

Best Sellers: 1900-1935. The Trend of Popular Reading Taste Since the Turn of the Century, by Frederick Lewis Allen. *Saturday Review*, Dec. 7, 1935
Analysis of American reading over an extended period. A similar analysis of the reading of the 1930's appears as a chapter in Mr. Allen's book, *Since Yesterday*, Harper, 1939.

Best Sellers in Fiction During the First Quarter of the Twentieth Century, by Irving Harlow Hart. *Publishers' Weekly*, Feb. 14, 1925

Best Sellers in Non-Fiction Since 1921, by Irving Harlow Hart. *Publishers' Weekly*, Feb. 4, 1933

Best Sellers of the Fifties, by Don C. Seitz. *Publishers' Weekly*, Feb. 28, 1931
Discusses *A Prince of the House of David*, by Joseph Holt Ingraham.

Best Sellers of Yesterday. *The Bookman*, 1910
Articles run throughout the year on such 19th-century best sellers as *St. Elmo, Innocents Abroad*, and *Mr. Barnes of New York*.

The Best Sellers Since 1875: Thirty-Five Books Have Had Sales of More Than 500,000 Copies Since 1875, by Edward A. Weeks. *Publishers' Weekly*, Apr. 4, 1934

Big Books: The Story of Best Sellers, by J. A. Goodman and Albert Rice. *Saturday Evening Post*, Nov. 17, 1934
The sales and marketing of big best sellers of the 1930's.

The Book in America. A History of the Making and Selling of Books in the United States, by Hellmut Lehmann-Haupt and others. 2nd ed. R. R. Bowker Co., 1951

Book Publishing in America, by Charles A. Madison. McGraw-Hill, 1966
Comprehensive coverage of the publishing scene from the Colonial beginnings through 1965, including a great deal of information on popular books.

Books, Their Place in a Democracy, by R. L. Duffus. Houghton Mifflin, 1930

The Book Trade in War Time, by Archibald G. Ogden. *Publishers' Weekly,* July 8, 1939
    Publishing and sales during World War I.

Books and Best Sellers, by Philip Van Doren Stern. *Virginia Quarterly Review,* Jan., 1942
    The making and importance of best sellers of the 1940's, with some historical background.

The Case of Erle Stanley Gardner, by Alva Johnston. Morrow, 1947

Chronicles of Barabbas, 1884-1934: Further Chronicles and Comment, 1952, by George H. Doran. Rinehart, 1952
    A famous American publisher included background and anecdotal material about many best-selling authors, W. Somerset Maugham, H. G. Wells, Hugh Walpole, Mary Roberts Rinehart, Ralph Connor, among them.

Classics and Best-Sellers, by Malcolm Cowley. *New Republic,* Dec. 22, 1947

The Comics, by Coulton Waugh. Macmillan, 1947
    "From the Katzenjammer Kids to the Sad Sack."

The Content Characteristics of Best-Selling Novels, by John Harvey. *Public Opinion Quarterly,* v. 17, no. 1
    A statistical approach to "the puzzle of literary success."

The Critical Period in American Literature, by Grant C. Knight. University of North Carolina Press, 1951
    Writers and changing popular taste, 1890-1900.

Death's Fair-haired Boy, by Richard W. Johnston. *Life,* June 23, 1952
    Pictures and text about the success of the Mickey Spillane "sex and slaughter" novels.

The Devil with James Bond, by Ann S. Boyd. John Knox Press, 1966
    About the theological significance of the Ian Fleming spy stories.

The Extinction of the Dime Novel, by Firmin Dredd. *The Bookman,* March, 1900

The Fiction Factory, by Quentin Reynolds. Random House, 1956
    The history of the magazine publishing firm of Street & Smith gives sidelights on such best-selling authors as Max Brand and Edgar Wallace.

Fiction Fashions from 1895 to 1926, by Irving Harlow Hart. *Publishers' Weekly,* Feb. 5, 1927

Forgotten Best Sellers That Influenced America. New York *Times Book Review,* 1944
    Ethan Allen, Author. (Ethan Allen's *A Narrative of Colonel Ethan Allen's Captivity.*) May 7
    A Southerner Who Maddened the South. (Hinton Rowland's *The Impending Crisis of the South.*) June 11
    Horatio Alger, Jr. and Ragged Dick. (Horatio Alger's *Ragged Dick.*) July 2
    An Outspoken Visitor. (Mrs. Trollope's *Domestic Manners of the Americans.*) July 9

A Congressman Rediscovers Atlantis. (Ignatius Donnelly's *Atlantis.*) July 30

Gen. Wallace and Ben Hur. (Lew Wallace's *Ben Hur.*) Aug. 6

Professor Coin, Financial Wizard. (William Hope Harvey's *Coin's Financial School.*) Oct. 15

Monk Hall, Shame of Philadelphia. (George Lippard's *The Quaker City, or the Monks of Monk Hall, a Romance of Philadelphia Life, Mystery and Crime.*) Oct. 22

How to Drive the Sheriff from the Homestead Door. (Susan Warner's *The Wide, Wide World.*) Dec. 24

From Rags to Riches, by John Tebbel. Macmillan, 1963
About Horatio Alger and the books he wrote.

Genteel Queen of Crime, by Nigel Dennis. *Life,* May 14, 1956
Agatha Christie's life and writing.

Golden Multitudes, by Frank Luther Mott. R. R. Bowker Co., 1947
A critical and anecdotal history of best sellers in this country from 1638 to 1947. The author evolved his own method of determining a best seller. The lists he made are based upon the formula of a book selling at least a number equal to "one per cent of the total population of continental United States for the decade in which the book was published."

"Heidi"—or the Story of a Juvenile Best Seller. *Publishers' Weekly,* July 25, 1953

The History of 'In His Steps' by Its Author Charles M. Sheldon. Privately Printed. 1938
The writing and the sales history of *In His Steps.*

Hoosiers Sell Best, by John H. Moriarty. *Indiana Quarterly for Bookmen.* Jan., 1947
The most popular authors on the yearly lists, 1895-1944 in the first edition of this book, *Fifty Years of Best Sellers,* with statistics of their geographical origins, by States.

The House of Beadle and Adams and Its Dime and Nickel Novels; The Story of a Vanished Literature, by Albert Johannsen. University of Oklahoma Press, 1950

How a Best-Seller Happens, by E. M. D. Watson. *Cosmopolitan,* August, 1959

Ian Fleming: The Spy Who Came in with the Gold, by Henry A. Zeiger. Duell, Sloan & Pearce, 1966
A biography of the creator of James Bond, Agent 007.

How Large Is Our Book-Reading Public? by Maxwell Aley. *Publishers' Weekly,* June 6, 1931

"In His Steps," the Story of a Best Seller. *Publishers' Weekly,* Mar. 2, 1946

"In Tune with the Infinite," Famous Best Seller, Now 50 Years Old. *Publishers' Weekly,* Feb. 22, 1947
The author, Ralph Waldo Trine, the book, and its history.

The Inside Story of the World of Perry Mason, by Frank E. Robbins. Morrow, 1950
About the chief characters created by Erle Stanley Gardner. Reprinted from the *Michigan Alumnus Quarterly Review.*

James Bond's World of Values, by Lycurgus M. Starkey, Jr. Abingdon, 1966
A severe criticism, from the standpoint of Christian ethic, of the James Bond character in the Ian Fleming novels.

Lew Wallace's 'Ben Hur' Gallops On, by Walter Moonfried. Milwaukee *Journal,* Feb. 27, 1955

The Life of Ian Fleming, by John Pearson. McGraw-Hill, 1966
Biography of the author of the James Bond thrillers.

Lincoln's Doctor's Dog, by George Stevens. Lippincott, 1939
Account of famous best sellers of the 1930's.

Margaret Mitchell of Atlanta, by Finis Farr. Morrow, 1965
The life of Margaret Mitchell and the writing of *Gone with the Wind.*

Miracle Books, by Leon Whipple. *Survey,* May 1, 1927
Reasons for the sales of big nonfiction best sellers of the 1920's.

The Most Popular Authors of Fiction Between 1900 and 1925, by Irving Harlow Hart. *Publishers' Weekly,* Feb. 21, 1925

The Most Popular Authors of Fiction in the Post-War Period, 1919-1926, by Irving Harlow Hart. *Publishers' Weekly,* Mar. 12, 1927

The Nation's Appetite for Fiction, by Herbert F. Jenkins. *Publishers' Weekly,* Sept. 24, 1921
Gives information and figures on the sale of many novels of the post-World War I period.

Of Making Many Books: A Hundred Years of Reading, Writing and Publishing, by Roger Burlingame. Scribner, 1946
A chapter on "Best-Sellers" is included in this 100th anniversary history of the publishing house of Charles Scribner's Sons as well as background material on such best-selling Scribner authors as Edith Wharton, F. Hopkinson Smith, S. S. Van Dine, Ernest Hemingway, John Galsworthy, James Boyd, Harold Frederic, and others.

The One Hundred "Best Sellers of the Last Quarter Century," by Irving Harlow Hart. *Publishers' Weekly,* Jan. 29, 1921

The One Hundred Leading Authors of Best Sellers in Fiction from 1895 to 1944, by Irving Harlow Hart. *Publishers' Weekly,* Jan. 19, 1946
This, like all Professor Hart's studies of best sellers in *Publishers' Weekly,* is based upon his intensive analysis, over the years, of the monthly best seller geographical charts issued at one time by the *Publishers' Weekly* office. These charts are no longer published.

Over the Tops, by Gilbert Seldes. *Saturday Evening Post,* Apr. 25, 1936
On the popularity of books, legitimate plays, musicals, road shows, moving pictures, sheet music, etc.

Paperback Books: A Pocket History, by John Tebbel. Pocket Books, 1964
History of the paperback publishing firm, Pocket Books.

The Paperbound Book in America, by Frank L. Schick. R. R. Bowker Co., 1958
The history of paperback publishing in the United States and its European background.

244

The Paper-Bound Book: Twentieth-Century Publishing Phenomenon, by Kurt Enoch. *Library Quarterly*, July, 1954

Paper-Bound Books in America, by Freeman Lewis. New York Public Library, 1952
The history of paperbound publishing up to 1952.

The Popular Book, by James D. Hart. Oxford University Press, 1950
Full of background material and facts about the popular and best-selling books from the beginning of American reading to 1950.

The Publisher, by Robert Sterling Yard. Houghton Mifflin, 1913
A chapter on "What Makes a Book Sell."

Mary Roberts Rinehart, by Geoffrey T. Hellman. *Life,* June 25, 1946

Some "Best Sellers" of Other Days, by Michael Sadleir. *Publishers' Weekly,* Mar. 26, 1927
Subject matter and quality of best sellers and their chances for survival.

The Story of the McGuffeys, by Alice McGuffey Ruggles. American Book Co., 1950
About the famous McGuffey readers.

The Strenuous Age in American Literature, by Grant C. Knight. University of North Carolina Press, 1954
A critical history of the books of the years 1900-1910, against the social background of the period.

Ten Best Sellers, by W. Somerset Maugham. *Good Housekeeping,* Sept., 1948
Discussion of the qualities that appealed to the public in ten famous 19th century novels.

There Were Giants in Those Days, by Mildred Catharine Smith. *Publishers' Weekly,* July 13, 1929
Quo Vadis and its advertising campaign.

This Was Publishing, by Donald Sheehan. Indiana University Press, 1952
The business, philosophy and problems of book publishing in the years from the close of the Civil War to the beginning of World War I. Information about many individual books and authors.

Twenty-five Years of Best-Sellers, by Harrison Smith. *The English Journal,* Oct., 1944
Analysis of literature and reading tastes, 1914-1944.

Twenty Years of Post-War Best-Sellers—Part II: United States of America, by Alice P. Hackett. Publishers' World, 1965
A survey of the hardbound best sellers in the years from the end of World War II through 1964.

What a New Englander Was Likely to Read in 1711, by John J. Winterich. *Publishers' Weekly,* Feb. 3, 1951

What Makes a Book Sell? by Robert Banker. *Publishers' Weekly,* Dec. 4, 1954

Why of the Best Seller, by William Lyon Phelps. *The Bookman,* Dec., 1921
The quality of best sellers, chiefly *Main Street* and the novels of Harold Bell Wright and Gene Stratton Porter.

The Wonderful Career of the Wonderful Wizard. *Publishers' Weekly,* Feb. 13, 1961
The publishing history of L. Frank Baum's *The Wonderful Wizard of Oz.*

Writing As a Career, by Thomas H. Uzzell. Harcourt, Brace, 1938
The chapter on "The Popular Novel" analyzes the literary quality of some novels which sold over half a million copies between 1875 and 1938.

Title and Author Index

TITLE AND AUTHOR INDEX

254

255

257

259

264

265

272

274

277